From Loss to Love

The Beginning of a Celtic Journey
through
The Spiritual Exercises of Saint Ignatius of Loyola

Timothy J. Ray

Copyright © 2021 Timothy J. Ray
All rights reserved.
ISBN: 9798485582975

To
Per Mollerup

who shared my journey,
nourishing me with his wisdom and his faith,
in times of darkness and of light

Table of Contents

Finding Your Place of Resurrection: a foreword	i
Preface for *From Loss to Love*	iii
Acknowledgements	v

Accepting the Gift of God's Love

Accepting the Gift of God's Love	3

From Loss to Love

Considerations	7
Prelude: Praying with Jesus and St. Patrick	14
1. Reliance upon God's Plan	17
1.1a O Splendour Of God's Face	18
1.1b Preparation for Prayer	24
1.2 Jeremiah 29:11-14	26
1.3 Isaiah 55:1-13	29
1.4 Romans 8:28-39	32
1.5 Repetition of Isaiah 55:1-13	35
1.6 An Application of the Senses	38
1.7 Review of Prayer	40
2. Living for God's Glory	43
2.1a O Word Of Might, That Springing Forth	44
2.1b Preparation for Prayer	50
2.2 Principle and Foundation	52
2.3 Ephesians 1:3-14	54
2.4 Isaiah 43:1-7	57
2.5 Repetition of Isaiah 43:1-7	60
2.6 An Application of the Senses	63
2.7 Review of Prayer	65
3. Rebellion Against God's Desires	67
3.1a Shamed And Shaken Sore With Terror	68
3.1b Preparation for Prayer	74
3.2 Luke 15:11-32	76
3.3 2 Peter 2:2-22	79
3.4 Genesis 3:1-24	82
3.5 Repetition of Luke 15:11-32	85
3.6 An Application of the Senses	88

	3.7	Review of Prayer	90
4.	The Personal Nature of Sin		93
	4.1a	I Call On You To Save Me	94
	4.1b	Preparation for Prayer	100
	4.2	A Consideration of Personal Sins	102
	4.3	Matthew 13:1-9,18-23	105
	4.4	Matthew 13:24-30	108
	4.5	Matthew 13:24-30,36-43	111
	4.6	An Application of the Senses	114
	4.7	Review of Prayer	116
5.	The Contemplation of Hell		119
	5.1a	Loving Jesus, Hear Me Calling	120
	5.1b	Preparation for Prayer	126
	5.2	Jeremiah 18:1-11	128
	5.3	Isaiah 5:1-6	131
	5.4	Matthew 22:1-14	134
	5.5	Repetition of Matthew 22:1-14	137
	5.6	An Application of the Senses	140
	5.7	Review of Prayer	142
6.	Sin and Sorrow		145
	6.1a	I Am Not Worthy, O God	146
	6.1b	Preparation for Prayer	152
	6.2	Matthew 25:31-46	154
	6.3	Ephesians 4:17-24	157
	6.4	Colossians 1:15-20	160
	6.5	Repetition of Ephesians 4:17-24	163
	6.6	An Application of the Senses	166
	6.7	Review of Prayer	168
7.	The Gift of God's Love and Forgiveness		171
	7.1a	Redeemer, Sole-Begotten Son, You Are My Hope	172
	7.1b	Preparation for Prayer	178
	7.2	John 10:1-18	180
	7.3	Luke 15:1-10	183
	7.4	Ephesians 2:1-10	186
	7.5	Repetition of Luke 15:1-10	189
	7.6	An Application of the Senses	192
	7.7	Review of Prayer	194
8.	Trusting in God's Love and Forgiveness		197
	8.1a	Let My Tongue Be Free From Blame	198
	8.1b	Preparation for Prayer	204

8.2	John 8:2-11	206
8.3	Luke 6:17-38	209
8.4	John 6:32-58	212
8.5	Repetition of Luke 6:17-38	215
8.6	An Application of the Senses	218
8.7	Review of Prayer	220
9.	Responding to God's Love and Forgiveness	223
9.1a	Jesus, My Love, My Saviour	224
9.1b	Preparation for Prayer	230
9.2	Romans 8:1-17	232
9.3	Ephesians 6:10-18	235
9.4	Jeremiah 29:11-14	238
9.5	"The Deer's Cry"	241
9.6	An Application of the Senses	243
9.7	Review of Prayer	245

The Call of the King of Heaven

The Call of the King of Heaven	249
A Contemplation of the Kingdom of Jesus Christ	250

Manifesting God's Mercy

Introduction	255
Spiritual Practices	261
Traditional Prayers	263
Preparing a Personal Penitential	269
Sacred Citizenship	283
Patrick the Apostle – Kyrie Eleison	285
Saint Patrick's "Letter to the Soldiers of Coroticus"	289
Articulate Witness	295
Discerning Your Passions	297

Textual Resources

From Saint Ignatius' *Spiritual Exercises*	309
The Principle and Foundation	309
A Meditation on Personal Sin	309
A Contemplation of the Kingdom of Jesus Christ	310
Rules for the Discernment of Spirits, Week 1	312

From Celtic Sources	317
A Description of Saint Patrick	317
Stories about Saint Patrick	317
The Leper and the Floating Stone	317
Patrick Receives the Staff of Jesus	317
God Protects Patrick from His Enemies	318
Patrick is Betrayed for a Cauldron	318
Failge Tries to Kill Patrick	319
The Conversion of Dichu	319
Patrick's Wedding Night	320
Patrick Converts Daire	320
The Young Patrick and the Flooded House	321
The Young Patrick and the Wolf	321
"The Deer's Cry"	321

Resources for Prayer

Considerations	327
A Morning Prayer of Encircling	329
An Evening Prayer of Review	331
Notes on the Prayerful Review of the Day	334
Imaginative Contemplation	336
The Application of the Senses	339
Approaching Prayer during this Retreat	341
Honoring Holy Ground: rituals for creating a sacred space	348

Finding Your Place of Resurrection: a foreword

A commitment to the spiritual life involves a journey of unfolding possibilities and new awarenesses. Each new discovery in our relationship with God reveals a deeper experience of divine love as well as further opportunities to serve God through our involvement with other people and various causes in our world, which in turn invites further prayer and reflection about these new expressions of God's activity in our lives. This is a journey into ever-deepening awareness of God's love for us and our need to respond in kind – a love that invites a reciprocal response of love. It is an unending pilgrimage into the mystery of creation that does not end until we find our rest within God's loving consciousness.

For the ancient Celtic saints, this pilgrimage is a journey towards the individual's "place of resurrection" – that place in the world where a person discovers his or her relationship to God and their purpose in life. For the ancient Celts, this was an actual location a man or woman sought out through prayer (and often quite dangerous travel) where he or she would wait for death and subsequent resurrection while committing themselves to rigorous spiritual disciplines and prayers. In the modern world, this "place of resurrection" might better be understood as an earthly situation or type of ministry where a person feels closest to God through prayerful and social activities intended to foster the renewal of God's creation (both human and nonhuman) and the establishment of the kingdom of God.

Centuries later, Saint Ignatius of Loyola would create in his *Spiritual Exercises* an ordered set of meditations designed to help men and women open themselves with ever-increasing generosity to the love God demonstrates towards them and the world around them. At the heart of these Ignatian exercises lies an ideal that Ignatius called *"magis"*, "the more" by which God invites an individual – through an incremental and ongoing process of revelation and invitation – to greater and more challenging opportunities to become instruments of God's love in the world. Like the Celtic saints before him, Ignatius understood the spiritual life as an unfolding journey of possibilities to be embraced in response to the individual's tangible experience of God's love in his or her life.

The recognition of this shared vision between the ancient Celtic saints and St. Ignatius of Loyola forms the foundation for the books in this series. Each book presents a self-directed retreat addressing a portion of *The Spiritual Exercises of Saint Ignatius of Loyola* accompanied by materials by or about a particular Celtic saint whose vision complements Ignatius' exercises. Each book in the series also provides resources from both the Celtic and Ignatian spiritual traditions to facilitate further prayer and reflection as well as exercises developed from Celtic spiritual practices related to the themes of each retreat. Used together, these retreats and their companion materials cultivate habits of prayer and action intended to nurture a holistic spirituality embracing spiritual discipline, sacred citizenship and articulate witness in the world.

So, as you begin this pilgrimage of faith and love, you should walk with confidence in the knowledge that many have walked before you and others will follow after you. You are being invited into an intimate relationship with God through which your faults and failings are forgiven as you become an instrument of love and reconciliation in a world often bereft of hope. The examples of the ancient Celtic saints and the followers of the Ignatian spiritual tradition offer you a supportive companionship as you strive to find your own "place of resurrection" – embracing the increasingly wonderful gifts God presents to you and expressing your gratitude through generous acts of self-giving service to God's other children and creatures.

Preface for *From Loss to Love*

Through the prayers and reflections of this first book in the "Finding your Place of Resurrection" series, you will experience the fullness of God's forgiving love for you. Ensnared by the power of sin, you separated yourself from God and – if you are honest with yourself – came to believe that your human nature is inherently sinful. However, through the prayers and reflections in *From Loss to Love*, you will contemplate the tremendous love God has for you (and the rest of creation) and recognize the forgiveness you are being offered despite your own intransigence. Accepting that forgiveness and love will liberate you, offering you hope and a desire to serve God in gratitude.

> *Note: Saint Ignatius of Loyola believed their experience was so important that he says this portion of his* Spiritual Exercises *may be offered as a stand-alone experience, even though he hoped men and women would desire to carry through to the end of his exercises. So, if you decide to focus exclusively on the retreat in this book, you should remain confident in your decision.*
>
> *However, remember that the invitation to complete the full* Spiritual Exercises *remains open to you.*

From Loss to Love begins with a self-guided retreat (conducted over nine days or nine weeks, depending on how you approach it) focused on the first portion of *The Spiritual Exercises of Saint Ignatius of Loyola*, often referred to as the "First Week". The designation of a week is somewhat confusing since Ignatius divides his *Spiritual Exercises* into four irregular thematic sections. So, it might be easier to think of this portion as the first movement of a musical composition – one that can be appreciated for itself while also contributing to the larger work. As mentioned earlier, the focus of this first portion or movement of the Ignatian exercises is sin and forgiveness. This may be a difficult topic for you to confront, but it is extremely important that you open yourself as fully as possible to the spiritual gifts God will provide as you explore your own sinfulness and your capacity to reciprocate the love God has for you.

However, it is important for you to remember as you begin the retreat presented in this book that this is only the beginning of a process of reconciliation between God, you, and the world around you. Through

God's grace, you will explore the depths of your personal identity and the various behaviors that attract you toward God or distract you from God's desires for you. The prayers and meditations of this retreat are intended to help you accept that you are worthy of the love and forgiveness God offers you. In this way, the retreat might be seen as opening a door and allowing God to enter your life in a new way. So, just as each new visit – even by the most familiar guest or visitor – reveals a unique and fresh experience (depending on its timing and circumstances), the significance of your encounters with God in *From Loss to Love* will only be fully revealed through the unfolding generosity of God in which each new act of divine love and forgiveness invites you move forward in your life with greater confidence and gratitude.

The reflections and exercises provided in *From Loss to Love* will help you develop an awareness of the unique patterns of God's love in your own life so you will be able to respond to that love through acts of gratitude and service. The retreat and resource materials in this book draw upon the stories and prayers of Saint Patrick of Armagh as well as prayers and hymns he would recognize, either because he was familiar with them or they share in his understanding of God's activity in the world. Some of these materials may be familiar to you, but many of them will not. As with the retreat, pray that your heart and mind may be opened to the loving presence of God expressed through these resources. Again, you should know that you will never be alone during this journey.

So, as you move forward into the retreat and reflections of *From Loss to Love*, pray for the patience to learn the disciplines of prayer and to persevere as the seeds planted in this book mature and bear fruit over time – carrying with you the promise offered by God through Isaiah 55:10-11:

For as the rain and the snow come down from heaven,
   and do not return there until they have watered the earth,
making it bring forth and sprout,
   giving seed to the sower and bread to the eater,
so shall my word be that goes out from my mouth;
   it shall not return to me empty,
but it shall accomplish that which I purpose,
   and succeed in the thing for which I sent it.

Acknowledgements

This book represents a personal journey that would not have been possible without the generous companionship of numerous friends and spiritual companions who, to varying degrees and for different lengths of time, supported and encouraged me to persevere in this pilgrimage.

Among these friends, I remain especially grateful to Kathleen Deignan, Edward Egros, Rosalyn Knowles Ferrell, Douglas Galbraith, Patrick Henry, Susan Rakoczy, Jim Swonger and George Theodoridis.

In addition, I am very grateful for:
- the permission of *The Capuchin Annual* and the King estate to reproduce Richard King's image of Saint Patrick on the cover of this book.
- the permission of Johnston McMaster to excerpt "Saint Patrick – Kyrie Eleison" from his *A Passion for Justice: Social Ethics in the Celtic Tradition* (Edinburgh: Dunedin Academic Press Ltd., 2008).
- the inclusion (under the provisions of fair use) of "Grant Me Tears, O Lord" from *Celtic Spirituality*, edited by Oliver Davies (New York: Paulist Press, 1999) in The Classics of Western Spirituality series.

The prayer sequences presented in this book were developed using ancient Christian hymns and traditional Irish prayers from the following public domain books, all of which are available on the Internet Archive:
- *Early Christian Hymns; translations of the verses of the most notable Latin writers of the early and middle ages* (1908), edited by Daniel Joseph Donahoe.
- *Early Christian Hymns, Series II: translations of the verses of the early and middle ages* (1911), edited by Daniel Joseph Donahoe.
- *Hymns of the Early Church* (1896), edited by John Brownlie.
- *The Irish "Liber hymnorum", Volume 2* (1908), edited by John Henry Bernard Robert Atkinson.
- *The Religious Songs of Connacht: A collection of poems, stories, prayers, satires, ranns, charms, etc., Volume One* (1906) by Douglas Hyde.
- *The Religious Songs of Connacht: A collection of poems, stories, prayers, satires, ranns, charms, etc., Volume Two* (1906) by Douglas Hyde.

- *The Story of Iona* (1909) by Edward Craig Trenholme.

These prayer sequences are adaptations of these sources – not transcriptions or translations – so any fault in their literary quality lies with the author.

Also, excerpts from the following public domain books have been included in this retreat, its reflection materials, and its resources:
- *The Epistles and Hymn of Saint Patrick* (1876), edited by Thomas Olden.
- *Lives of Saints from The Book of Lismore* (1890), edited by Whitley Stokes.
- *Selections from Ancient Irish Poetry* (1911), translated by Kuno Meyer.
- *The Spiritual Exercises of Saint Ignatius of Loyola* (1847), edited by Charles Seager.
- *Three Middle-Irish homilies on the lives of Saints Patrick, Brigit and Columba* (1877), edited by Whitley Stokes.

All these books are available on the Internet Archive.

Finally, some material in this book has been excerpted (with some variations) from the author's earlier *A Pilgrimage to the Land of the Saints* and *Nurturing the Courage of Pilgrims*.

Accepting the Gift of God's Love

embracing God's transformative love

Accepting the Gift of God's Love
embracing God's transformative love

One of the most challenging aspects of the spiritual life involves our ability to accept the love God offers each of us. Most of us are fully aware of our own sinful tendencies as well as the challenges we have faced in trying to overcome them. So, the idea that God loves us despite these failings and offers us forgiveness might seem delusional. However, we cannot proceed beyond the early stages of a relationship with God until we recognize and embrace the unconditional love God has for each of us. This reluctance to accept God's love never disappears completely since our future sins will also separate us from God's love through self-doubt and shame, but the knowledge that God still loves us despite our sinful choices will teach us patterns of humility and repentance.

The ancient Celtic saints recognized this dilemma as well as the discipline needed to continuously open ourselves to God's love. Many scholars note that the largest group of surviving writings from the early Celtic church were penitentials, manuals listing various types of sins and the penances most appropriate to each. However, the same scholars also recognize that the use of these penitential manuals created a redemptive path into the love of God through a cycle of confession, penance, and absolution. While the penalties prescribed in the penitentials could be harsh, they fostered an attitude of humility and atonement that returned the sinner to the loving embrace of God.

The ancient Celtic saints believed in the intrinsic goodness of creation and in the love of God that shaped it. The ancient Celts lived precarious lives, yet they could see and appreciate the intricate network of care shaping the natural environment. This, along with their pre-Christian admiration and reverence for nature, made the world around them a parable of God's love. Also, through their study and prayerful use of the Old and New Testaments, the ancient Celtic saints understood the love and concern God expressed for all of creation – especially in the Psalms which were so central to worship in the ancient Celtic church. By seeing these patterns of love in the world around them and in the sacred Scriptures, the ancient Celtic saints were able to humbly present themselves before God with both repentance and hope.

Centuries later, Ignatius of Loyola presents in his *Spiritual Exercises* a very similar vision of hopeful repentance. He begins these exercises with a powerful statement of God's love and an invitation to participate in the cosmic plan emerging from these desires. Then, he invites men and women to recognize the forces actively seeking to undermine this plan – both on a cosmic level and within each of them. Saint Ignatius demonstrates how temptation and self-doubt make it impossible to participate in the unfolding possibilities of God's love without actively accepting the divine forgiveness and assistance made possible through the Incarnation, Passion and Resurrection of Jesus Christ.

For both Saint Ignatius and the ancient Celtic saints, the love and forgiveness offered by God presents new opportunities for participating in God's cosmic plan with each act of humble repentance. In the Ignatian spiritual tradition shaped by the journey through his *Spiritual Exercises*, this unfolding sequence of opportunities for greater service to God is referred to as *"magis"* (or "more") since each loving encounter with God invites a more intense desire to offer oneself and one's abilities to the fulfillment of God's cosmic plan. In a similar manner, the ancient Celtic cycle of sin, repentance, penance, and absolution fostered in an individual greater gratitude and resolution in remaining true to God's desires, both for that person and for all of creation. Both Ignatius and the ancient Celtic saints understood, in the words of 1 John 4:19, "We love because he first loved us."

So, as you begin this journey of faith, pray for the humility to repent your sins and to accept the love God will offer when you have the courage to ask. Approach these coming prayers with confidence, knowing God is waiting to embrace you once again. Acknowledge the many ways you have failed to return the love God has offered you throughout your life, knowing the burdens of your sins will be lifted and you will be able to encounter hitherto unknown possibilities for your life. In the days or weeks ahead, remember the words of Micah 6:8:
>   *He has told you, O mortal, what is good;*
>   *and what does the Lord require of you*
>   *but to do justice, and to love kindness,*
>   *and to walk humbly with your God?*

From Loss to Love

Considerations

Note: These considerations focus on the practical concerns of approaching this self-guided retreat (e.g., in seclusion or in daily life, alone or with others, etc.). If you would like more information (and a few suggestions) concerning the spiritual practices and resources which will shape your retreat experience, please read "Approaching Prayer during this Retreat" (found on page 341).

A retreat is a journey of prayer and, like any journey, it requires proper preparation. You need to decide where you are going, how long you will be traveling, what you need to bring with you and – just as important – what you need to leave behind. An experienced traveler will travel light but also remain aware that there are certain things that must be brought along if your travels are to be comfortable and sustainable. As you prepare for this spiritual journey, you will need to consider these questions as well. You will need to give careful thought to your desires for this retreat, how long you want to be on retreat, the rhythms of prayer best suited to your personal situation and finally whether you wish to make this retreat alone or with companions.

This self-guided retreat presents the first of three distinct but interrelated journeys through the meditations outlined in *The Spiritual Exercises of Saint Ignatius* using resources from the early Celtic saints and surviving remnants of Celtic spirituality. However, Ignatius points out that the portion of his *Spiritual Exercises* presented in this book may either stand alone or establish a foundation for the retreats that follow it. You may find it helpful to ask if you are only interested in the journey encompassed in this retreat or if you wish to see it as the beginning of longer and more challenging travels. You may change your mind after completing this retreat but having a sense of how much time and energy you wish to commit to your prayers over the coming weeks or months will help you clarify your desires as well as force you to consider practical issues involved in making this commitment.

Once you have made this decision (which, as I have said, you may decide to change after the retreat), you need to consider how you will approach this retreat. You have the option of completing the retreat through nine days of secluded prayer or through nine weeks of prayer in daily life. Praying in seclusion offers little time between prayers, so the presence of God permeates your entire consciousness and makes each moment a sacred encounter. On the other hand, praying in daily life requires that you dedicate a portion of your day to encountering God and often draws the mundane events of each day into your prayer.

If you decide to make this retreat in daily life, you will need to separate your prayers from your daily routines. It will be important that you release yourself from these day-to-day concerns and personal problems before entering the sacred space of your prayer. You will need to make certain that you come to your prayer without being tired or overstimulated by the events of your day. You should develop tools intended to separate your place and time of prayer from distractions – creating transitions from daily life into your time of prayer (such as the rituals described in "Honoring Holy Ground", found on page 348), dedicating a particular time each day to your prayer, and creating an environment that is most conducive to quiet prayer.

When making this retreat in daily life, you need to devote approximately one-and-a-half hours of each day to prayer. Of this time, 45 to 50 minutes of your day should be dedicated to the preparation exercises, the formal contemplations and meditations, the application of the senses, and the weekly review of your prayer. In addition, you should spend 10 to 15 minutes after your contemplations, meditations and application of the senses reviewing the specific aspects of your prayer and recording them in your journal so these moments remain clear during your later (more comprehensive) review at the end of the week. Finally, you will need to set aside 15 minutes at the beginning and end of your day to each of the examens.

Note: *To foster an awareness of the special nature of these moments with God, and to cultivate a sense of anticipation toward these moments, you will also find it helpful to commit specific times in your day to each of these types of prayer. Also, to nurture the efficacy of your paper (and, therefore, your desire to enter it) you should avoid the temptation to either lengthen your prayer when it is going well or shortening it when you feel distracted.*

It is also very important during our daily life retreat to consecrate a specific place to your prayer. You should create a comfortable and contemplative atmosphere in which to pray and preserve the distinctive character of this place so that you may enter it with a sense of reverence and devotion. You may choose to use locations that you have always found prayerful, such as a chapel or a secluded outdoor bench, or you may decide to create spaces within your home dedicated specifically (and only) to your prayer. Whether you choose to pray in a specific and consistent place or to pray in various places during your retreat, remember that this is the space you choose to share with God and it should be approached with reverence, generosity, and humility.

Note: You need to ensure that the place of your prayer remains consciously devoted to prayer by creating either a permanent focal point in these places (e.g., a statue, an icon or cross, a candle, etc.) or by developing rituals in which this focal point is established at the beginning of your prayer.

However, if you make this retreat in seclusion, the rhythm of your prayer will be sustained by your four or five daily conversations with God that will dominate and define your day. As in the daily life retreat, you need to devote 45 to 50 minutes of your day to the formal contemplations, meditations, and application of the senses as well as 10 to 15 minutes after each prayer period to your preliminary review. Also, you will need to be consistent in the times when you pray and remove any impediments to honoring these specific times. Finally, to intensify your awareness of the emotional and spiritual undercurrents of your prayer, you may find it useful to integrate the examens into your preparation at the beginning of your day and the review of your prayer at the end of your day.

Note: During a retreat in seclusion, it is especially important that you not allow your prayers or reflections to become burdensome or exhausting. So, if you find that the amount of recommended prayer makes you tired, you may decide during your preparations to temporarily remove one of the contemplations or meditations from your day.

Also, the nature of secluded prayer requires that you create a calm environment both for your prayer and the time around it since the entirety of your day is immersed in the sacred. You will need to choose whether you want to make your retreat at home or somewhere else, and each of these options presents its own unique obstacles. Praying at home will require you to create a quiet and solitary place for your time with God, creating specific places for your formal prayer and removing any distracting elements from your home and daily routine (including making your friends and neighbors aware of your need for privacy). Praying away from home will require you to make the necessary arrangements to create the stillness needs during your retreat.

If you make a secluded retreat at home, you also will need to limit your normal daily activities as well as your contact with other people. You should preserve any activities you find restful or reflective but put those that distract or tire you. For example, you should devote time to mindfully cooking if you enjoy it but plan simple meals (or delivery) if cooking is tiresome to you. Also, activities such as exercise that you enjoy but which may tire you should be curtailed as well as any activities that provoke their own emotional response (e.g., reading, listening to the radio, watching television, etc.). Also, make certain that anyone who might contact you knows that you will be unavailable and leave a message about this on your devices. Finally, you should arrange for someone to receive any emergency messages for you during your retreat.

However, if you do not feel comfortable praying so intensely at home, you may decide to live a secluded life away from home. This may include camping (if you find this restful and enjoyable) or staying at a beach house or cabin (and observing the same precautions you would use if you were in your home). This might also involve staying at a bed-and-breakfast or hotel and making the necessary arrangements to be given your privacy both during the day and during meals (including telling housekeeping not to disturb you during your stay and to arrange for linens to be changed in the least disruptive manner possible). Also, if choosing to pray away from home, you should bring with you some familiar prayer objects to serve as focal points during your retreat.

Note: Whether you pray at home or away from home, it also would be good to have access to beautiful places during your retreat (e.g., parks, beaches, woodlands, etc.) where you might choose to pray or simply spend quiet time between your prayer periods.

After making these important preliminary decisions about this retreat – deciding (if only temporarily) that this retreat is a discrete event or part of a longer journey as well as whether you will pray in daily life or in seclusion – you should consider whether making this journey with companions will enrich your prayer or detract from it. The prayers of this retreat will be quite intense, and you might benefit from spiritual conversation with companions concerning your experiences in prayer. However, if you choose to make this retreat with companions, you will need to make certain decisions about where and when you will conduct the retreat and make certain that everyone's physical emotional and spiritual needs are addressed before, during and after the retreat.

If you choose to make this spiritual journey with others, you should meet before the retreat to discuss your various hopes and desires. You should pay careful attention to the amount of time each of you wants to spend in prayer and the places where each of you prefers to pray. You should decide practical matters concerning the retreat as well as housekeeping (e.g., preparing meals, washing dishes, etc.) and matters concerning the sequences (e.g., timing, choice of music, individual duties, etc.), and the types of faith-sharing you may want related to the retreat. During these conversations, you should try to maximize your collective spiritual experience while still ensuring that each member of your group does not feel pressured beyond his or her capabilities.

Note: This conversation should also address your individual responsibilities during the retreat, such as who will lead the readings (including the selection of music) during the sequences as well as if you will incorporate faith-sharing during or after the retreat (e.g., as part of the sequences, in special meetings, etc.).

It may be simpler to make your retreat in daily life if you decide to include spiritual companions. Using the resources of a local church or prayer group, you may find it helpful to meet on a specific day to pray the prayer sequence for the coming week together. This space should be large enough for all of you and your companions to gather comfortably while remaining intimate enough that all of you remain connected to one another. However, if this is not possible, you will need to find (or create) another location where you and your companions may conduct your shared prayers.

However, if you and your companions decide to make a secluded retreat away from home, you will need to find a quiet place in which each of you is able to focus on his or her individual prayer. As with finding a private place for a secluded retreat, this might be somewhere able to care for all your material needs (e.g., a retreat house, a small inn, etc.) or one where you and your companions need to take care of yourselves (e.g., a cabin, a beach house, etc.). So, as you select this place, make certain it meets all the needs for the creation of a contemplative space outlined earlier as well as offers enough space to allow you and your companions to pray – both alone in each person's unique manner as well as together – without feeling confined.

Also, if you decide to make your retreat in seclusion with companions, you should discuss the practical concerns of being together in this new environment. To avoid disturbing each other, you will find it helpful to maintain silence for as much of the retreat as possible so you should decide before the retreat how much of your time together during the retreat is silent. You should also discuss how you and your companions will handle living accommodations (e.g., private rooms, shared spaces, etc.), personal daily routines (e.g., showers, sleep patterns, etc.) and any chores that may arise during your retreat (e.g., cooking, laundry, setting out meals, cleaning dishes, etc.).

Note: *You and your companions may also find it very helpful to discuss ways to resolve any conflicts that may arise during your retreat, such as finding themselves attracted to the same prayer spaces or encountering annoying patterns of behavior in another person (since your emotional sensitivity will be heightened during the retreat). In these matters, try to be generous and respectful with one another.*

Finally, after deciding on the kind of retreat experience you want to have, you would find it helpful to review the resources for prayer found at the end of this book (especially "Approaching Prayer during this Retreat" which addresses many of the technical concerns of the retreat such as scheduling and pacing your prayer, recording your spiritual experiences, and selecting the version of the Bible for your retreat). If you are approaching this retreat after completing the journey with Brendan and his companions presented in *A Pigrimage to the Land of the Saints* (or have already made in Ignatian retreat in the past) much of this material will seem familiar but you still will find it helpful to make certain you remain comfortable and confident with these techniques as you approach this retreat.

Still, while the retreat meditations presented in this book will guide you and the various reflection exercises offered after the retreat will nourish the spiritual gifts you receive during the retreat, always remember that God is traveling with you as a loving and nurturing companion. So, proceed confident in the knowledge that you are entering into a profound conversation with a loving and nurturing God. You may face spiritual and emotional challenges during this retreat, but you need to trust in the holy desires that will fill your heart and mind. This is a moment for generosity, so may you have the courage to allow God changes during your journey together and through that transformation become an instrument of divine.

In the words of Saint Paul:
I bow my knees before the Father, from whom every family in heaven and on earth takes its name. I pray that, according to the riches of his glory, he may grant that you may be strengthened in your inner being with power through his Spirit, and that Christ may dwell in your hearts through faith, as you are being rooted and grounded in love. I pray that you may have the power to comprehend, with all the saints, what is the breadth and length and height and depth, and to know the love of Christ that surpasses knowledge, so that you may be filled with all the fullness of God.
(Ephesians 3:14-19)

Prelude
Praying with Jesus and Saint Patrick

During the days or weeks of this retreat, you will be accompanied by two companions: Jesus and Saint Patrick. So, it is important for you to have a clear image in your mind of how they look, speak and act.

Note: It is important to remember that these images are not intended to be historically accurate. Instead, they provide you with an image of how you perceive these two individuals and how you think they will act while you are with them.

Begin by calming yourself and putting aside all other concerns.

Then, when you are ready, allow an image of Jesus to come into your mind. He is alone, either standing or sitting. Look at him carefully, noting his physical features and demeanor as he looks back at you. Take your time with this first encounter and become aware of the love and care Jesus radiates toward you. After a short while, watch as a person approaches Jesus and observe how he interacts with that individual. Then, watch and listen as a crowd gathers around Jesus. Observe any nuances of his behavior that seem particularly unexpected and hear his voice as he speaks to different people.

Take as long as you need to make these observations. Then, remaining in your imagination, listen as Jesus instructs you, "Pray then in this way... Our Father in heaven, hallowed be your name. Your kingdom come. Your will be done, on earth as it is in heaven. Give us this day our daily bread. And forgive us our debts, as we also have forgiven our debtors. And do not bring us to the time of trial, but rescue us from the evil one." (Matthew 6:9-13)

Take a moment to linger in the sounds and resonances of Jesus' voice, then allow this image to fade from your consciousness before summarizing your impressions, reactions, and observations in your workbook.

Then, read the description of Saint Patrick presented on page 317.

Gradually, guided by the description, allow an image of Saint Patrick to emerge in your mind. He also is alone, either standing or sitting. Note his physical features and demeanor while he looks back at you. Again, take your time with this first encounter and be aware of how you feel in Patrick's presence. Consider power of his personality, how it manifests itself and his gaze toward you. Then, see other people approach Patrick – first a few and then many. Watch and listen as he engages these different people and speaks with them, noting any nuances in Patrick's behavior that seem unexpected while listening to the sound of his voice as he speaks with these different people.

As with your time with Jesus, take as long as you need to make these observations of Saint Patrick. Then, while remaining in your imagination as much as possible, listen to Patrick's voice as you read "The Deer's Cry" (found on page 321). Allow the rhythm and pace of your reading to be guided by Patrick's voice.

Linger in the sounds and resonances of Saint Patrick's voice for a moment. Then, allow this image to fade from your consciousness before summarizing your impressions, reactions, and observations in your workbook.

Note: It is important to remember that these impressions are intended as an aid to helping you imagine Jesus and Patrick during your periods of prayer. If you find your images of Jesus and Patrick changing during the retreat, you should embrace these transitions and record these new perceptions in your workbook as they occur.

1. Reliance upon God's Plan

1.1a   O Splendour Of God's Face
a prayer of gratitude for the Triune God's generosity

Take a moment to quiet your spirit, becoming completely present to this time and place. Allow all other thoughts and concerns to fall away as you come into the presence of God. Then, when you are ready, begin.

O Splendour of God's face,
Bringer of glory from above,
    True light, and Fount of every grace,
    Illume my day with faith and love.

Pour on my way, O Sun Divine,
Your holy truth with rays serene,
    And let the heavenly spirit shine
    With purging fires to make me clean.

A Hymn, sung or heard (optional)

O God, I believe in you; strengthen my belief.
I trust in you; confirm my trust.
    I love you; double my love.
    I repent that I angered you,
    Increase my repentance.

I adore you as first-beginning of my life.
I desire you as my last end.
    I give thanks to you as my ever-helper.
    I call upon you as my strong-defender.

Fill you my heart with awe without despair;
With hope, without over-confidence;
    With piety without infatuation;
    And with joy without excess.

My God, consent to guide me by your wisdom;
To constrain me by your right;
    To comfort me by your mercy;
    And to protect me by your power.

I offer to you all my thoughts, words, deeds and sufferings.
So that from hence-forward I may think on you faithfully,
> May converse of you lovingly, may labour for you devotedly,
> And may suffer for you cheerfully.

Read or recite Psalm 20.

Holy Triune God,
> Father, Son and Spirit

Under my thoughts may I God-thoughts find.
Half of my sins escape my mind.
> For what I said, or did not say,
> Pardon me, O Lord, I pray.

Read Romans 8: 28-39, aloud or quietly.

O Holy God,
> Father, Son and Spirit

If I were in Heaven my harp I would sound
With apostles and angels and saints all around,
> Praising and thanking the Son *who is* crowned,
> May the poor race of Eve for that heaven be bound!

I cry out to you, O Triune God.
Both morning and night.
> Come to me, guide me,
> And save me from fright,

And make me repentant
And wash me with tears,
> And lead me to heaven
> When spent are my years.

O Holy God,
> Father, Son and Spirit

For me is many a snare designed,
To fill my mind with doubts and fears;
> Far from the land of holy saints,
> I dwell within my vale of tears.

Let faith, let hope, let love –
Traits far above the cold world's way –
    With patience, humility, and awe,
    Become my guides from day to day.

I acknowledge, the evil I have done.
From the day of my birth till the day of my death,
    Through the sight of my eyes,
Through the hearing of my ears,
    Through the sayings of my mouth,
Through the thoughts of my heart,
    Through the touch of my hands,
Through the course of my way,
    Through all I said and did not,
Through all I promised and fulfilled not,
    Through all the laws and holy commandments I broke.
I ask even now absolution of you,
In the sweet name of Jesus Christ,
    For fear I may have never asked it as was right,
    And that I might not live to ask it again,

O Divine Majesty,
    Father, Son and Spirit
May you not let my soul stray from you,
May you keep me in a good state,
    May you turn me toward what is good to do,
    May you protect me from dangers, small and great.
May you fill my eyes with tears of repentance,
    So I may avoid the sinner's awful sentence.
May the Grace of the God for ever be with me,
    And whatever my needs, may the Triune God give me.

Select one of the following options for the Lord's Prayer.

Option A

O God,
Father, Son and Spirit,
Help me pray as Jesus himself taught:
    "Our Father in heaven,

> *hallowed be your name.*
> *Your kingdom come.*
> *Your will be done,*
> *on earth as it is in heaven.*
> *Give us this day our daily bread.*
> *And forgive us our debts,*
> *as we also have forgiven our debtors.*
> *And do not bring us to the time of trial,*
> *but rescue us from the evil one."*
> *(Matthew 6:9-13)*

From the foes of my land,
from the foes of my faith,
From the foes who would us dissever,
> O Trinity preserve me, in life, in death,
> With the Sign of the Cross for ever.
> *For the kingdom, the power, and the glory*
> *are yours now and for ever. Amen.*

Please proceed with "I beseech the wonderful and blessed Trinity,...," found after Option B.

Option B

O God,
Father, Son and Spirit,
Help me pray as Jesus himself taught:
> *Our Father in heaven,*
> *hallowed be your name,*
> *your kingdom come,*
> *your will be done,*
> *on earth as in heaven.*
> *Give us today our daily bread.*
> *Forgive us our sins*
> *as we forgive those who sin against us.*
> *Lead us not into temptation*
> *but deliver us from evil.*

From the foes of my land,
from the foes of my faith,
From the foes who would us dissever,
> O Trinity preserve me, in life, in death,

With the Sign of the Cross for ever.
*For the kingdom, the power, and the glory
are yours now and for ever. Amen.*

I beseech the wonderful and blessed Trinity,
God in Heaven, unsurpassed in power and might;
    Be behind me, Be on my left,
    Be before me, Be on my right!
Against each danger, God is my help;
In distress, upon the Divine Majesty I call.
    In dark times, may my God sustain me
    And lift me up again when I fall.
Lord over heaven and of earth,
The Triune God knows my offenses.
    Yet, listening to my pleadings,
    Guides me away from sinful pretenses.
Lord of all creation and the many creatures,
My God bestows on me many earthly treasures.
    Revealing love in each life and season,
    My God shares with me heavenly pleasures.
May the Holy Trinity arouse me
In moments both of joy and of strife;
    God the Father, with Mary's mighty Son,
    And the noble Spirit, bring me new life!

A Hymn, sung or heard (optional)

O Divine Majesty,
Three in one Godhead, without division.
    You are my riches, my store, my provision,
My star through the years
When troubles rend me,
    Through times of strife and tears,
    O God, defend me.

Confirm me in your love divine,
Smooth for my feet life's rugged way;
    My will with yours entwine,
    Lest evil lead my steps astray.

Be with me still as guard and guide,
Keep me in holy sanctity,
    Let my firm faith on you abide,
    From fraud and error hold me free.

End this time of prayer by taking some time to bring to mind the various ways God shields you from harm or guides you through the world's tumult. Then, when you are ready, conclude by saying:

O Holy Triune God,
Father, Son and Spirit,
I place myself at the edge of your grace,
    On the floor of your house myself I place,
And to banish the sin of my heart away,
    I lower my knee to you this day.
Through life's torrents of pain may you bring me whole,
    And, O Blessed Trinity, preserve also my soul. Amen.

1.1b Preparation for Prayer

Consideration of the Readings

After reciting or prayerfully reading the prayer sequence for this day or week:
- Read Jeremiah 29:11-14. Allow yourself to linger on any thoughts or phrases that seem particularly meaningful to you or especially relevant to your life. Then, record these highlights in your workbook so you will remember them during the meditations on these readings during this day or week of prayer.
- Read Isaiah 55:1-13. Again, pay careful attention to any phrases or images that seem particularly meaningful to you. Then, record these highlights in your workbook so you will remember them during this day or week of prayer.
- Read Romans 8:28-39. Again, note any phrases or images that seem particularly meaningful to you and record these highlights in your workbook.

Note: *You also should take a moment to consider any aspect of the prayer sequence from this day or week that seemed particularly significant to you.*

Contemplation of Your Needs

When you are ready, concentrating on your breath or an object near you, allow any distractions to fade from your consciousness as you become aware of your desire to live in God's goodness. Feel yourself yearning to properly use the many gifts God has given you, to experience God's continuing care, and to be open to the immense love God shows for you, then:
- Read "The Leper and the Floating Stone" (found on page 317). Allow yourself to linger on any thoughts, phrases or images that seem particularly meaningful or significant to your earlier preparations or prayer.
- Pray for your desires in the coming day or week. Ask that the divine presence all around you may be revealed so all your intentions and actions may be directed purely to the service and praise of God.

Ask also to feel a deepening desire to recognize and to be open to God's activity in your life.
• Conclude by praying for the faith to trust in God's plan for you and the love and protection at the heart of God's presence in your life.
Then, take a moment record any significant thoughts, emotions, or reactions from these moments in your workbook.

After this, put your notes aside. Without straining your memory, consider in turn each of the readings for the coming day or week and allow them to take shape in your imagination – even if all you remember are small fragments. Prayerfully ponder how each reading affects you emotionally without overtly thinking about their content, asking God to illuminate the spiritual gifts offered in each reading – quieting your mind and creating a receptive space in yourself to see or hear the response.

Finally, conclude by allowing these desires to fade from your consciousness as you offer this traditional Irish prayer collected by Douglas Hyde in *The Religious Songs of Connacht*:
> O God, I believe in you; strengthen my belief.
> I trust in you; confirm my trust.
> I love you; double my love.
> I repent that I angered you,
> Increase my repentance.
> Fill you my heart with awe without despair;
> With hope, without over-confidence;
> With piety without infatuation;
> And with joy without excess.
> My God, consent to guide me by your wisdom;
> To constrain me by your right;
> To comfort me by your mercy;
> And to protect me by your power. Amen.

Allow these words to linger on your mind and in your heart for a few moments and then, while they are still fresh in your memory, write the most important thoughts, feelings, and desires from this preparatory time in your workbook.

1.2   A Meditation on Jeremiah 29:11-14

In this meditation on Jeremiah 29:11-14, you will see and hear Saint Patrick teaching his disciples to trust in God's plan for them.

[1]   Begin by reading the biblical selection and reviewing your notes on it from your earlier preparations.

[2]   Then, focus on this specific time and place as you allow all other concerns to fall away. Then, when you are ready, consider the people and place in this moment of prayer.

- Allow an image of Patrick to emerge in your imagination, noting his physical characteristics and mannerisms. Look at what he is wearing or carrying, observing his clothing and any objects he is holding. Make a note of whether he is sitting, standing, or walking. Ponder this mental image, allowing any other observations about Patrick to form in your mind.

- Then, observe the disciples around Saint Patrick. Note how many disciples are with Patrick, making a mental note of their appearance and demeanor. Observe whether they are sitting, standing, or walking. Take a moment to ponder this mental image, allowing other impressions of these people to form. Become familiar with the men and women you will encounter during your prayer as well as their behavior.

- Gradually, allow yourself to become aware of the location of this moment of prayer. Observe whether it is inside or outside, paying attention to its physical characteristics and the arrangement of the people in it. As you ponder this mental image, look around the place and notice more details about it – noting if it is in dim or bright light, if it is still and silent or filled with noise, if it has an unusual smell or not, etc. Become familiar with the location of your upcoming prayer.

- Take a moment to remain in this place with these people, then allow these images to fade from your consciousness.

[3]   After you become still, become aware of your desires during this moment of prayer. Remember your desire to experience the divine presence all around you and to trust in God's plan for you, asking that all your intentions and actions may be directed purely to the service and praise of God. Reassert your trust in the love and protection at the heart of God's presence in your life while reaffirming your desire to open yourself to God's plan for you.

As these desires fill your consciousness, let all other concerns fall aside as you focus on this specific time and place of prayer.

[4]   Again, when you are ready, allow the image of Saint Patrick and his disciples to reemerge in your imagination.

• Watch as the group assembles around Patrick. Listen to the sounds of this moment and become comfortable as you prepare to hear Patrick speak. Feel the anticipation of the people around you and share in that enthusiasm.

• As you hear Patrick invite his companions to pray, ask God to help you share in their prayer – either by joining them as they pray or by listening quietly to them. Focus your attention on Saint Patrick, noting his physical appearance and his emotional demeanor.

• Then, watch and listen as Patrick speaks the words of Jeremiah. You may want to quietly read the passage while remaining prayerfully aware of your mental image of Patrick or you may choose to stay completely within the imagined realm of your prayer. Whichever you choose, know that God will offer you the words from the biblical passage that you need to hear – even if only in fragments.

• Afterward, hear Patrick explain the passage. Listen to him as he explains the meaning and significance of God's promise expressed in Jeremiah's words.

– Again, look around as Patrick speaks and see the reactions of his disciples. Become aware of their feelings and how they behave toward Patrick and one another.

– Remember that Patrick is speaking to men and women struggling to remain faithful to God's desires and promises while living difficult lives which challenge their faith. Remember that he also is speaking to you.

• After Saint Patrick finishes speaking, allow his image and this place to fade from your imagination as you become aware of the phrases and images from this moment of prayer which touched you most deeply. Recall the emotions and memories – including any sounds or smells – evoked during your prayer. Allow these seminal aspects of your meditation to linger on your mind and in your heart, making a mental note of any special feelings evoked by them.

[5]   When you are ready, become aware of God's presence – experienced in your imagination either as a single entity or as the Holy Trinity – with you in this moment and begin an open and informal conversation about this prayer period and how the passage from Jeremiah expresses your own needs or desires as you begin this retreat.

> <u>Note:</u> *This type of intimate conversation – either with God or Jesus – will be a distinguishing feature of your journey through the Spiritual Exercises. Saint Ignatius calls this conversational prayer a colloquy, saying it should "be made similarly to the language of a friend to a friend, or of a servant to his Lord; now by asking some favour, now by accusing myself of some fault; sometimes by communicating my own affairs of any kind, and asking counsel or help concerning them (Sp.Ex. #54)."*

In this conversation, be completely honest about your desires and fears in prayer and in your life outside the retreat while also making certain to give space for God to respond or to highlight different aspects from the biblical selection and your experiences during this meditation. Then, gradually allow your thoughts to recede as you focus on God's broader presence in your life and in the world around you.

[6] Finally, conclude by allowing these desires to fade from your consciousness as you offer this traditional Irish prayer collected by Douglas Hyde in *The Religious Songs of Connacht*:

> *Confirm me in your love divine,*
> *Smooth for my feet life's rugged way;*
> *My will with yours entwine,*
> *Lest evil lead my steps astray.*
> *Be with me still as guard and guide,*
> *Keep me in holy sanctity,*
> *Let my firm faith on you abide,*
> *From fraud and error hold me free. Amen.*

[7] Afterward, take 10-15 minutes in a quiet space to reflect on the most significant moments from this time of prayer and record your reflections in your retreat journal.

1.3   A Contemplation of Isaiah 55:1-13

In this contemplation of Isaiah 55:1-13, you will see and hear Jesus preaching to a crowd about their need to remain faithful to God's plan for his children.

[1]   Begin by reading the biblical selection and reviewing your notes on it from your earlier preparations.

[2]   Then, focus on this specific time and place as you allow all other concerns to fall away. Then, when you are ready, consider the people and place in this moment of prayer.

- Allow an image of Jesus to emerge in your imagination, noting his physical characteristics and mannerisms. Look at what he is wearing or carrying, observing his clothing and any objects he is holding. Make a note of whether he is sitting, standing, or walking. Ponder this mental image, allowing any other observations about Jesus to form in your mind.

- Then, observe the people around Jesus. Note how many people are with Jesus, making a mental note of their appearance and demeanor. Look at Jesus' disciples, observing where they are standing and how they behave toward Jesus. Look at the crowd, noting their attitude and behavior toward Jesus. Observe whether the people are sitting, standing, or walking. Take a moment to ponder this mental image, allowing other impressions of these men and women to form. Become familiar with the men and women you will encounter during your prayer as well as their behavior.

- Gradually, allow yourself to become aware of the location of this moment of prayer. Pay attention to its physical characteristics and the arrangement of the people in it. As you ponder this mental image, look around the place and notice more details about it – noting if it is in dim or bright light, if it is still and silent or filled with noise, if it has an unusual smell or not, etc. Become familiar with the location of your upcoming prayer.

- Take a moment to remain in this place with these people, then allow these images to fade from your consciousness.

[3]   After you become still, become aware of your desires during this moment of prayer. Remember your desire to experience the divine presence all around you and to trust in God's plan for you, asking that all your intentions and actions may be directed purely to the service and praise of God. Reassert your trust in the love and protection at the

heart of God's presence in your life while reaffirming your desire to open yourself to God's plan for you.

As these desires fill your consciousness, let all other concerns fall aside as you focus on this specific time and place of prayer.

[4]   Again, when you are ready, allow the image of Jesus and his disciples to reemerge in your imagination.

• Watch as the group assembles around Jesus. Listen to the sounds of this moment and become comfortable as you prepare to hear Jesus speak. Feel the anticipation of the people around you and share in that enthusiasm.

• As you hear Jesus begin to calm the crowd, ask God to help you share in their experience – either by joining them or by listening quietly to them. Focus your attention on Jesus, noting his physical appearance and his emotional demeanor.

• Then, watch and listen as Jesus speaks the words of Isaiah. You may want to quietly read the passage while remaining prayerfully aware of your mental image of Jesus or you may choose to stay completely within the imagined realm of your prayer. Whichever you choose, know that God will offer you the words from the biblical passage that you need to hear – even if only in fragments.

• Afterward, hear Jesus explain the passage. Listen to him as he explains the meaning and significance of God's promise expressed in Isaiah's words.

– Again, look around as Jesus speaks and see the reactions of his disciples and the people in the crowd. Become aware of their feelings and how they behave toward Jesus and one another.

– Remember that Jesus is speaking to men and women struggling to remain faithful to God's desires and promises while living difficult lives which challenge their faith. Remember that he also is speaking to you.

• After Jesus finishes speaking, allow his image and this place to fade from your imagination as you become aware of the phrases and images from this moment of prayer which touched you most deeply. Recall the emotions and memories – including any sounds or smells – evoked during your prayer. Allow these seminal aspects of your meditation to linger on your mind and in your heart, making a mental note of any special feelings evoked by them.

[5]   When you are ready, become aware of God's presence – again, experienced in your imagination either as a single entity or as the Holy Trinity – with you in this moment and begin an open and informal

conversation about this prayer period and how the passage from Isaiah expresses your own needs or desires. Remember Saint Ignatius' admonition that this colloquy should reflect "the language of a friend to a friend, or of a servant to his Lord; now by asking some favour, now by accusing myself of some fault; sometimes by communicating my own affairs of any kind, and asking counsel or help concerning them." Again, be certain to give space for God to respond or to highlight different aspects from the biblical selection and your experiences during this contemplation. Then, gradually allow your thoughts to recede as you focus on God's broader presence in your life and in the world around you.

[6]   Finally, conclude by allowing these desires to fade from your consciousness as you offer this traditional Irish prayer collected by Douglas Hyde in *The Religious Songs of Connacht*:

> *Confirm me in your love divine,*
> *Smooth for my feet life's rugged way;*
> *My will with yours entwine,*
> *Lest evil lead my steps astray.*
> *Be with me still as guard and guide,*
> *Keep me in holy sanctity,*
> *Let my firm faith on you abide,*
> *From fraud and error hold me free. Amen.*

[7]   Afterward, take 10-15 minutes in a quiet space to reflect on the most significant moments from this time of prayer and record your reflections in your retreat journal.

1.4   A Meditation on Romans 8:28-39

In this meditation on Romans 8:28-39, you will see and hear Saint Patrick preaching to a crowd about their need to trust in God's loving providence.

[1]   Begin by reading the biblical selection and reviewing your notes on it from your earlier preparations.

[2]   Then, focus on this specific time and place as you allow all other concerns to fall away. Then, when you are ready, consider the people and place in this moment of prayer.

- Allow an image of Patrick to emerge in your imagination, noting his physical characteristics and mannerisms. Look at what he is wearing or carrying, observing his clothing and any objects he is holding. Make a note of whether he is sitting, standing, or walking. Ponder this mental image, allowing any other observations about Patrick to form in your mind.

- Then, observe the people around Saint Patrick. Note how many people are with Patrick, making a mental note of their appearance and demeanor. Look at Patrick's disciples, observing where they are standing and how they behave toward Patrick. Look at the crowd, noting their attitude and behavior toward Saint Patrick. Observe whether the people are sitting, standing, or walking. Take a moment to ponder this mental image, allowing other impressions of these people to form. Become familiar with the men and women you will encounter during your prayer as well as their behavior.

- Gradually, allow yourself to become aware of the location of this encounter with Patrick. Pay attention to its physical characteristics and the arrangement of the people in it. As you ponder this mental image, look around the place and notice more details about it – noting if it is in dim or bright light, if it is still and silent or filled with noise, if it has an unusual smell or not, etc. Become familiar with the location of your upcoming prayer.

- Take a moment to remain in this place with these people, then allow these images to fade from your consciousness.

[3]   After you become still, become aware of your desires during this moment of prayer. Remember your desire to experience the divine presence all around you and to trust in God's plan for you, asking that all your intentions and actions may be directed purely to the service and praise of God. Reassert your trust in the love and protection at the

heart of God's presence in your life while reaffirming your desire to open yourself to God's plan for you.

As these desires fill your consciousness, let all other concerns fall aside as you focus on this specific time and place of prayer.

[4]   Again, when you are ready, allow the image of Saint Patrick and his disciples to reemerge in your imagination.

• Watch as the group assembles around Patrick. Listen to the sounds of this moment and become comfortable as you prepare to hear Patrick speak. Feel the anticipation of the people around you and share in that enthusiasm.

• As you hear Saint Patrick begin to calm the crowd, ask God to help you share in their experience – either by joining them or by listening quietly to them. Focus your attention on Patrick, noting his physical appearance and his emotional demeanor.

• Then, watch and listen as Patrick speaks the words of Saint Paul's letter to the Romans. You may want to quietly read the passage while remaining prayerfully aware of your mental image of Patrick or you may choose to stay completely within the imagined realm of your prayer. Whichever you choose, know that God will offer you the words from the biblical passage that you need to hear – even if only in fragments.

• Afterward, hear Saint Patrick explain the passage. Listen to him as he explains the meaning and significance of God's promise expressed in Paul's epistle.

– Again, look around as Patrick speaks and see the reactions of his disciples and the people in the crowd. Become aware of their feelings and how they behave toward Patrick and one another.

– Remember that Patrick is speaking to men and women struggling to remain faithful to God's desires and promises while living difficult lives which challenge their faith. Remember that he also is speaking to you.

• After Patrick finishes speaking, allow his image and this place to fade from your imagination as you become aware of phrases and images from this moment of prayer which touched you most deeply. Recall the emotions and memories – including any sounds or smells – evoked during your prayer. Allow these seminal aspects of your meditation to linger on your mind and in your heart, making a mental note of any special feelings evoked by them.

[5]   When you are ready, become aware of God's presence – again, experienced either as a single entity or as the Holy Trinity – with you

in this moment and begin an open and informal conversation about this prayer period and how the passage from Paul's epistle expresses your own needs or desires. Again, remember Saint Ignatius' admonition that this colloquy should reflect "the language of a friend to a friend, or of a servant to his Lord" as you give space for God to respond or to highlight different aspects from the biblical selection and your experiences during this meditation. Then, gradually allow your thoughts to recede as you focus on God's broader presence in your life and in the world around you.

[6] Finally, conclude by allowing these desires to fade from your consciousness as you offer this traditional Irish prayer collected by Douglas Hyde in *The Religious Songs of Connacht*:

> *Confirm me in your love divine,*
> *Smooth for my feet life's rugged way;*
> *My will with yours entwine,*
> *Lest evil lead my steps astray.*
> *Be with me still as guard and guide,*
> *Keep me in holy sanctity,*
> *Let my firm faith on you abide,*
> *From fraud and error hold me free. Amen.*

[7] Afterward, take 10-15 minutes in a quiet space to reflect on the most significant moments from this time of prayer and record your reflections in your retreat journal.

1.5 A Repeated Contemplation of Isaiah 55:1-13

In this repeated contemplation of Isaiah 55:1-13, you again will see and hear Jesus preaching to a crowd about their need to remain faithful to God's plan for his children.

[1] Begin by re-reading the biblical selection and reviewing your notes on it from your earlier preparations as well as the notes from your earlier prayer on this passage.

[2] Then, focus on this specific time and place as you allow all other concerns to fall away. Then, when you are ready, consider the people and place in this moment of prayer.

- Allow an image of Jesus to emerge in your imagination, noting his physical characteristics and mannerisms. Look at what he is wearing or carrying, observing his clothing and any objects he is holding. Make a note of whether he is sitting, standing, or walking. Ponder this mental image, allowing any other observations about Jesus to form in your mind.

- Then, observe the people around Jesus. Note how many people are with Jesus, making a mental note of their appearance and demeanor. Look at Jesus' disciples, observing where they are standing and how they behave toward Jesus. Look at the crowd, noting their attitude and behavior toward Jesus. Observe whether the people are sitting, standing, or walking. Take a moment to ponder this mental image, allowing other impressions of these people to form. Become familiar with the men and women you will encounter during your prayer as well as their behavior.

- Gradually, allow yourself to become aware of the location of this moment of prayer. Pay attention to its physical characteristics and the arrangement of the people in it. As you ponder this mental image, look around the place and notice more details about it – noting if it is in dim or bright light, if it is still and silent or filled with noise, if it has an unusual smell or not, etc. Become familiar with the location of your upcoming prayer.

- Take a moment to remain in this place with these people, then allow these images to fade from your consciousness.

[3] After you become still, become aware of your desires during this moment of prayer. Remember your desire to experience the divine presence all around you and to trust in God's plan for you, asking that all your intentions and actions may be directed purely to the service

and praise of God. Reassert your trust in the love and protection at the heart of God's presence in your life while reaffirming your desire to open yourself to God's plan for you.

As these desires fill your consciousness, let all other concerns fall aside as you focus on this specific time and place of prayer.

[4]   Again, when you are ready, allow the image of Jesus and his disciples to reemerge in your imagination.

- Watch as the group assembles around Jesus. Listen to the sounds of this moment and become comfortable as you prepare to hear Jesus speak. Feel the anticipation of the people around you and share in that enthusiasm.

- As you hear Jesus begin to calm the crowd, ask God to help you share in their experience – either by joining them or by listening quietly to them. Focus your attention on Jesus, noting his physical appearance and his emotional demeanor.

- Then, watch and listen as Jesus speaks the words of Isaiah. You may want to quietly read the passage while remaining prayerfully aware of your mental image of Jesus or you may choose to stay completely within the imagined realm of your prayer. Whichever you choose, know that God will offer you the words from the biblical passage that you need to hear – even if only in fragments.

- Afterward, hear Jesus explain the passage. Listen to him as he explains the meaning and significance of God's promise expressed in Isaiah.

– Again, look around as Jesus speaks and see the reactions of his disciples and the people in the crowd. Become aware of their feelings and how they behave toward Jesus and one another.

– Remember that Jesus is speaking to men and women struggling to remain faithful to God's desires and promises while living difficult lives which challenge their faith. Remember that he also is speaking to you.

- After Jesus finishes speaking, allow his image and this place to fade from your imagination as you become aware of the phrases and images from this moment of prayer which touched you most deeply. Recall the emotions and memories – including any sounds or smells – evoked during your prayer. Allow these seminal aspects of your meditation to linger on your mind and in your heart, making a mental note of any special feelings evoked by them.

[5]   When you are ready, become aware of God's presence – either as a single entity or as the Holy Trinity – with you in this moment and

have an open and informal conversation about this prayer period and how the passage from Isaiah expresses your own needs or desires – giving space for God to respond or to highlight different aspects from the biblical selection and your experiences during this contemplation. Then, gradually allow your thoughts to recede as you focus on God's broader presence in your life and in the world around you.

[6]   Finally, conclude by allowing these desires to fade from your consciousness as you offer this traditional Irish prayer collected by Douglas Hyde in *The Religious Songs of Connacht*:

> *Confirm me in your love divine,*
> *Smooth for my feet life's rugged way;*
> *My will with yours entwine,*
> *Lest evil lead my steps astray.*
> *Be with me still as guard and guide,*
> *Keep me in holy sanctity,*
> *Let my firm faith on you abide,*
> *From fraud and error hold me free. Amen.*

[7]   Afterward, take 10-15 minutes in a quiet space to reflect on the most significant moments from this time of prayer and record your reflections in your retreat journal.

1.6 An Application of the Senses

[1]   Become aware of your prayerful desires during this day or week. Bring to mind your desire to experience the divine presence all around you and to trust in God's plan for you. Focus on your desire that all your intentions and actions may be directed purely to the service and praise of God. Finally, recognize your need to trust in the love and protection at the heart of God's presence in your life to open yourself fully to God's plan for you.

[2]   When you are ready, in your imagination, call to mind the various prayers of the preceding day or days. Allow the images and words of these prayers to linger and then slowly fade from your consciousness.

• Remember your meditation on Jeremiah 29:11-14. Consider the images and feelings evoked in you during your prayer, feeling God's presence in these memories and becoming aware of the specific sensations associated with each image.

• Recall your contemplations of Isaiah 55:1-13, considering them in the same way as your memories of Jeremiah 29.

• Review your meditation on Romans 8:28-39 in the same manner as the previous meditations.

As these prayers enter your memory, make a mental note of which senses are most active. You may see an image or a color, hear a sound or a phrase, or smell a scent or a fragrance. You may even taste a flavor or feel a sensation on your skin.

[3]   Then, relax and allow these various memories and experiences to quietly enter and leave your consciousness without being controlled – whether they are clear or diffuse, whether they come quickly or slowly. Linger on the sensory images and memories being evoked in you – noticing any images or colors, any sounds or phrases, any scents or fragrances, any flavors or physical sensations associated with each prayer.

[4]   When you are ready, become completely still and clear your mind of all thoughts and concerns. Allow an image of a special personal space to form in your imagination, a place where you are completely comfortable and alone. Then, watch as God enters that place and forms a small image or object for you that expresses the thought or awareness that you most need to carry with you into your life.

Reverently pick up the object or image, a reflection of the most important gift you have been given during this time of prayer. Look at it carefully and become aware of the divine presence contained within it. Take a moment to register what it looks like and how it feels in your hand. Then, feel the joy and confidence that comes from touching the presence of God as you accept this gift, offering a short prayer of gratitude while you relax into the pleasure of this moment.

[5]   Then, conclude by allowing these images to fade from your consciousness as you offer this traditional Irish prayer collected by Douglas Hyde in *The Religious Songs of Connacht*:

> *Confirm me in your love divine,*
> *Smooth for my feet life's rugged way;*
> *My will with yours entwine,*
> *Lest evil lead my steps astray.*
> *Be with me still as guard and guide,*
> *Keep me in holy sanctity,*
> *Let my firm faith on you abide,*
> *From fraud and error hold me free. Amen.*

[6]   While your experiences are still fresh in your mind, record the most significant impressions or sensations from this time of prayer in your retreat journal.

1.7 Review of Prayer

[1]   Remember your desires during the preceding day or week of prayer. Become aware of our desire to experience the divine presence all around you and to trust in God's plan for you. Recall your desire that all your intentions and actions may be directed purely to the service and praise of God. Finally, reaffirm your need to trust in the love and protection at the heart of God's presence in your life.

After bringing these thoughts and desires into your consciousness, ask God once again to fulfill these desires in your own life and in your interactions with others.

[2]   Then, take a moment to allow the words, thoughts, and feelings from your prayers during the last day or week to linger – on your mind and in your heart – before asking God to reveal the fulfillment of your deepest desires in these various memories.

- Think about the prayer sequence at the beginning of this day or week. Make a mental note of any words, insights or images that remain particularly significant or meaningful to you.
- Ponder the story, "The Leper and the Floating Stone". Note any words, insights, or images from it that remain particularly significant or meaningful to you.
- Remember your meditation on Jeremiah 29:11-14.

– Consider the most powerful images, phrases, or feelings from your prayer. Ask yourself what gifts God gave to you through these moments, perhaps offering you new insights or perhaps affirming an important aspect of your faith. Ask yourself how God may be calling you to change through these moments, being as specific as possible.

– Examine your disposition as you prayed, noting whether prayer came easily or with resistance. Recall the easiest moments in your prayer and any moments of joy you may have experienced. Remember also if you encountered any difficulty opening yourself to God or if you felt any sadness as you prayed. Ask God to help you understand why these feelings surfaced.

– Bring to mind any moments when you added personal elements (e.g., familiar places or people from your life) or connected your prayers to other scriptures or spiritual writings. Ask yourself how these additions helped or hindered you as you prayed. Again, if you do not know why this happened, ask God to help you understand.

- Recall your contemplations of Isaiah 55:1-13. Then, review your prayer in the same way as your earlier reflection on Jeremiah 29.

- Review your meditation on Romans 8:28-39 in the same manner as the previous prayers.
- Reflect on the ebb and flow of sensory impressions and feelings that marked your application of the senses. Isolate the most memorable moments and sensory impressions from your prayer and reflect on how God used these moments to give you a particular gift, perhaps offering you new insights or changing you in some way.

[3]   Finally, ponder the times when images or feelings from the readings of this day or week surfaced outside these prayer periods. Consider those moments or events in which God's presence or guidance was especially strong as well as any moments when you were struggling. Think about the most memorable aspects of these experiences, asking God to explain their significance.

[4]   Take a moment to allow the words, thoughts, and feelings of these prayers to linger on your mind and in your heart. Finally, conclude by allowing these desires to fade from your consciousness as you offer this traditional Irish prayer collected by Douglas Hyde in *The Religious Songs of Connacht*:

> *O God, I believe in you; strengthen my belief.*
> *I trust in you; confirm my trust.*
> *I love you; double my love.*
> *I repent that I angered you,*
> *Increase my repentance.*
> *Fill you my heart with awe without despair;*
> *With hope, without over-confidence;*
> *With piety without infatuation;*
> *And with joy without excess.*
> *My God, consent to guide me by your wisdom;*
> *To constrain me by your right;*
> *To comfort me by your mercy;*
> *And to protect me by your power. Amen.*

[5]   After finishing these prayers, summarize your reflections on the gifts or graces you received during the prayers of this last day or week and record these thoughts in your retreat journal.

2. Living for God's Glory

2.1a   O Word Of Might, That Springing Forth
a prayer of gratitude and commitment to Jesus

Take a moment to quiet your spirit, becoming completely present to this time and place. Allow all other thoughts and concerns to fall away as you come into the presence of God. Then, when you are ready, begin.

O Word of Might, that springing forth
From out the Father's heart, was born
    To raise my fallen state on earth,
    Bring help, and leave me not forlorn.

Illume my breast with heavenly light,
And set my soul aflame with love,
    That I, forsaking things of night,
    Shall lift my hopes to joys above.

A Hymn, sung or heard (optional)

O Lord, make me wise in the things that pass near me.
    Valiant in danger, patient in tribulation,
    And humble in going forward through the world.

May I never forget
To put heed in my prayers,
    Moderation in my ways,
    Earnestness in my cares,
    And perseverance in the things I set before me.

O Lord, Jesus the Christ,
Stir me up to keep a right conscience,
    Give me courtesy on the out-side,
    Profitable conversation, and orderly bearing.

Vouchsafe me always
To get the upper hand of my natural disposition
    By inclining to your graces,
    By fulfilling your commandments,
    And by working out my salvation.

Show me, Lord, the nothingness of this world,
The majesty of heaven above,
> The shortness of time
> And the length of eternity.

Grant me to put myself into a state of fitness for death,
To be afraid of your judgment,
> To shun condemnation,
> And at last to gain heaven.

Read or recite Psalm 103.

Holy Lord,
Under my thoughts may I God-thoughts find.
Half of my sins escape my mind.
> For what I said, or did not say,
> Pardon me, O Lord, I pray.

Read Ephesians 1: 3-14, aloud or quietly.

O Lord, Jesus the Christ,
If I were in Heaven my harp I would sound
With apostles and angels and saints all around,
> Praising and thanking you who is crowned above,
> May the poor race of Eve for that heaven be bound!

Holy Lord,
In your hands I do lay my soul.
Let it not fall out of your control,
> Countenance brighter than the sun,
> Shield me from pain when the race is run.

The will of God be done by me,
The law of God be kept surely,
> My evil will controlled by me,
> My tongue in check be held securely,

Repentance timely made by me,
Your passion understood contritely,

Each sinful crime be shunned by me,
And my sins be mused nightly.

O Holy Lord,
    God with the Father and the Spirit,
For me is many a snare designed,
To fill my mind with doubts and fears;
    Far from the land of holy saints,
    I dwell within my vale of tears.
Let faith, let hope, let love –
Traits far above the cold world's way –
    With patience, humility, and awe,
    Become my guides from day to day.

I acknowledge, the evil I have done.
From the day of my birth till the day of my death,
    Through the sight of my eyes,
Through the hearing of my ears,
    Through the sayings of my mouth,
Through the thoughts of my heart,
    Through the touch of my hands,
Through the course of my way,
    Through all I said and did not,
Through all I promised and fulfilled not,
    Through all the laws and holy commandments I broke.
I ask even now absolution of you,
    For fear I may have never asked it as was right,
    And that I might not live to ask it again,

O Holy Lord, my King in Heaven,
May you not let my soul stray from you,
May you keep me in a good state,
    May you turn me toward what is good to do,
    May you protect me from dangers, small and great.
May you fill my eyes with tears of repentance,
    So I may avoid the sinner's awful sentence.
May the Grace of the God for ever be with me,
    And whatever my needs, may the Triune God give me.

Select one of the following options for the Lord's Prayer.

Option A

O Jesus Christ,
Lord of heaven and earth,
Help me pray as you yourself taught:
> "Our Father in heaven,
> hallowed be your name.
> Your kingdom come.
> Your will be done,
> on earth as it is in heaven.
> Give us this day our daily bread.
> And forgive us our debts,
> as we also have forgiven our debtors.
> And do not bring us to the time of trial,
> but rescue us from the evil one."
> *(Matthew 6:9-13)*

From the foes of my land,
from the foes of my faith,
From the foes who would us dissever,
> O Lord, preserve me, in life and in death,
> With the Sign of the Cross for ever.
> *For the kingdom, the power, and the glory*
> *are yours now and for ever. Amen.*

Please proceed with "I beseech you, O Lord...," found after Option B.

Option B

O Jesus Christ,
Lord of heaven and earth,
Help me pray as you yourself taught:
> *Our Father in heaven,*
> *hallowed be your name,*
> *your kingdom come,*
> *your will be done,*
> *on earth as in heaven.*
> *Give us today our daily bread.*
> *Forgive us our sins*

as we forgive those who sin against us.
Lead us not into temptation
but deliver us from evil.
From the foes of my land,
from the foes of my faith,
From the foes who would us dissever,
    O Lord, preserve me, in life and in death,
    With the Sign of the Cross for ever.
For the kingdom, the power, and the glory
are yours now and for ever. Amen.

I beseech you, O Lord.
God in Heaven, unsurpassed in power and might;
    Be behind me, Be on my left,
    Be before me, Be on my right!
Against each danger, you are my help;
In distress, upon you I call.
    In dark times, may you sustain me
    And lift me up again when I fall.
Lord over heaven and of earth,
You know my offenses.
    Yet, listening to my pleadings,
    You guide me away from sinful pretenses.
Lord of all creation and the many creatures,
You bestow on me many earthly treasures.
    Revealing love in each life and season,
    You share with me heavenly pleasures.
May you arouse me
In moments both of joy and of strife;
    Most holy Lord, bring me new life!

A Hymn, sung or heard (optional)

O Jesus Christ,
    Lord of heaven and earth,
You are my riches, my store, my provision,
    My star through the years
When troubles rend me,
    Through times of strife and tears,
    Sweet Jesus, defend me.

The faith that fires the holy heart,
The true believer's blessed hope,
    And perfect love, these powers impart,
    The strength with evil force to cope.

To me your tender mercy lend,
And hear the humble prayers I raise;
    In holy love my voice blend;
    Make strong my heart to sing your praise.

End this time of prayer by taking some time to bring to mind the various ways God shields you from harm or guides you through the world's tumult. Then, when you are ready, conclude by saying:

O Word of Might,
O Holy Lord, King in Heaven,
I place myself at the edge of your grace,
    On the floor of your house myself I place,
And to banish the sin of my heart away,
    I lower my knee to you this day.
Through life's torrents of pain may you bring me whole,
    And, O Lord Jesus Christ, preserve also my soul. Amen.

2.1b Preparation for Prayer

Consideration of the Readings

After reciting or prayerfully reading the prayer sequence for this day or week:

- Read the "Principle and Foundation" from *The Spiritual Exercises of Saint Ignatius* (found on page 309). Allow yourself to linger on any thoughts or phrases that seem particularly meaningful to you or especially relevant to your life. Then, record these highlights in your workbook so you will remember them during the meditations on these readings during this day or week of prayer.
- Read Ephesians 1:3-14. Again, pay careful attention to any phrases or images that seem particularly meaningful to you. Then, record these highlights in your workbook so you will remember them during this day or week of prayer.
- Read Isaiah 43:1-7. Again, note any phrases or images that seem particularly meaningful to you and record these highlights in your workbook.

Note: You also should take a moment to consider any aspect of the prayer sequence from this day or week that seemed particularly significant to you.

Contemplation of Your Needs

When you are ready, concentrating on your breath or an object near you, allow any distractions to fade from your consciousness as you become aware of your desire to live in God's goodness. Feel yourself yearning to properly use the many gifts God has given you, to experience God's continuing care, and to be open to the immense love God shows for you, then:

- Read "Patrick Receives the Staff of Jesus" (found on page 317). Allow yourself to linger on any thoughts, phrases or images that seem particularly meaningful or significant to your earlier preparations or prayer.
- Pray for your desires in the coming day or week. Ask that the divine presence all around you may be revealed so all your intentions and actions may be directed purely to the service and praise of God.

Ask also for the wisdom to recognize the invitation to live for God's glory through your life choices and to respond faithfully as God calls you to action.
- Conclude by praying for the strength and trust to respond to God's desires for you.

Then, take a moment record any significant thoughts, emotions, or reactions from these moments in your workbook.

After this, put your notes aside. Without straining your memory, consider in turn each of the readings for the coming day or week and allow them to take shape in your imagination – even if all you remember are small fragments. Prayerfully ponder how each reading affects you emotionally without overtly thinking about their content, asking God to illuminate the spiritual gifts offered in each reading – quieting your mind and creating a receptive space in yourself to see or hear the response.

Finally, conclude by allowing these desires to fade from your consciousness as you offer this traditional Irish prayer collected by Douglas Hyde in *The Religious Songs of Connacht*:

> O God, I believe in you; strengthen my belief.
> I trust in you; confirm my trust.
> I love you; double my love.
> I repent that I angered you,
> Increase my repentance.
> Fill you my heart with awe without despair;
> With hope, without over-confidence;
> With piety without infatuation;
> And with joy without excess.
> My God, consent to guide me by your wisdom;
> To constrain me by your right;
> To comfort me by your mercy;
> And to protect me by your power. Amen.

Allow these words to linger on your mind and in your heart for a few moments and then, while they are still fresh in your memory, write the most important thoughts, feelings, and desires from this preparatory time in your workbook.

2.2 A Consideration of the Principle and Foundation

In this consideration, you will reflect upon the words and spiritual vision of the "Principle and Foundation" presented in *The Spiritual Exercises of Saint Ignatius*.

[1]   Begin by reading the "Principle and Foundation" in *The Spiritual Exercises of Saint Ignatius* (found on page 309) and reviewing your notes on it from your preparations.

[2]   Then, focus on this specific time and place as you allow all other concerns to fall away. As you become still, become aware of your desires during this moment of prayer. Remember your desire to experience the divine presence all around you so all your intentions and actions may be directed purely to the service and praise of God. Reassert your desire to live for God's glory through your life choices, to respond faithfully as God calls you to action. Finally, recall your need for divine assistance to fulfill God's desires for you.

As these desires fill your consciousness, let all other concerns fall aside as you focus on this specific time and place of prayer.

[3]   Then, slowly and deliberately, re-read the "Principle and Foundation".

- As you read, take time to stop and ponder each statement within it as you read. When you pause, allow images shaped by the words and thoughts of the passages to form in your imagination. See and hear the way each statement expresses a need or desire in your life.

- Take more time with passages that seem particularly significant or meaning to you. Become aware of the passages from the "Principle and Foundation" which you accept easily and any of those which cause you difficulty. Clarify these thoughts and feeling as much as possible while remaining focused on each specific statement within the "Principle and Foundation".

- After finishing the reading, allow the various words and images of your prayer to flow freely in your consciousness without being controlled. Become aware of those aspects of the "Principle and Foundation" that arouse positive desires in you, toward God and toward others (including nonhuman creatures). Become aware of those aspects of the reading that make you feel shame for those times you fall short of these ideals.

- When you are ready, allow these thoughts and images to fade from your consciousness and become aware of God's presence with you in this moment. Then, have an open and informal conversation about your experience of the Principle and Foundation. Speak candidly about how it expresses your own desires and fears, giving space for God to respond to your concerns or to explain the divine desires expressed in the Principle and Foundation.

• Then, gradually allow your thoughts to recede as you focus on God's broader presence in your life and in the world around you.

[4] Finally, conclude by allowing these desires to fade from your consciousness as you offer this traditional Irish prayer collected by Douglas Hyde in *The Religious Songs of Connacht*:

Confirm me in your love divine,
Smooth for my feet life's rugged way;
My will with yours entwine,
Lest evil lead my steps astray.
Be with me still as guard and guide,
Keep me in holy sanctity,
Let my firm faith on you abide,
From fraud and error hold me free. Amen.

[5] Afterward, take 10-15 minutes in a quiet space to reflect on the most significant moments from this time of prayer and record your reflections in your retreat journal.

2.3   A Meditation on Ephesians 1:3-14

In this meditation on Ephesians 1:3-14, you will see and hear Saint Patrick admonish his disciples to live as sons and daughters of God.

[1]   Begin by reading the biblical selection and reviewing your notes on it from your earlier preparations.

[2]   Then, focus on this specific time and place as you allow all other concerns to fall away. Then, when you are ready, consider the people and place in this moment of prayer.

- Allow an image of Patrick to emerge in your imagination, noting his physical characteristics and mannerisms. Look at what he is wearing or carrying, observing his clothing and any objects he is holding. Make a note of whether he is sitting, standing, or walking. Ponder this mental image, allowing any other observations about Patrick to form in your mind.

- Then, observe the disciples around Saint Patrick. Note how many people are with Patrick, making a mental note of their appearance and demeanor. Observe whether they are sitting, standing, or walking. Take a moment to ponder this mental image, allowing other impressions of these people to form. Become familiar with the men and women you will encounter during your prayer as well as their behavior.

- Gradually, allow yourself to become aware of the location of this moment of prayer. Observe whether it is inside or outside, paying attention to its physical characteristics and the arrangement of the people in it. As you ponder this mental image, look around the place and notice more details about it – noting if it is in dim or bright light, if it is still and silent or filled with noise, if it has an unusual smell or not, etc. Become familiar with the location of your upcoming prayer.

- Take a moment to remain in this place with these people, then allow these images to fade from your consciousness.

[3]   After you become still, become aware of your desires during this moment of prayer. Remember your desire to experience the divine presence all around you so all your intentions and actions may be directed purely to the service and praise of God. Reassert your desire to live for God's glory through your life choices, to respond faithfully as God calls you to action. Finally, recall your need for divine assistance to fulfill God's desires for you.

As these desires fill your consciousness, let all other concerns fall aside as you focus on this specific time and place of prayer.

[4]   Again, when you are ready, allow the image of Saint Patrick and his disciples to reemerge in your imagination.

• Watch as the group assembles around Patrick. Listen to the sounds of this moment and become comfortable as you prepare to hear Patrick speak. Feel the anticipation of the people around you and share in that enthusiasm.

• As you hear Patrick quiet his companions, ask God to help you share in their experience – either by joining them or by listening quietly to them. Focus your attention on Saint Patrick, noting his physical appearance and his emotional demeanor.

• Then, watch and listen as Patrick speaks the words of Saint Paul's letter to the Ephesians. You may want to quietly read the passage while remaining prayerfully aware of your mental image of Patrick or you may choose to stay completely within the imagined realm of your prayer. Whichever you choose, know that God will offer you the words from the biblical passage that you need to hear – even if only in fragments.

• Afterward, hear Patrick explain the passage. Listen to him as he explains the meaning and significance of God's promise expressed in Saint Paul's epistle.

– Again, look around as Patrick speaks and see the reactions of his disciples and the people in the crowd. Become aware of their feelings and how they behave toward Patrick and one another.

– Remember that Patrick is speaking to men and women struggling to remain faithful to God's desires and promises while living difficult lives which challenge their faith. Remember that he also is speaking to you.

• After Saint Patrick finishes speaking, allow his image and this place to fade from your imagination as you become aware of the phrases and images from this moment of prayer which touched you most deeply. Recall the emotions and memories – including any sounds or smells – evoked during your prayer. Allow these seminal aspects of your meditation to linger on your mind and in your heart, making a mental note of any special feelings evoked by them.

[5]   When you are ready, become aware of God's presence with you in this moment and have an open and informal conversation about this prayer period and how the passage from Paul's epistle expresses your own needs or desires – giving space for God to respond or to

highlight different aspects from the biblical selection and your experiences during this meditation. Then, gradually allow your thoughts to recede as you focus on God's broader presence in your life and in the world around you.

[6] Finally, conclude by allowing these desires to fade from your consciousness as you offer this traditional Irish prayer collected by Douglas Hyde in *The Religious Songs of Connacht*:

> *Confirm me in your love divine,*
> *Smooth for my feet life's rugged way;*
> *My will with yours entwine,*
> *Lest evil lead my steps astray.*
> *Be with me still as guard and guide,*
> *Keep me in holy sanctity,*
> *Let my firm faith on you abide,*
> *From fraud and error hold me free. Amen.*

[7] Afterward, take 10-15 minutes in a quiet space to reflect on the most significant moments from this time of prayer and record your reflections in your retreat journal.

2.4 A Meditation on Isaiah 43:1-7

In this meditation on Isaiah 43:1-7, you will see and hear Saint Patrick preaching to a crowd about their need to trust in God's loving providence.

[1] Begin by reading the biblical selection and reviewing your notes on it from your earlier preparations.

[2] Then, focus on this specific time and place as you allow all other concerns to fall away. Then, when you are ready, consider the people and place in this moment of prayer.

- Allow an image of Patrick to emerge in your imagination, noting his physical characteristics and mannerisms. Look at what he is wearing or carrying, observing his clothing and any objects he is holding. Make a note of whether he is sitting, standing, or walking. Ponder this mental image, allowing any other observations about Patrick to form in your mind.

- Then, observe the people around Saint Patrick. Note how many people are with Patrick, making a mental note of their appearance and demeanor. Look at Patrick's disciples, observing where they are standing and how they behave toward Patrick. Look at the crowd, noting their attitude and behavior toward Saint Patrick. Observe whether the people are sitting, standing, or walking. Take a moment to ponder this mental image, allowing other impressions of these people to form. Become familiar with the men and women you will encounter during your prayer as well as their behavior.

- Gradually, allow yourself to become aware of the location of this encounter with Patrick. Pay attention to its physical characteristics and the arrangement of the people in it. As you ponder this mental image, look around the place and notice more details about it – noting if it is in dim or bright light, if it is still and silent or filled with noise, if it has an unusual smell or not, etc. Become familiar with the location of your upcoming prayer.

- Take a moment to remain in this place with these people, then allow these images to fade from your consciousness.

[3] After you become still, become aware of your desires during this moment of prayer. Remember your desire to experience the divine presence all around you so all your intentions and actions may be directed purely to the service and praise of God. Reassert your desire to live for God's glory through your life choices, to respond faithfully

as God calls you to action. Finally, recall your need for divine assistance to fulfill God's desires for you.

As these desires fill your consciousness, let all other concerns fall aside as you focus on this specific time and place of prayer.

[4]   Again, when you are ready, allow the image of Saint Patrick and his disciples to reemerge in your imagination.

- Watch as the group assembles around Patrick. Listen to the sounds of this moment and become comfortable as you prepare to hear Patrick speak. Feel the anticipation of the people around you and share in that enthusiasm.

- As you hear Saint Patrick quieting the crowd, ask God to help you share in their experience – either by joining them or by listening quietly to them. Focus your attention on Patrick, noting his physical appearance and his emotional demeanor.

- Then, watch and listen as Patrick speaks the words of Isaiah. You may want to quietly read the passage while remaining prayerfully aware of your mental image of Patrick or you may choose to stay completely within the imagined realm of your prayer. Whichever you choose, know that God will offer you the words from the biblical passage that you need to hear – even if only in fragments.

- Afterward, hear Saint Patrick explain the passage. Listen to him as he explains the meaning and significance of God's promise expressed in the words of Isaiah.

– Again, look around as Patrick speaks and see the reactions of his disciples and the people in the crowd. Become aware of their feelings and how they behave toward Patrick and one another.

– Remember that Patrick is speaking to men and women struggling to remain faithful to God's desires and promises while living difficult lives which challenge their faith. Remember that he also is speaking to you.

- After Patrick finishes speaking, allow his image and this place to fade from your imagination as you become aware of the phrases and images from this moment of prayer which touched you most deeply. Recall the emotions and memories – including any sounds or smells – evoked during your prayer. Allow these seminal aspects of your meditation to linger on your mind and in your heart, making a mental note of any special feelings evoked by them.

[5]   When you are ready, become aware of God's presence with you in this moment and have an open and informal conversation about this prayer period and how the passage from Isaiah expresses your own

needs or desires – giving space for God to respond or to highlight different aspects from the biblical selection and your experiences during this meditation. Then, gradually allow your thoughts to recede as you focus on God's broader presence in your life and in the world around you.

[6] Finally, conclude by allowing these desires to fade from your consciousness as you offer this traditional Irish prayer collected by Douglas Hyde in *The Religious Songs of Connacht*:

Confirm me in your love divine,
Smooth for my feet life's rugged way;
My will with yours entwine,
Lest evil lead my steps astray.
Be with me still as guard and guide,
Keep me in holy sanctity,
Let my firm faith on you abide,
From fraud and error hold me free. Amen.

[7] Afterward, take 10-15 minutes in a quiet space to reflect on the most significant moments from this time of prayer and record your reflections in your retreat journal.

2.5 A Repeated Meditation on Isaiah 43:1-7

In this repeated meditation on Isaiah 43:1-7, you again will see and hear Saint Patrick preaching to a crowd about their need to trust in God's loving providence.

[1]   Begin by re-reading the biblical selection and reviewing your notes on it from your earlier preparations.

[2]   Then, focus on this specific time and place as you allow all other concerns to fall away. Then, when you are ready, consider the people and place in this moment of prayer.

• Allow an image of Patrick to emerge in your imagination, noting his physical characteristics and mannerisms. Look at what he is wearing or carrying, observing his clothing and any objects he is holding. Make a note of whether he is sitting, standing, or walking. Ponder this mental image, allowing any other observations about Patrick to form in your mind.

• Then, observe the people around Saint Patrick. Note how many people are with Patrick, making a mental note of their appearance and demeanor. Look at Patrick's disciples, observing where they are standing and how they behave toward Patrick. Look at the crowd, noting their attitude and behavior toward Saint Patrick. Observe whether the people are sitting, standing, or walking. Take a moment to ponder this mental image, allowing other impressions of these people to form. Become familiar with the men and women you will encounter during your prayer as well as their behavior.

• Gradually, allow yourself to become aware of the location of this encounter with Patrick. Pay attention to its physical characteristics and the arrangement of the people in it. As you ponder this mental image, look around the place and notice more details about it – noting if it is in dim or bright light, if it is still and silent or filled with noise, if it has an unusual smell or not, etc. Become familiar with the location of your upcoming prayer.

• Take a moment to remain in this place with these people, then allow these images to fade from your consciousness.

[3]   After you become still, become aware of your desires during this moment of prayer. Remember your desire to experience the divine presence all around you so all your intentions and actions may be directed purely to the service and praise of God. Reassert your desire to live for God's glory through your life choices, to respond faithfully

as God calls you to action. Finally, recall your need for divine assistance to fulfill God's desires for you.

As these desires fill your consciousness, let all other concerns fall aside as you focus on this specific time and place of prayer.

[4]   Then, when you are ready, allow the image of Saint Patrick and his disciples to reemerge in your imagination.

- Watch as the group assembles around Patrick. Listen to the sounds of this moment and become comfortable as you prepare to hear Patrick speak. Feel the anticipation of the people around you and share in that enthusiasm.

- As you hear Saint Patrick quieting the crowd, ask God to help you share in their experience – either by joining them or by listening quietly to them. Focus your attention on Patrick, noting his physical appearance and his emotional demeanor.

- Then, watch and listen as Patrick speaks the words of Isaiah. You may want to quietly read the passage while remaining prayerfully aware of your mental image of Patrick or you may choose to stay completely within the imagined realm of your prayer. Whichever you choose, know that God will offer you the words from the biblical passage that you need to hear – even if only in fragments.

- Afterward, hear Saint Patrick explain the passage. Listen to him as he explains the meaning and significance of God's promise expressed in Isaiah.

– Again, look around as Patrick speaks and see the reactions of his disciples and the people in the crowd. Become aware of their feelings and how they behave toward Patrick and one another.

– Remember that Patrick is speaking to men and women struggling to remain faithful to God's desires and promises while living difficult lives which challenge their faith. Remember that he also is speaking to you.

- After Patrick finishes speaking, allow his image and this place to fade from your imagination as you become aware of the phrases and images from this moment of prayer which touched you most deeply. Recall the emotions and memories – including any sounds or smells – evoked during your prayer. Allow these seminal aspects of your meditation to linger on your mind and in your heart, making a mental note of any special feelings evoked by them.

[5]   When you are ready, become aware of God's presence with you in this moment and have an open and informal conversation about this prayer period and how the passage from Isaiah expresses your own

needs or desires – giving space for God to respond or to highlight different aspects from the biblical selection and your experiences during this meditation. Then, gradually allow your thoughts to recede as you focus on God's broader presence in your life and in the world around you.

[6]   Finally, conclude by allowing these desires to fade from your consciousness as you offer this traditional Irish prayer collected by Douglas Hyde in *The Religious Songs of Connacht*:

> *Confirm me in your love divine,*
> *Smooth for my feet life's rugged way;*
> *My will with yours entwine,*
> *Lest evil lead my steps astray.*
> *Be with my still as guard and guide,*
> *Keep me in holy sanctity,*
> *Let my firm faith on you abide,*
> *From fraud and error hold me free. Amen.*

[7]   Afterward, take 10-15 minutes in a quiet space to reflect on the most significant moments from this time of prayer and record your reflections in your retreat journal.

2.6 An Application of the Senses

[1]   Become aware of your prayerful desires during this day or week. Bring to mind to experience the divine presence all around you so all your intentions and actions may be directed purely to the service and praise of God. Focus on your desire to live for God's glory through your life choices, to respond faithfully as God calls you to action. Finally, recognize your need for divine assistance to fulfill God's desires for you.

[2]   When you are ready, in your imagination, call to mind the various prayers of the preceding day or days. Allow the images and words of these prayers to linger and then slowly fade from your consciousness.

- Remember your meditation on the "Principle and Foundation" from *The Spiritual Exercises of Saint Ignatius*. Consider the images and feelings evoked in you during your prayer, feeling God's presence in these memories and becoming aware of the specific sensations associated with each image.

- Recall your meditation on Ephesians 1:3-14, considering them in the same way as your memories of the Principle and Foundation.

- Review your meditations on Isaiah 43:1-7 in the same manner as the previous meditations.

As these prayers enter your memory, make a mental note of which senses are most active. You may see an image or a color, hear a sound or a phrase, or smell a scent or a fragrance. You may even taste a flavor or feel a sensation on your skin.

[3]   Then, relax and allow these various memories and experiences to quietly enter and leave your consciousness without being controlled – whether they are clear or diffuse, whether they come quickly or slowly. Linger on the sensory images and memories being evoked in you – noticing any images or colors, any sounds or phrases, any scents or fragrances, any flavors or physical sensations associated with each prayer.

[4]   When you are ready, become completely still and clear your mind of all thoughts and concerns. Allow an image of a special personal space to form in your imagination, a place where you are completely comfortable and alone. Then, watch as God enters that place and forms a small image or object for you that expresses the

thought or awareness that you most need to carry with you into your life.

Reverently pick up the object or image, a reflection of the most important gift you have been given during this time of prayer. Look at it carefully and become aware of the divine presence contained within it. Take a moment to register what it looks like and how it feels in your hand. Then, feel the joy and confidence that comes from touching the presence of God as you accept this gift, offering a short prayer of gratitude while you relax into the pleasure of this moment.

[5]   Then, conclude by allowing these images to fade from your consciousness as you offer this traditional Irish prayer collected by Douglas Hyde in *The Religious Songs of Connacht*:

>   *Confirm me in your love divine,*
>   *Smooth for my feet life's rugged way;*
>   *My will with yours entwine,*
>   *Lest evil lead my steps astray.*
>   *Be with me still as guard and guide,*
>   *Keep me in holy sanctity,*
>   *Let my firm faith on you abide,*
>   *From fraud and error hold me free. Amen.*

[6]   While your experiences are still fresh in your mind, record the most significant impressions or sensations from this time of prayer in your retreat journal.

2.7 Review of Prayer

[1] Remember your desires during the preceding day or week of prayer. Become aware of our desire to experience the divine presence all around you and to trust in God's plan for you so that all your intentions and actions may be directed purely to the service and praise of God. Recall your desire to recognize the invitation to live for God's glory through your life choices and to respond faithfully as God calls you to action. Finally, reaffirm your desire for the strength and trust to respond to God's desires for you.

After bringing these thoughts and desires into your consciousness, ask God once again to fulfill these desires in your own life and in your interactions with others.

[2] Then, take a moment to allow the words, thoughts, and feelings from your prayers during the last day or week to linger – on your mind and in your heart – before asking God to reveal the fulfillment of your deepest desires in these various memories.

- Think about the prayer sequence at the beginning of this day or week. Make a mental note of any words, insights or images that remain particularly significant or meaningful to you.

- Ponder the story, "Patrick Receives the Staff of Jesus". Note any words, insights, or images from it that remain particularly significant or meaningful to you.

- Remember your meditation on the "Principle and Foundation" from *The Spiritual Exercises of Saint Ignatius*.

– Consider the most powerful images, phrases, or feelings from your prayer. Ask yourself what gifts God gave to you through these moments, perhaps offering you new insights or perhaps affirming an important aspect of your faith. Ask yourself how God may be calling you to change through these moments, being as specific as possible.

– Examine your disposition as you prayed, noting whether prayer came easily or with resistance. Recall the easiest moments in your prayer and any moments of joy you may have experienced. Remember also if you encountered any difficulty opening yourself to God or if you felt any sadness as you prayed. Ask God to help you understand why these feelings surfaced.

– Bring to mind any moments when you added personal elements (e.g., familiar places or people from your life) or connected your prayers to other scriptures or spiritual writings. Ask yourself how

these additions helped or hindered you as you prayed. Again, if you do not know why this happened, ask God to help you understand.

- Recall your meditation on Ephesians 1:3-14. Then, review your prayer in the same way as your earlier reflection on the Principle and Foundation.

- Review your meditations on Isaiah 43:1-7 in the same manner as the previous prayers.

- Reflect on the ebb and flow of sensory impressions and feelings that marked your application of the senses. Isolate the most memorable moments and sensory impressions from your prayer and reflect on how God used these moments to give you a particular gift, perhaps offering you new insights or changing you in some way.

[3]   Finally, ponder the times when images or feelings from the readings of this day or week surfaced outside these prayer periods. Consider those moments or events in which God's presence or guidance was especially strong as well as any moments when you were struggling. Think about the most memorable aspects of these experiences, asking God to explain their significance.

[4]   Take a moment to allow the words, thoughts, and feelings of these prayers to linger on your mind and in your heart. Finally, conclude by allowing these desires to fade from your consciousness as you offer this traditional Irish prayer collected by Douglas Hyde in *The Religious Songs of Connacht*:

> O God, I believe in you; strengthen my belief.
> I trust in you; confirm my trust.
> I love you; double my love.
> I repent that I angered you,
> Increase my repentance.
> Fill you my heart with awe without despair;
> With hope, without over-confidence;
> With piety without infatuation;
> And with joy without excess.
> My God, consent to guide me by your wisdom;
> To constrain me by your right;
> To comfort me by your mercy;
> And to protect me by your power. Amen.

[5]   After finishing these prayers, summarize your reflections on the gifts or graces you received during the prayers of this last day or week and record these thoughts in your retreat journal.

3. Rebellion Against God's Desires

3.1a Shamed And Shaken Sore With Terror
a sinner's prayer of remorse

Take a moment to quiet your spirit, becoming completely present to this time and place. Allow all other thoughts and concerns to fall away as you come into the presence of God. Then, when you are ready, begin.

Shamed and shaken sore with terror,
Lo! I fall before your face,
    Every grievous wrong and error
    Filling me with deep disgrace;
From the gulf deliver me;
    Cleanse me, Christ, and make me free.

I have walked in carnal pleasure,
Lived for worldly joys alone,
    Never sought your living treasure,
    Nought to please your will have done;
All my crimes in grief I see;
    Lord, be merciful to me.

A Hymn, sung or heard (optional)

Cast from the highest heights of heaven,
Far from the angels' shining state,
    Faded from glory, Lucifer,
    Falling in scorn infatuate.
Angels apostate share his fall,
Steeled with his hate and fired with pride,
    Banished from their fellows bright,
    Who in the heavenly seats abide.

Against Satan's wiles and hell's assault
Our primal parents could not stand:
    And into new abysses fell
    The leader and his horrid band:
Fierce forms, with noise of beating wings,
Too dread for sight of mortal eye,
    Who, fettered, far from human ken,

Within their prison houses lie.

Lucifer, banished from his first estate,
The Lord cast out for evermore;
    And now his wild and rebel crew
    In upper air together soar.
Invisible lest men should gaze
On wickedness without a name,
    And, breaking every barrier down,
    Defile themselves in open shame.

Read or recite Psalm 8.

Holy Lord,
Under my thoughts may I God-thoughts find.
Half of my sins escape my mind.
    For what I said, or did not say,
    Pardon me, O Lord, I pray.

Read Luke 15: 11-32, aloud or quietly.

O Lord, Jesus the Christ,
If I were in Heaven my harp I would sound
With apostles and angels and saints all around,
    Praising and thanking the Son who is crowned,
    May the poor race of Eve for that heaven be bound!

Holy Lord,
O King of heaven who did create
The man who ate of that sad tree.
    To you I cry, "Oh turn your face,
    Show heavenly grace this day to me".

From the sin of the apple, the crime of two,
Our virtues are few, our lust runs free;
    For my riotous appetite Christ alone
    From his mercy's throne can pardon me.

O Holy Lord,
    God with the Father and the Spirit,

For me is many a snare designed,
To fill my mind with doubts and fears;
    Far from the land of holy saints,
    I dwell within my vale of tears.
Let faith, let hope, let love –
Traits far above the cold world's way –
    With patience, humility, and awe,
    Become my guides from day to day.

I acknowledge, the evil I have done.
From the day of my birth till the day of my death,
    Through the sight of my eyes,
Through the hearing of my ears,
    Through the sayings of my mouth,
Through the thoughts of my heart,
    Through the touch of my hands,
Through the course of my way,
    Through all I said and did not,
Through all I promised and fulfilled not,
    Through all the laws and holy commandments I broke.
I ask even now absolution of you,
    For fear I may have never asked it as was right,
    And that I might not live to ask it again,

O Holy Lord, my King in Heaven,
May you not let my soul stray from you,
May you keep me in a good state,
    May you turn me toward what is good to do,
    May you protect me from dangers, small and great.
May you fill my eyes with tears of repentance,
    So I may avoid the sinner's awful sentence.
May the Grace of the God for ever be with me,
    And whatever my needs, may the Triune God give me.

Select one of the following options for the Lord's Prayer.

Option A

O Jesus Christ,
Lord of heaven and earth,

Help me pray as you yourself taught:
> "Our Father in heaven,
> hallowed be your name.
> Your kingdom come.
> Your will be done,
> on earth as it is in heaven.
> Give us this day our daily bread.
> And forgive us our debts,
> as we also have forgiven our debtors.
> And do not bring us to the time of trial,
> but rescue us from the evil one."
> (Matthew 6:9-13)

From the foes of my land,
from the foes of my faith,
From the foes who would us dissever,
> O Lord, preserve me, in life and in death,
> With the Sign of the Cross for ever.
> *For the kingdom, the power, and the glory*
> *are yours now and for ever. Amen.*

Please proceed with "I beseech you, O Lord...," found after Option B.

Option B

O Jesus Christ,
Lord of heaven and earth,
Help me pray as you yourself taught:
> *Our Father in heaven,*
> *hallowed be your name,*
> *your kingdom come,*
> *your will be done,*
> *on earth as in heaven.*
> *Give us today our daily bread.*
> *Forgive us our sins*
> *as we forgive those who sin against us.*
> *Lead us not into temptation*
> *but deliver us from evil.*

From the foes of my land,
from the foes of my faith,

From the foes who would us dissever,
>   O Lord, preserve me, in life and in death,
>   With the Sign of the Cross for ever.
>   *For the kingdom, the power, and the glory*
>   *are yours now and for ever. Amen.*

I beseech you, O Lord.
God in Heaven, unsurpassed in power and might;
>   Be behind me, Be on my left,
>   Be before me, Be on my right!
Against each danger, you are my help;
In distress, upon you I call.
>   In dark times, may you sustain me
>   And lift me up again when I fall.
Lord over heaven and of earth,
You know my offenses.
>   Yet, listening to my pleadings,
>   You guide me away from sinful pretenses.
Lord of all creation and the many creatures,
You bestow on me many earthly treasures.
>   Revealing love in each life and season,
>   You share with me heavenly pleasures.
May you arouse me
In moments both of joy and of strife;
>   Most holy Lord, bring me new life!

A Hymn, sung or heard (optional)

O Jesus Christ,
>   Lord of heaven and earth,
>   You are my riches, my store, my provision,
My star through the years
When troubles rend me,
>   Through times of strife and tears,
>   Sweet Jesus, defend me.

Long in feasting and in riot,
In deceptions vile and vain,
>   I have walked with heart unquiet,
>   Fouled my soul with sinful stain ;

From the depths I cry to you.
    Lord, be merciful to me.

Jesus, Maker and Defender,
Sweet Redeemer of mankind,
    Hear me in your mercy tender,
    Let my soul your pardon find ;
From my woes deliver me ;
    Cleanse and raise me unto you.

End this time of prayer by taking some time to bring to mind the various ways God shields you from harm or guides you through the world's tumult. Then, when you are ready, conclude by saying:

O Holy Lord, King in Heaven,
I place myself at the edge of your grace,
    On the floor of your house myself I place,
And to banish the sin of my heart away,
    I lower my knee to you this day.
Through life's torrents of pain may you bring me whole,
    And, O Lord Jesus Christ, preserve also my soul. Amen.

3.1b   Preparation for Prayer

Consideration of the Readings

After reciting or prayerfully reading the prayer sequence for this day or week:

- Read about the prodigal son and his brother in Luke 15:11-32. Make a mental note of each person's appearance and actions during the episode as well as the key elements of the story and its setting. Again, consider any aspects of this story that speak strongly to you before recording these observations in your workbook.
- Read 2 Peter 2:2-22. Again, pay careful attention to any phrases or images that seem particularly meaningful to you. Then, record these highlights in your workbook so you will remember them during this day or week of prayer.
- Read about the sin of the first parents in Genesis 3:1-24. Again, note each person's appearance and actions during the episode as well as the key elements of the story and its setting, including the setting in your workbook. Then, record any aspects of this story that speak strongly to you.

Note: You also should take a moment to consider any aspect of the prayer sequence from this day or week that seemed particularly significant to you.

Contemplation of Your Needs

When you are ready, concentrating on your breath or an object near you, allow any distractions to fade from your consciousness as you become aware of your desire to live in God's goodness. Feel yourself yearning to properly use the many gifts God has given you, to experience God's continuing care, and to be open to the immense love God shows for you, then:

- Read "God Protects Patrick from His Enemies" (found on page 318). Allow yourself to linger on any thoughts, phrases or images that seem particularly meaningful or significant to your earlier preparations or prayer.
- Pray for your desires in the coming day or week. Ask that the divine presence all around you may be revealed so all your intentions

and actions may be directed purely to the service and praise of God. Ask also to acknowledge sin as a rebellion against God and to feel intense sorrow (and even tears) for your own sins as you consider the parable of the prodigal son and his brother, the sin of the angels and the sin of the first parents.
    • Conclude by praying for a deep "felt knowledge" of God's sorrow in response to the sinful rebellion of his creatures and children. Then, take a moment record any significant thoughts, emotions, or reactions from these moments in your workbook.

After this, put your notes aside. Without straining your memory, consider in turn each of the readings for the coming day or week and allow them to take shape in your imagination – even if all you remember are small fragments. Prayerfully ponder how each reading affects you emotionally without overtly thinking about their content, asking God to illuminate the spiritual gifts offered in each reading – quieting your mind and creating a receptive space in yourself to see or hear the response.

Finally, conclude by allowing these desires to fade from your consciousness as you offer this traditional Irish prayer collected by Douglas Hyde in *The Religious Songs of Connacht*:
> O God, I believe in you; strengthen my belief.
> I trust in you; confirm my trust.
> I love you; double my love.
> I repent that I angered you,
> Increase my repentance.
> Fill you my heart with awe without despair;
> With hope, without over-confidence;
> With piety without infatuation;
> And with joy without excess.
> My God, consent to guide me by your wisdom;
> To constrain me by your right;
> To comfort me by your mercy;
> And to protect me by your power. Amen.

Allow these words to linger on your mind and in your heart for a few moments and then, while they are still fresh in your memory, write the most important thoughts, feelings, and desires from this preparatory time in your workbook.

3.2 A Contemplation of Luke 15:11-32

In this contemplation of Luke 15:11-32, you will see and hear Jesus tell the story of the prodigal son and his brother.

[1]   Begin by reading the biblical selection and reviewing your notes on it from your earlier preparations.

[2]   Then, focus on this specific time and place as you allow all other concerns to fall away. Then, when you are ready, consider the people and place in this moment of prayer.

• Allow an image of Jesus to emerge in your imagination, noting his physical characteristics and mannerisms. Look at what he is wearing or carrying, observing his clothing and any objects he is holding. Make a note of whether he is sitting, standing, or walking. Ponder this mental image, allowing any other observations about Jesus to form in your mind.

• Then, observe the people around Jesus. Note how many people are with Jesus, making a mental note of their appearance and demeanor. Look at Jesus' disciples, observing where they are standing and how they behave toward Jesus. Look at the crowd, noting their attitude and behavior toward Jesus. Observe whether the people are sitting, standing, or walking. Take a moment to ponder this mental image, allowing other impressions of these men and women to form. Become familiar with the men and women you will encounter during your prayer as well as their behavior.

• Gradually, allow yourself to become aware of the location of this moment of prayer. Pay attention to its physical characteristics and the arrangement of the people in it. As you ponder this mental image, look around the place and notice more details about it – noting if it is in dim or bright light, if it is still and silent or filled with noise, if it has an unusual smell or not, etc. Become familiar with the location of your upcoming prayer.

• Consider allow an image to emerge in your imagination of the characters in the parable of the prodigal son and his brother as well as the locations described in the story. See the father and his two sons, noting their physical characteristics and mannerisms. Become aware of the locations in the story, looking around each place you remember and noticing details about each. Again, become familiar with the location of your upcoming prayer.

• Take a moment to remain immersed in these images and sensations, then allow these images to fade from your consciousness.

[3]   After you become still, become aware of your desires during this moment of prayer. Remember your desire to experience the divine presence all around you may be revealed so all your intentions and actions may be directed purely to the service and praise of God. Reassert your desire to acknowledge sin as a rebellion against God and to feel intense sorrow (and even tears) for your own sins as you contemplate the prodigal son and his brother. Finally, recall your desire for a deep "felt knowledge" of God's sorrow in response to the sinful rebellion of his creatures and children.

As these desires fill your consciousness, let all other concerns fall aside as you focus on this specific time and place of prayer.

[4]   Again, when you are ready, allow the image of Jesus and his disciples to reemerge in your imagination.

• Watch as the group assembles around Jesus. Listen to the sounds of this moment and become comfortable as you prepare to hear Jesus speak. Feel the anticipation of the people around you and share in that enthusiasm.

• As you hear Jesus begin to calm the crowd, ask God to help you share in their experience – either by joining them or by listening quietly to them. Focus your attention on Jesus, noting his physical appearance and his emotional demeanor.

• Then, watch and listen as Jesus tells the parable of the prodigal son and his brother. As Jesus speaks, look around and see the reactions of Jesus' disciples and the people in the crowd. Become aware of their feelings and how they behave toward Jesus and any another.

• Afterward, hear Jesus explain the parable. Listen to him as he explains the nature of human sin and describes God's promise of forgiveness expressed through the parable.

– Again, look around as Jesus speaks and see the reactions of his disciples and the people in the crowd. Become aware of their feelings and how they behave toward Jesus and one another.

– Remember that Jesus is speaking to men and women struggling to remain faithful to God's desires while struggling with their own sinfulness. Remember that he also is speaking to you.

• After Jesus finishes speaking, allow his image and this place to fade from your imagination as you become aware of the phrases and images from this moment of prayer which touched you most deeply.

Recall the emotions and memories – including any sounds or smells – evoked during your prayer. Allow these seminal aspects of your meditation to linger on your mind and in your heart, making a mental note of any special feelings evoked by them.

[5]   When you are ready, become aware of Jesus' presence with you in this moment and have an open and informal conversation about this prayer period and how the passage from Luke's gospel expresses your own needs or desires – giving space for Jesus to respond or to highlight different aspects from the biblical account and your experiences during this contemplation. Then, gradually allow your thoughts to recede as you focus on God's broader presence in your life and in the world around you.

[6]   Finally, conclude by allowing these desires to fade from your consciousness as you offer this traditional Irish prayer collected by Douglas Hyde in *The Religious Songs of Connacht*:

> Confirm me in your love divine,
> Smooth for my feet life's rugged way;
> My will with yours entwine,
> Lest evil lead my steps astray.
> Be with me still as guard and guide,
> Keep me in holy sanctity,
> Let my firm faith on you abide,
> From fraud and error hold me free. Amen.

[7]   Afterward, take 10-15 minutes in a quiet space to reflect on the most significant moments from this time of prayer and record your reflections in your retreat journal.

3.3 A Meditation on 2 Peter 2:2-22

In this meditation on 2 Peter 2:2-22, you will see and hear Saint Patrick preaching to a crowd about false prophets and the sin of the angels.

[1]   Begin by reading the biblical selection and reviewing your notes on it from your earlier preparations.

[2]   Then, focus on this specific time and place as you allow all other concerns to fall away. Then, when you are ready, consider the people and place in this moment of prayer.

• Allow an image of Patrick to emerge in your imagination, noting his physical characteristics and mannerisms. Look at what he is wearing or carrying, observing his clothing and any objects he is holding. Make a note of whether he is sitting, standing, or walking. Ponder this mental image, allowing any other observations about Patrick to form in your mind.

• Then, observe the people around Saint Patrick. Note how many people are with Patrick, making a mental note of their appearance and demeanor. Look at Patrick's disciples, observing where they are standing and how they behave toward Patrick. Look at the crowd, noting their attitude and behavior toward Saint Patrick. Observe whether the people are sitting, standing, or walking. Take a moment to ponder this mental image, allowing other impressions of these people to form. Become familiar with the men and women you will encounter during your prayer as well as their behavior.

• Gradually, allow yourself to become aware of the location of this encounter with Patrick. Pay attention to its physical characteristics and the arrangement of the people in it. As you ponder this mental image, look around the place and notice more details about it – noting if it is in dim or bright light, if it is still and silent or filled with noise, if it has an unusual smell or not, etc. Become familiar with the location of your upcoming prayer.

• Take a moment to remain in this place with these people, then allow these images to fade from your consciousness.

[3]   After you become still, become aware of your desires during this moment of prayer. Remember your desire to experience the divine presence all around you may be revealed so all your intentions and actions may be directed purely to the service and praise of God. Reassert your desire to acknowledge sin as a rebellion against God and

to feel intense sorrow (and even tears) for your own sins as you contemplate the prodigal son and his brother. Finally, recall your desire for a deep "felt knowledge" of God's sorrow in response to the sinful rebellion of his creatures and children.

As these desires fill your consciousness, let all other concerns fall aside as you focus on this specific time and place of prayer.

[4]   Again, when you are ready, allow the image of Saint Patrick and his disciples to reemerge in your imagination.

- Watch as the group assembles around Patrick. Listen to the sounds of this moment and become comfortable as you prepare to hear Patrick speak. Feel the anticipation of the people around you and share in that enthusiasm.

- As you hear Saint Patrick begin to calm the crowd, ask God to help you share in their experience – either by joining them or by listening quietly to them. Focus your attention on Patrick, noting his physical appearance and his emotional demeanor.

- Then, watch and listen as Patrick speaks the words of Saint Peter's letter. You may want to quietly read the passage while remaining prayerfully aware of your mental image of Patrick or you may choose to stay completely within the imagined realm of your prayer. Whichever you choose, know that God will offer you the words from the biblical passage that you need to hear – even if only in fragments.

- Afterward, hear Saint Patrick explain the sin of the angels and the nature of their rebellion against God. Listen to him as he speaks about God's sorrow and anger as it is expressed Saint Peter's epistle.

– Again, look around as Patrick speaks and see the reactions of Patrick's disciples and the people in the crowd. Become aware of their feelings and how they behave toward Patrick and one another.

– Remember that Patrick is speaking to men and women struggling to remain faithful to God's desires while struggling with their own sinfulness. Remember that he also is speaking to you.

- After Patrick finishes speaking, allow his image and this place to fade from your imagination as you become aware of the phrases and images from this moment of prayer which touched you most deeply. Recall the emotions and memories – including any sounds or smells – evoked during your prayer. Allow these seminal aspects of your meditation to linger on your mind and in your heart, making a mental note of any special feelings evoked by them.

[5] When you are ready, become aware of yourself standing below Jesus on the cross. Feel the depth of your grief for Jesus' suffering on the cross because of this cosmic rebellion against God's desires for creation and ask, "What have I done for Christ? What am I now doing for Christ? What more ought I do for Christ?" Allow Jesus and the Spirit to guide your thoughts and desires as you address each question in turn, highlighting different aspects from the biblical selection and your experiences during this meditation. Then, gradually allow your thoughts to recede as you focus on God's broader presence in your life and in the world around you.

[6] Finally, conclude by allowing these desires to fade from your consciousness as you offer this traditional Irish prayer collected by Douglas Hyde in *The Religious Songs of Connacht*:

> *Confirm me in your love divine,*
> *Smooth for my feet life's rugged way;*
> *My will with yours entwine,*
> *Lest evil lead my steps astray.*
> *Be with me still as guard and guide,*
> *Keep me in holy sanctity,*
> *Let my firm faith on you abide,*
> *From fraud and error hold me free. Amen.*

[7] Afterward, take 10-15 minutes in a quiet space to reflect on the most significant moments from this time of prayer and record your reflections in your retreat journal.

3.4 A Meditation on Genesis 3:1-24

In this meditation on Genesis 3:1-24, you will see and hear Saint Patrick preaching to a crowd about the sins of the first parents.

[1]   Begin by reading the biblical selection and reviewing your notes on it from your earlier preparations.

[2]   As you begin, focus on this specific time and place as you allow all other concerns to fall away. Then, when you are ready, consider the people and place in this moment of prayer.

• Allow an image of Patrick to emerge in your imagination, noting his physical characteristics and mannerisms. Look at what he is wearing or carrying, observing his clothing and any objects he is holding. Make a note of whether he is sitting, standing, or walking. Ponder this mental image, allowing any other observations about Patrick to form in your mind.

• Then, observe the people around Saint Patrick. Note how many people are with Patrick, making a mental note of their appearance and demeanor. Look at Patrick's disciples, observing where they are standing and how they behave toward Patrick. Look at the crowd, noting their attitude and behavior toward Saint Patrick. Observe whether the people are sitting, standing, or walking. Take a moment to ponder this mental image, allowing other impressions of these people to form. Become familiar with the men and women you will encounter during your prayer as well as their behavior.

• Gradually, allow yourself to become aware of the location of this encounter with Patrick. Pay attention to its physical characteristics and the arrangement of the people in it. As you ponder this mental image, look around the place and notice more details about it – noting if it is in dim or bright light, if it is still and silent or filled with noise, if it has an unusual smell or not, etc. Become familiar with the location of your upcoming prayer.

• Take a moment to remain in this place with these people, then allow these images to fade from your consciousness.

[3]   After you become still, become aware of your desires during this moment of prayer. Remember your desire to experience the divine presence all around you may be revealed so all your intentions and actions may be directed purely to the service and praise of God. Reassert your desire to acknowledge sin as a rebellion against God and to feel intense sorrow (and even tears) for your own sins as you

contemplate the prodigal son and his brother. Finally, recall your desire for a deep "felt knowledge" of God's sorrow in response to the sinful rebellion of his creatures and children.

As these desires fill your consciousness, let all other concerns fall aside as you focus on this specific time and place of prayer.

[4]   Then, when you are ready, allow the image of Saint Patrick and his disciples to reemerge in your imagination.

- Watch as the group assembles around Patrick. Listen to the sounds of this moment and become comfortable as you prepare to hear Patrick speak. Feel the anticipation of the people around you and share in that enthusiasm.

- As you hear Saint Patrick quieting the crowd, ask God to help you share in their experience – either by joining them or by listening quietly to them. Focus your attention on Patrick, noting his physical appearance and his emotional demeanor.

- Then, watch and listen as Patrick tells the story of Adam and Eve in Genesis. You may want to quietly read the passage while remaining prayerfully aware of your mental image of Patrick or you may choose to stay completely within the imagined realm of your prayer. Whichever you choose, know that God will offer you the words from the biblical passage that you need to hear – even if only in fragments.

- Hear Saint Patrick explain the sin of the First Parents and the rebellion against God's it entails, a sin in which all men and women share. Listen to him as he explains the meaning and significance of God's sorrow and anger as it is expressed in Genesis.

– Again, look around as Patrick speaks and see the reactions of his disciples and the people in the crowd. Become aware of their feelings and how they behave toward Patrick and one another.

– Remember that Patrick is speaking to men and women struggling to remain faithful to God's desires while struggling with their own sinfulness. Remember that he also is speaking to you.

- After Patrick finishes speaking, allow his image and this place to fade from your imagination as you become aware of the phrases and images from this moment of prayer which touched you most deeply. Recall the emotions and memories – including any sounds or smells – evoked during your prayer. Allow these seminal aspects of your meditation to linger on your mind and in your heart, making a mental note of any special feelings evoked by them.

[5] When you are ready, become aware of yourself standing below Jesus on the cross. Feel the depth of your grief for Jesus' suffering on the cross because of this human rebellion against God's desires for creation and ask, "What have I done for Christ? What am I now doing for Christ? What more ought I do for Christ?" Allow Jesus and the Spirit to guide your thoughts and desires as you address each question in turn, highlighting different aspects from the biblical selection and your experiences during this meditation. Then, gradually allow your thoughts to recede as you focus on God's broader presence in your life and in the world around you.

[6] Finally, conclude by allowing these desires to fade from your consciousness as you offer this traditional Irish prayer collected by Douglas Hyde in *The Religious Songs of Connacht*:

> *Confirm me in your love divine,*
> *Smooth for my feet life's rugged way;*
> *My will with yours entwine,*
> *Lest evil lead my steps astray.*
> *Be with me still as guard and guide,*
> *Keep me in holy sanctity,*
> *Let my firm faith on you abide,*
> *From fraud and error hold me free. Amen.*

[7] Afterward, take 10-15 minutes in a quiet space to reflect on the most significant moments from this time of prayer and record your reflections in your retreat journal.

3.5 A Repeated Contemplation of Luke 15:11-32

In this repeated contemplation of Luke 15:11-32, you again will see and hear Jesus tell the story of the prodigal son and his brother.

[1]   Begin by re-reading the biblical selection and reviewing your notes on it from your earlier preparations.

[2]   Then, focus on this specific time and place as you allow all other concerns to fall away. Then, when you are ready, consider the people and place in this moment of prayer.

- Allow an image of Jesus to emerge in your imagination, noting his physical characteristics and mannerisms. Look at what he is wearing or carrying, observing his clothing and any objects he is holding. Make a note of whether he is sitting, standing, or walking. Ponder this mental image, allowing any other observations about Jesus to form in your mind.

- Then, observe the people around Jesus. Note how many people are with Jesus, making a mental note of their appearance and demeanor. Look at Jesus' disciples, observing where they are standing and how they behave toward Jesus. Look at the crowd, noting their attitude and behavior toward Jesus. Observe whether the people are sitting, standing, or walking. Take a moment to ponder this mental image, allowing other impressions of these people to form. Become familiar with the men and women you will encounter during your prayer as well as their behavior.

- Gradually, allow yourself to become aware of the location of this moment of prayer. Pay attention to its physical characteristics and the arrangement of the people in it. As you ponder this mental image, look around the place and notice more details about it – noting if it is in dim or bright light, if it is still and silent or filled with noise, if it has an unusual smell or not, etc. Become familiar with the location of your upcoming prayer.

- Consider allow an image to emerge in your imagination of the characters in the parable of the prodigal son and his brother as well as the locations described in the story. See the father and his two sons, noting their physical characteristics and mannerisms. Become aware of the locations in the story, looking around each place you remember and noticing details about each. Again, become familiar with the location of your upcoming prayer.

- Take a moment to remain immersed in these images and sensations, then allow these images to fade from your consciousness.

[3] After you become still, become aware of your desires during this moment of prayer. Remember your desire to experience the divine presence all around you may be revealed so all your intentions and actions may be directed purely to the service and praise of God. Reassert your desire to acknowledge sin as a rebellion against God and to feel intense sorrow (and even tears) for your own sins as you contemplate the prodigal son and his brother. Finally, recall your desire for a deep "felt knowledge" of God's sorrow in response to the sinful rebellion of his creatures and children.

As these desires fill your consciousness, let all other concerns fall aside as you focus on this specific time and place of prayer.

[4] Again, when you are ready, allow the image of Jesus and his disciples to reemerge in your imagination.

- Watch as the group assembles around Jesus. Listen to the sounds of this moment and become comfortable as you prepare to hear Jesus speak. Feel the anticipation of the people around you and share in that enthusiasm.

- As you hear Jesus begin to calm the crowd, ask God to help you share in their experience – either by joining them or by listening quietly to them. Focus your attention on Jesus, noting his physical appearance and his emotional demeanor.

- Then, watch and listen as Jesus tells the parable of the prodigal son and his brother. As Jesus speaks, look around and see the reactions of Jesus' disciples and the people in the crowd. Become aware of their feelings and how they behave toward Jesus and any another.

- Afterward, hear Jesus explain the parable. Listen to him as he explains the nature of human sin and describes God's promise of forgiveness expressed through the parable.

– Again, look around as Jesus speaks and see the reactions of Jesus' disciples and the people in the crowd. Become aware of their feelings and how they behave toward Jesus and one another.

– Remember that Jesus is speaking to men and women struggling to remain faithful to God's desires while struggling with their own sinfulness. Remember that he also is speaking to you.

- After Jesus finishes speaking, allow his image and this place to fade from your imagination as you become aware of the phrases and images from this moment of prayer which touched you most deeply.

Recall the emotions and memories – including any sounds or smells – evoked during your prayer. Allow these seminal aspects of your meditation to linger on your mind and in your heart, making a mental note of any special feelings evoked by them.

[5] When you are ready, become aware of yourself standing below Jesus on the cross. Feel the depth of your grief for Jesus' suffering on the cross because of your own rebellion against God's desires for creation and ask, "What have I done for Christ? What am I now doing for Christ? What more ought I do for Christ?" Allow Jesus and the Spirit to guide your thoughts and desires as you address each question in turn, highlighting different aspects from the biblical selection and your experiences during this meditation. Then, gradually allow your thoughts to recede as you focus on God's broader presence in your life and in the world around you.

[6] Finally, conclude by allowing these desires to fade from your consciousness as you offer this traditional Irish prayer collected by Douglas Hyde in *The Religious Songs of Connacht*:

> *Confirm me in your love divine,*
> *Smooth for my feet life's rugged way;*
> *My will with yours entwine,*
> *Lest evil lead my steps astray.*
> *Be with me still as guard and guide,*
> *Keep me in holy sanctity,*
> *Let my firm faith on you abide,*
> *From fraud and error hold me free. Amen.*

[7] Afterward, take 10-15 minutes in a quiet space to reflect on the most significant moments from this time of prayer and record your reflections in your retreat journal.

3.6 An Application of the Senses

[1] Become aware of your prayerful desires during this day or week. Bring your desire to experience the divine presence all around you may be revealed so all your intentions and actions may be directed purely to the service and praise of God. Focus on your desire to acknowledge sin as a rebellion against God and to feel intense sorrow (and even tears) for your own sins. Finally, reaffirm your desire for a deep "felt knowledge" of God's sorrow in response to the sinful rebellion of his creatures and children.

[2] When you are ready, in your imagination, call to mind the various prayers of the preceding day or days. Allow the images and words of these prayers to linger and then slowly fade from your consciousness.

- Remember your imaginative contemplations of Luke 15:11-32. Consider the images and feelings evoked in you during your prayer, feeling God's presence in these memories and becoming aware of the specific sensations associated with each image.
- Recall your meditation on 2 Peter 2:2-22, considering them in the same way as considering them in the same way as your memories of Luke 15.
- Review your meditation on Genesis 3:1-24 in the same manner as the previous prayers.

As these prayers enter your memory, make a mental note of which senses are most active. You may see an image or a color, hear a sound or a phrase, or smell a scent or a fragrance. You may even taste a flavor or feel a sensation on your skin.

[3] Then, relax and allow these various memories and experiences to quietly enter and leave your consciousness without being controlled – whether they are clear or diffuse, whether they come quickly or slowly. Linger on the sensory images and memories being evoked in you – noticing any images or colors, any sounds or phrases, any scents or fragrances, any flavors or physical sensations associated with each prayer.

[4] When you are ready, become completely still and clear your mind of all thoughts and concerns. Allow an image of a special personal space to form in your imagination, a place where you are completely comfortable and alone. Then, watch as God enters that place and forms a small image or object for you that expresses the

thought or awareness that you most need to carry with you into your life.

Reverently pick up the object or image, a reflection of the most important gift you have been given during this time of prayer. Look at it carefully and become aware of the divine presence contained within it. Take a moment to register what it looks like and how it feels in your hand. Then, feel the joy and confidence that comes from touching the presence of God as you accept this gift, offering a short prayer of gratitude while you relax into the pleasure of this moment.

[5]   Then, conclude by allowing these images to fade from your consciousness as you offer this traditional Irish prayer collected by Douglas Hyde in *The Religious Songs of Connacht*:

> *Confirm me in your love divine,*
> *Smooth for my feet life's rugged way;*
> *My will with yours entwine,*
> *Lest evil lead my steps astray.*
> *Be with me still as guard and guide,*
> *Keep me in holy sanctity,*
> *Let my firm faith on you abide,*
> *From fraud and error hold me free. Amen.*

[6]   While your experiences are still fresh in your mind, record the most significant impressions or sensations from this time of prayer in your retreat journal.

3.7   Review of Prayer

[1]   Remember your desires during the preceding day or week of prayer. Become aware of our desire to experience the divine presence all around you and to trust in God's plan for you so that all your intentions and actions may be directed purely to the service and praise of God. Recall your desire to acknowledge sin as a rebellion against God and to feel intense sorrow (and even tears) for your own sins as you consider the parable of the prodigal son and his brother, the sin of the angels and the sin of the first parents. Finally, reaffirm your desire for a deep "felt knowledge" of God's sorrow in response to the sinful rebellion of his creatures and children.

After bringing these thoughts and desires into your consciousness, ask God once again to fulfill these desires in your own life and in your interactions with others.

[2]   Then, take a moment to allow the words, thoughts, and feelings from your prayers during the last day or week to linger – on your mind and in your heart – before asking God to reveal the fulfillment of your deepest desires in these various memories.

• Think about the prayer sequence at the beginning of this day or week. Make a mental note of any words, insights or images that remain particularly significant or meaningful to you.

• Ponder the story, "God Protects Patrick from His Enemies". Note any words, insights, or images from it that remain particularly significant or meaningful to you.

• Remember your imaginative contemplations of Luke 15:11-32.

– Consider the most powerful images, phrases, or feelings from your prayer. Ask yourself what gifts God gave to you through these moments, perhaps offering you new insights or perhaps affirming an important aspect of your faith. Ask yourself how God may be calling you to change through these moments, being as specific as possible.

– Examine your disposition as you prayed, noting whether prayer came easily or with resistance. Recall the easiest moments in your prayer and any moments of joy you may have experienced. Remember also if you encountered any difficulty opening yourself to God or if you felt any sadness as you prayed. Ask God to help you understand why these feelings surfaced.

– Bring to mind any moments when you added personal elements (e.g., familiar places or people from your life) or connected your prayers to other scriptures or spiritual writings. Ask yourself how these additions helped or hindered you as you prayed. Again, if you do not know why this happened, ask God to help you understand.

- Recall your meditation on 2 Peter 2:2-22. Then, review your prayer in the same way as your earlier reflection on Luke 15.
- Review your meditation on Genesis 3:1-24 in the same manner as the previous prayers.
- Reflect on the ebb and flow of sensory impressions and feelings that marked your application of the senses. Isolate the most memorable moments and sensory impressions from your prayer and reflect on how God used these moments to give you a particular gift, perhaps offering you new insights or changing you in some way.

[3] Finally, ponder the times when images or feelings from the readings of this day or week surfaced outside these prayer periods. Consider those moments or events in which God's presence or guidance was especially strong as well as any moments when you were struggling. Think about the most memorable aspects of these experiences, asking God to explain their significance.

[4] Take a moment to allow the words, thoughts, and feelings of these prayers to linger on your mind and in your heart. Finally, conclude by allowing these desires to fade from your consciousness as you offer this traditional Irish prayer collected by Douglas Hyde in *The Religious Songs of Connacht*:

> *O God, I believe in you; strengthen my belief.*
> *I trust in you; confirm my trust.*
> *I love you; double my love.*
> *I repent that I angered you,*
> *Increase my repentance.*
> *Fill you my heart with awe without despair;*
> *With hope, without over-confidence;*
> *With piety without infatuation;*
> *And with joy without excess.*
> *My God, consent to guide me by your wisdom;*
> *To constrain me by your right;*
> *To comfort me by your mercy;*
> *And to protect me by your power. Amen.*

[5] After finishing these prayers, summarize your reflections on the gifts or graces you received during the prayers of this last day or week and record these thoughts in your retreat journal.

4. The Personal Nature of Sin

4.1a   I Call On You To Save Me
a prayer for redemption from sin

Take a moment to quiet your spirit, becoming completely present to this time and place. Allow all other thoughts and concerns to fall away as you come into the presence of God. Then, when you are ready, begin.

I call on you to save me,
From grovelling deeds of shame;
    O make me yours by grace divine,
    To love and bless your name.

Drive from my heart all darkness,
All evil from my mind;
    Forever be my joy in you,
    O Saviour of mankind.

A Hymn, sung or heard (optional)

Sweet Jesus, help the foolish sinner
Who strays, with none to guard.
    He rises up in the morning's light
    But thinks not on his God.

Prayer and the blessed word of God
He never hears them read,
    And when he leaves this world at last,
    Ah, where shall be his bed?

You Christians, do you hear me?
Be thinking of the Death.
    The night to it is as the day
    To sweep away your breath.

And he who mocked at penitence
When he was on the world,
    To frost and cold outside the fold
    Too soon shall he be hurled.

When the soul shall go up to the gate of heaven
That has made not its peace with the Son of God,
> The angels shall cry and the saints shall say
> you did not, soul, foresee this day,
> When alive upon earth's green sod.

Read or recite Psalm 36.

Holy Lord,
Under my thoughts may I God-thoughts find.
Half of my sins escape my mind.
> For what I said, or did not say,
> Pardon me, O Lord, I pray.

Read Matthew 13:1-9, aloud or quietly.

O Lord, Jesus the Christ,
If I were in Heaven my harp I would sound
With apostles and angels and saints all around,
> Praising and thanking the Son who is crowned,
> May the poor race of Eve for that heaven be bound!

Holy Lord,
May you show mercy upon me with your grace.
> Showing forgiveness and mercy to my soul.
May you put nothing in my heart
> That may take my share of the eternal glory of the heavens from me.
May you saye me from the showers of calamity,
> And from the diseases of the year.
May you nurture in me, in life and in health,
> The love of God and of my neighbours.

O Holy Lord,
> God with the Father and the Spirit,
For me is many a snare designed,
To fill my mind with doubts and fears;
> Far from the land of holy saints,
> I dwell within my vale of tears.
Let faith, let hope, let love –

Traits far above the cold world's way –
    With patience, humility, and awe,
    Become my guides from day to day.

I acknowledge, the evil I have done.
From the day of my birth till the day of my death,
    Through the sight of my eyes,
Through the hearing of my ears,
    Through the sayings of my mouth,
Through the thoughts of my heart,
    Through the touch of my hands,
Through the course of my way,
    Through all I said and did not,
Through all I promised and fulfilled not,
    Through all the laws and holy commandments I broke.
I ask even now absolution of you,
    For fear I may have never asked it as was right,
    And that I might not live to ask it again,

O Holy Lord, my King in Heaven,
May you not let my soul stray from you,
May you keep me in a good state,
    May you turn me toward what is good to do,
    May you protect me from dangers, small and great.
May you fill my eyes with tears of repentance,
    So I may avoid the sinner's awful sentence.
May the Grace of the God for ever be with me,
    And whatever my needs, may the Triune God give me.

Select one of the following options for the Lord's Prayer.

Option A

O Jesus Christ,
Lord of heaven and earth,
Help me pray as you yourself taught:
    "Our Father in heaven,
    hallowed be your name.
    Your kingdom come.
    Your will be done,

on earth as it is in heaven.
Give us this day our daily bread.
And forgive us our debts,
as we also have forgiven our debtors.
And do not bring us to the time of trial,
but rescue us from the evil one."
(Matthew 6:9-13)
From the foes of my land,
from the foes of my faith,
From the foes who would us dissever,
    O Lord, preserve me, in life and in death,
    With the Sign of the Cross for ever.
    For the kingdom, the power, and the glory
    are yours now and for ever. Amen.

Please proceed with "I beseech you, O Lord...," found after Option B.

Option B

O Jesus Christ,
Lord of heaven and earth,
Help me pray as you yourself taught:
    Our Father in heaven,
    hallowed be your name,
    your kingdom come,
    your will be done,
    on earth as in heaven.
    Give us today our daily bread.
    Forgive us our sins
    as we forgive those who sin against us.
    Lead us not into temptation
    but deliver us from evil.
From the foes of my land,
from the foes of my faith,
From the foes who would us dissever,
    O Lord, preserve me, in life and in death,
    With the Sign of the Cross for ever.
    For the kingdom, the power, and the glory
    are yours now and for ever. Amen.

I beseech you, O Lord.
God in Heaven, unsurpassed in power and might;
    Be behind me, Be on my left,
    Be before me, Be on my right!
Against each danger, you are my help;
In distress, upon you I call.
    In dark times, may you sustain me
    And lift me up again when I fall.
Lord over heaven and of earth,
You know my offenses.
    Yet, listening to my pleadings,
    You guide me away from sinful pretenses.
Lord of all creation and the many creatures,
You bestow on me many earthly treasures.
    Revealing love in each life and season,
    You share with me heavenly pleasures.
May you arouse me
In moments both of joy and of strife;
    Most holy Lord, bring me new life!

A Hymn, sung or heard (optional)

O Jesus Christ,
    Lord of heaven and earth,
    You are my riches, my store, my provision,
My star through the years
When troubles rend me,
    Through times of strife and tears,
    Sweet Jesus, defend me.

Lo, though my heart is evil,
Though strong the tempter's power,
    I dare to raise my voice in praise,
    And seek you every hour.

Drive from my heart all darkness,
All evil from my mind;
    Forever be my joy in you,
    O Saviour of mankind.

End this time of prayer by taking some time to bring to mind the various ways God shields you from harm or guides you through the world's tumult. Then, when you are ready, conclude by saying:

O Holy Lord, King in Heaven,
I place myself at the edge of your grace,
    On the floor of your house myself I place,
And to banish the sin of my heart away,
    I lower my knee to you this day.
Through life's torrents of pain may you bring me whole,
    And, O Lord Jesus Christ, preserve also my soul. Amen.

4.1b   Preparation for Prayer

Consideration of the Readings

After reciting or prayerfully reading the prayer sequence for this day or week:
- Read about Jesus telling the parable of the sower in Matthew 13:1-9,18-23. Make a mental note of Jesus' appearance and actions during the episode, the people hearing the parable, and the key elements of the story and its setting. Again, consider any aspects of this story that speak strongly to you before recording these observations in your workbook.
- Read about Jesus telling the parable of the weeds among the wheat in Matthew 13:24-30. Again, note each person's appearance and actions during the episode as well as the key elements of the story and its setting. Then, record any aspects of this story that speak strongly to you.
- Read about Jesus explaining the parable of the weeds among the wheat in Matthew 13:36-43. Again, note each person's appearance and actions during the episode as well as the key elements of the story and its setting before recording in your workbook any aspects of this story that speak strongly to you.

Note: *You also should consider any aspect of the prayer sequence from this day or week that seemed particularly significant to you.*

Contemplation of Your Needs

When you are ready, allow any distractions to fade from your consciousness as you become aware of your desire to live in God's goodness. Feel yourself yearning to properly use the many gifts God has given you, to experience God's continuing care, and to be open to the immense love God shows for you, then:
- Read "Patrick is Betrayed for a Cauldron" (found on page 318). Allow yourself to linger on any thoughts, phrases or images that seem particularly meaningful or significant to your earlier preparations or prayer.

- Pray for your desires in the coming day or week. Ask that the divine presence all around you may be revealed so all your intentions and actions may be directed purely to the service and praise of God. Ask also to open yourself to feel your own rebellion against God as you review your life – experiencing increased and intense sorrow (and even tears) for your sins.
- Conclude by praying for the courage to acknowledge and repent these sins wholeheartedly.

Then, record any significant thoughts, emotions, or reactions from these moments in your workbook.

After this, put your notes aside. Without straining your memory, consider in turn each of the readings for the coming day or week and allow them to take shape in your imagination. Prayerfully ponder how each reading affects you emotionally without overtly thinking about their content, asking God to illuminate the spiritual gifts offered in each reading – quieting your mind and creating a receptive space in yourself to see or hear the response.

Finally, conclude by allowing these desires to fade from your consciousness as you offer this traditional Irish prayer:

O God, I believe in you; strengthen my belief.
I trust in you; confirm my trust.
I love you; double my love.
I repent that I angered you,
Increase my repentance.
Fill you my heart with awe without despair;
With hope, without over-confidence;
With piety without infatuation;
And with joy without excess.
My God, consent to guide me by your wisdom;
To constrain me by your right;
To comfort me by your mercy;
And to protect me by your power. Amen.

Allow these words to linger on your mind and in your heart for a few moments and then, while they are still fresh in your memory, write the most important thoughts, feelings, and desires from this preparatory time in your workbook.

4.2 A Consideration of Personal Sins

In this consideration, you will review your sins in the manner presented in *The Spiritual Exercises of Saint Ignatius*.

[1]   Begin by focusing on this specific time and place as you allow all other concerns to fall away.
[2]   As you become still, become aware of your desires during this moment of prayer. Remember your desire to experience the divine presence all around you and to trust in God's plan for you, asking that all your intentions and actions may be directed purely to the service and praise of God. Reassert your desire to open yourself to feel your own rebellion against God as you review your life – experiencing increased and intense sorrow (and even tears) for your sins. Finally, recall your need for God's gift of courage to acknowledge and repent these sins wholeheartedly.

As these desires fill your consciousness, let all other concerns fall aside as you focus on this specific time and place of prayer.

Note: At this point, you may want to read the text of this exercise as Ignatius presented it is in his Spiritual Exercises *(see page 309). This review might offer you different perspectives on various aspects of this exercise, illuminate your reflections and open you to a broader awareness of God's activity during your prayer. However, you should feel free to ignore this suggestion if it distracts you from your prayers.*

[3]   Then, review your life and the many sins you have committed.
  • In your memory, review the span of your life, the places you have lived and the many people with whom you have interacted. Going year-by-year or period-by-period (e.g., childhood, adolescence, early adulthood, etc.), consider the events of your life. Consider the various people you have met in your life and your interactions with them. Consider the various occupations and activities during your life. Then ask: How and when did you sin during these times, places, and activities with these people?
  • Ponder the varying degrees of sinfulness you expressed during the events of your life and in your interactions with others. Consider the moments when you deliberately sinned and harmed either yourself or others. Also consider the moments when you harmed yourself or

others unintentionally. Then ask: Have you expressed sorrow for these sins and sought to redress them?

• Reflect on how your sins have separated you from God and all of those who have lived righteous lives. Reflect on the ways that your sins – both large and small, intentional and unintentional, conscious and unconscious – have festered and corrupted your choices in life and your relationships with others (including God). Then ask: How have you endured this state of life that emerged from placing your desires above those of God and others, despite know the effects of these choices?

• Consider how God's attributes and behaviors contrast so completely from your sinful nature and choices. Reflect on the goodness and power that God displays in sustaining the world around you and in nurturing virtuous behaviors (e.g., kindness, justice, etc.) in the world while your actions undermine God's efforts and desires. Then ask: What makes God so loving and merciful toward you when you consistently choose to sin and place your desires above those of God and others?

• Express your dismay that God has continued to support and sustain you when your choices and actions deserve condemnation. Consider the many ways that God's creation makes your life possible despite your disdainful and sinful behavior toward it. Ponder how you are treated despite your contemptuous behavior toward God's actions on your behalf. Then ask: Why have you not been consigned to Hell for your numerous sinful choices and actions?

[4] When you are ready, become aware of yourself standing below Jesus on the cross. Feel the depth of your grief for Jesus suffering on the cross because of your many sins and ask, "What have I done for Christ? What am I now doing for Christ? What more ought I do for Christ?" Allow Jesus and the Spirit to guide your thoughts and desires as you address each question in turn, highlighting different aspects of your experiences during this consideration. Then, gradually allow your thoughts to recede as you focus on God's forgiving presence in your life and in the world around you.

[5] Conclude by allowing these desires to fade from your consciousness as you offer this traditional Irish prayer:

Confirm me in your love divine,
Smooth for my feet life's rugged way;
My will with yours entwine,
Lest evil lead my steps astray.

Be with me still as guard and guide,
Keep me in holy sanctity,
Let my firm faith on you abide,
From fraud and error hold me free. Amen.

[6]   Afterward, take 10-15 minutes in a quiet space to reflect on the most significant moments from this time of prayer and record your reflections in your retreat journal.

4.3 A Contemplation of Matthew 13:1-9,18-23

In this contemplation of Matthew 13:1-9,18-23, you will see and hear Jesus telling a crowd the parable of the sower.

[1]   Begin by reading the biblical selection and reviewing your notes on it from your earlier preparations.

[2]   Focus on this specific time and place as you allow all other concerns to fall away. Then, when you are ready, consider the people and place of this moment of prayer.

• Allow an image of Jesus to emerge in your imagination, noting his physical characteristics and mannerisms. Look at what he is wearing or carrying. Make a note of whether he is sitting, standing, or walking. Ponder this mental image, allowing any other observations about Jesus to form in your mind.

• Note how many people are with Jesus, making a mental note of their appearance and demeanor. Look at Jesus' disciples, observing where they are standing and how they behave toward Jesus. Look at the crowd, noting their attitude and behavior toward Jesus. Observe whether the people are sitting, standing, or walking. Take a moment to ponder this mental image, allowing other impressions of these people to form. Become familiar with the men and women you will encounter during your prayer as well as their behavior.

• Allow yourself to become aware of the location of this moment of prayer. Observe whether it is inside or outside, paying attention to its physical characteristics and the arrangement of the people in it. Look around the place and notice more details about it – if it is in dim or bright light, if it is still and silent or filled with noise, if it has an unusual smell or not, etc. Become familiar with the location of your upcoming prayer.

• Take a moment to remain in this place with these people before allowing these images to fade from your consciousness.

[3]   Become aware of your desires during this moment of prayer. Remember your desire to experience the divine presence all around you and to trust in God's plan for you, asking that all your intentions and actions may be directed purely to the service and praise of God. Reassert your desire to open yourself to feel your own rebellion against God as you review your life – experiencing increased and intense sorrow (and even tears) for your sins. Finally, recall your need for God's gift of courage to acknowledge and repent these sins wholeheartedly.

As these desires fill your consciousness, let all other concerns fall aside as you focus on this time and place of prayer.

[4]   Allow the image of Jesus and the crowd to reemerge in your imagination.

- Watch as the group assembles around Jesus. Listen to the sounds of this moment and become comfortable as you prepare to hear Jesus speak. Feel the anticipation of the people around you and share in that enthusiasm.

- As you hear Jesus begin to calm the crowd, ask God to help you enter this moment – either by joining these events or by listening quietly to them. Focus your attention on Jesus, noting his physical appearance and his demeanor.

- Then, watch and listen as Jesus tells the parable of the sower. You may want to quietly read the passage while remaining prayerfully aware of your mental image of Jesus or you may choose to stay completely within the imagined realm of your prayer. Whichever you choose, know that God will offer you the words from the biblical passage that you need to hear – even if only in fragments.

- Hear Jesus explain the parable. Listen to him as he explains the meaning and significance of God's promise expressed in this story.

– Again, look around as Jesus speaks and see the reactions of his disciples and the people in the crowd. Become aware of their feelings and how they behave toward Jesus and one another.

– Remember that Jesus is speaking to men and women striving to remain faithful to God's desires and promises while struggling with their sinfulness. Remember that he also is speaking to you.

- After Jesus finishes speaking, allow his image and this place to fade from your imagination as you become aware of the phrases and images from this moment which touched you most deeply. Recall the emotions and memories – including any sounds or smells – evoked during your prayer. Allow these seminal aspects of your meditation to linger on your mind and in your heart, noting any special feelings evoked by them.

[5]   When you are ready, become aware of Jesus' presence with you in this moment and have an open and informal conversation about this prayer period and how the passage from Matthew's gospel expresses your own needs or desires – giving space for Jesus to respond or to highlight different aspects from the biblical selection and your experiences during this contemplation. Then, gradually allow your

thoughts to recede as you focus on God's broader presence in your life and in the world around you.

[6]   Conclude by allowing these desires to fade from your consciousness as you offer this traditional Irish prayer:

> *Confirm me in your love divine,*
> *Smooth for my feet life's rugged way;*
> *My will with yours entwine,*
> *Lest evil lead my steps astray.*
> *Be with me still as guard and guide,*
> *Keep me in holy sanctity,*
> *Let my firm faith on you abide,*
> *From fraud and error hold me free. Amen.*

[7]   Afterward, take 10-15 minutes in a quiet space to reflect on the most significant moments from this time of prayer and record your reflections in your retreat journal.

4.4 A Contemplation of Matthew 13:24-30

In this contemplation of Matthew 13:24-30, you will see and hear Jesus telling a crowd the parable of the weeds among the wheat.

[1] Begin by reading the biblical selection and reviewing your notes on it from your earlier preparations.

[2] Then, focus on this specific time and place as you allow all other concerns to fall away. When you are ready, consider the people and place of this moment of prayer.

- Allow an image of Jesus to emerge in your imagination, noting his physical characteristics and mannerisms. Look at what he is wearing or carrying. Make a note of whether he is sitting, standing, or walking. Ponder this mental image, allowing any other observations about Jesus to form in your mind.

- Note how many people are with Jesus, making a mental note of their appearance and demeanor. Look at Jesus' disciples, observing where they are standing and how they behave toward Jesus. Look at the crowd, noting their attitude and behavior toward Jesus. Observe whether the people are sitting, standing, or walking. Take a moment to ponder this mental image, allowing other impressions of these people to form. Become familiar with the men and women you will encounter during your prayer as well as their behavior.

- Allow yourself to become aware of the location of this moment of prayer. Observe whether it is inside or outside, paying attention to its physical characteristics and the arrangement of the people in it. Look around the place and notice more details about it – if it is in dim or bright light, if it is still and silent or filled with noise, if it has an unusual smell or not, etc. Become familiar with the location of your upcoming prayer.

- Take a moment to remain in this place with these people before allowing these images to fade from your consciousness.

[3] Become aware of your desires during this moment of prayer. Remember your desire to experience the divine presence all around you and to trust in God's plan for you, asking that all your intentions and actions may be directed purely to the service and praise of God. Reassert your desire to open yourself to feel your own rebellion against God as you review your life – experiencing increased and intense sorrow (and even tears) for your sins. Finally, recall your need for God's gift of courage to acknowledge and repent these sins wholeheartedly.

As these desires fill your consciousness, let all other concerns fall aside as you focus on this time and place of prayer.

[4]   Allow the image of Jesus and the crowd to reemerge in your imagination.

- Watch as the group assembles around Jesus. Listen to the sounds of this moment and become comfortable as you prepare to hear Jesus speak. Feel the anticipation of the people around you and share in that enthusiasm.

- As you hear Jesus begin to calm the crowd, ask God to help you enter this moment – either by joining these events or by listening quietly to them. Focus your attention on Jesus, noting his physical appearance and his demeanor.

- Then, watch and listen as Jesus tells the parable of the weeds among the wheat. You may want to quietly read the passage while remaining prayerfully aware of your mental image of Jesus or you may choose to stay completely within the imagined realm of your prayer. Whichever you choose, know that God will offer you the words from the biblical passage that you need to hear – even if only in fragments.

– Again, look around as Jesus speaks and see the reactions of his disciples and the people in the crowd. Become aware of their feelings and how they behave toward Jesus and one another.

– Remember that Jesus is speaking to men and women striving to remain faithful to God's desires and promises while struggling with their sinfulness. Remember that he also is speaking to you.

- After Jesus finishes speaking, allow his image and this place to fade from your imagination as you become aware of the phrases and images from this moment which touched you most deeply. Recall the emotions and memories – including any sounds or smells – evoked during your prayer. Allow these seminal aspects of your meditation to linger on your mind and in your heart, noting any special feelings evoked by them.

[5]   When you are ready, become aware of Jesus' presence with you in this moment and have an open and informal conversation about this prayer period and how the passage from Matthew's gospel expresses your own needs or desires – giving space for Jesus to respond or to highlight different aspects from the biblical account and your experiences during this contemplation. Then, gradually allow your thoughts to recede as you focus on God's broader presence in your life and in the world around you.

[6]   Conclude by allowing these desires to fade from your consciousness as you offer this traditional Irish prayer:
> *Confirm me in your love divine,*
> *Smooth for my feet life's rugged way;*
> *My will with yours entwine,*
> *Lest evil lead my steps astray.*
> *Be with me still as guard and guide,*
> *Keep me in holy sanctity,*
> *Let my firm faith on you abide,*
> *From fraud and error hold me free. Amen.*

[7]   Afterward, take 10-15 minutes in a quiet space to reflect on the most significant moments from this time of prayer and record your reflections in your retreat journal.

4.5 A Contemplation of Matthew 13:24-30,36-43

In this contemplation of Matthew 13:24-30,36-43, you will see and hear Jesus explaining the parable of the weeds among the wheat.

[1] Begin by reading the biblical selection and reviewing your notes on it from your earlier preparations.

[2] Then, focus on the specific time and place as you allow all other concerns to fall away. When you are ready, consider the people and place of this moment of prayer.

• Allow an image of Jesus to emerge in your imagination, noting his physical characteristics and mannerisms. Look at what he is wearing or carrying. Make a note of whether he is sitting, standing, or walking. Ponder this mental image, allowing any other observations about Jesus to form in your mind.

• Note how many people are with Jesus, making a mental note of their appearance and demeanor. Look at Jesus' disciples, observing where they are standing and how they behave toward Jesus. Look at the crowd, noting their attitude and behavior toward Jesus. Observe whether the people are sitting, standing, or walking. Take a moment to ponder this mental image, allowing other impressions of these people to form. Become familiar with the men and women you will encounter during your prayer as well as their behavior.

• Allow yourself to become aware of the location of this moment of prayer. Observe whether it is inside or outside, paying attention to its physical characteristics and the arrangement of the people in it. Look around the place and notice more details about it – if it is in dim or bright light, if it is still and silent or filled with noise, if it has an unusual smell or not, etc. Become familiar with the location of your upcoming prayer.

• Take a moment to remain in this place with these people before allowing these images to fade from your consciousness.

[3] Become aware of your desires during this moment of prayer. Remember your desire to experience the divine presence all around you and to trust in God's plan for you, asking that all your intentions and actions may be directed purely to the service and praise of God. Reassert your desire to open yourself to feel your own rebellion against God as you review your life – experiencing increased and intense sorrow (and even tears) for your sins. Finally, recall your need for God's gift of courage to acknowledge and repent these sins wholeheartedly.

As these desires fill your consciousness, let all other concerns fall aside as you focus on this time and place of prayer.

[4]   Allow the image of Jesus and the crowd to reemerge in your imagination.

• Watch as the group assembles around Jesus. Listen to the sounds of this moment and become comfortable as you prepare to hear Jesus speak. Feel the anticipation of the people around you and share in that enthusiasm.

• As you hear Jesus begin to calm the crowd, ask God to help you share in this experience – either by joining them or by listening quietly to them. Focus your attention on Jesus, noting his physical appearance and his demeanor.

• Then, watch and listen as Jesus explains the parable of the weeds among the wheat. You may want to quietly read the passage while remaining prayerfully aware of your mental image of Jesus or you may choose to stay completely within the imagined realm of your prayer. Whichever you choose, know that God will offer you the words from the biblical passage that you need to hear – even if only in fragments.

• Hear Jesus explain the parable. Listen to him as he explains the meaning and significance of God's promise expressed in this story.

– Again, look around as Jesus speaks and see the reactions of his disciples and the people in the crowd. Become aware of their feelings and how they behave toward Jesus and one another.

– Remember that Jesus is speaking to men and women striving to remain faithful to God's desires and promises while struggling with their sinfulness. Remember that he also is speaking to you.

• After Jesus finishes speaking, allow his image and this place to fade from your imagination as you become aware of the phrases and images from this moment which touched you most deeply. Recall the emotions and memories – including any sounds or smells – evoked during your prayer. Allow these seminal aspects of your meditation to linger on your mind and in your heart, noting any special feelings evoked by them.

[5]   When you are ready, become aware of Jesus' presence with you in this moment and have an open and informal conversation about this prayer period and how the passage from Matthew's gospel expresses your own needs or desires – giving space for Jesus to respond or to highlight different aspects from the biblical account and your experiences during this contemplation. Then, gradually allow your

thoughts to recede as you focus on God's broader presence in your life and in the world around you.

[6]   Conclude by allowing these desires to fade from your consciousness as you offer this traditional Irish prayer:

> *Confirm me in your love divine,*
> *Smooth for my feet life's rugged way;*
> *My will with yours entwine,*
> *Lest evil lead my steps astray.*
> *Be with me still as guard and guide,*
> *Keep me in holy sanctity,*
> *Let my firm faith on you abide,*
> *From fraud and error hold me free. Amen.*

[7]   Afterward, take 10-15 minutes in a quiet space to reflect on the most significant moments from this time of prayer and record your reflections in your retreat journal.

4.6   An Application of the Senses

[1]   Become aware of your prayerful desires during this day or week. Bring to mind your desire that the divine presence all around you may be revealed so all your intentions and actions may be directed purely to the service and praise of God. Focus on your desire to acknowledge your own rebellion against God as you review your life – experiencing increased and intense sorrow (and even tears) for your sins. Finally, reaffirm your desire to acknowledge and repent these sins wholeheartedly

[2]   When you are ready, call to mind the various prayers of the preceding day or days. Allow the images and words of these prayers to linger and then slowly fade from your consciousness.

- Remember the consideration of your personal sins from *The Spiritual Exercises of Saint Ignatius*. Consider the images and feelings evoked in you during your prayer, feeling God's presence in these memories and becoming aware of the specific sensations associated with each image.
- Recall your imaginative contemplation of Matthew 13:1-9,18-23, considering it in the same way as the memories of your meditation on sin.
- Review your imaginative contemplation of Matthew 13:24-30 in the same manner as the previous prayers.
- Reflect on your imaginative contemplation of Matthew 13:24-30,36-43 before reviewing it in the same manner as the previous prayers.

Make a mental note of which senses are most active. You may see an image or a color, hear a sound or a phrase, or smell a scent or a fragrance. You may even taste a flavor or feel a sensation on your skin.

[3]   Then, relax and allow these various memories and experiences to quietly enter and leave your consciousness without being controlled. Linger on the sensory images and memories being evoked in you – noticing any images or colors, any sounds or phrases, any scents or fragrances, any flavors or physical sensations associated with each prayer.

[4]   When you are ready, become completely still and clear your mind of all thoughts and concerns. Allow an image of a special personal space to form in your imagination. Then, watch as God enters that place and forms a small image or object for you that expresses the

thought or awareness that you most need to carry with you into your life.

Reverently pick up the object or image, a reflection of the most important gift you have been given during this time of prayer. Look at it carefully and become aware of the divine presence contained within it. Take a moment to register what it looks like and how it feels in your hand. Then, feel the joy and confidence that comes from touching the presence of God as you accept this gift, offering a short prayer of gratitude while you relax into the pleasure of this moment.

[5]   Then, conclude by allowing these images to fade from your consciousness as you offer this traditional Irish prayer:

> *Confirm me in your love divine,*
> *Smooth for my feet life's rugged way;*
> *My will with yours entwine,*
> *Lest evil lead my steps astray.*
> *Be with me still as guard and guide,*
> *Keep me in holy sanctity,*
> *Let my firm faith on you abide,*
> *From fraud and error hold me free. Amen.*

[6]   While your experiences are still fresh in your mind, record the most significant impressions or sensations from this time of prayer in your retreat journal.

4.7   Review of Prayer

[1]   Remember your desires during the preceding day or week of prayer. Become aware of our desire to experience the divine presence all around you and to trust in God's plan for you so that all your intentions and actions may be directed purely to the service and praise of God. Recall your desire to open yourself to feel your own rebellion against God as you review your life – experiencing increased and intense sorrow (and even tears) for your sins. Finally, reaffirm your desire to acknowledge and repent these sins wholeheartedly.

After bringing these thoughts and desires into your consciousness, ask God once again to fulfill these desires in your own life and in your interactions with others.

[2]   Then, take a moment to allow the words, thoughts, and feelings from your prayers during the last day or week to linger before asking God to reveal the fulfillment of your deepest desires in these various memories.

• Think about the prayer sequence at the beginning of this day or week. Make a mental note of any words, insights or images that remain particularly significant or meaningful to you.

• Ponder the story, "Patrick is Betrayed for a Cauldron". Note any words, insights, or images from it that remain particularly significant or meaningful to you.

• Remember the consideration of your personal sins from *The Spiritual Exercises of Saint Ignatius*.

– Consider the most powerful images, phrases, or feelings from your prayer. Ask yourself what gifts God gave to you through these moments, perhaps offering you new insights or perhaps affirming an important aspect of your faith. Ask yourself how God may be calling you to change through these moments, being as specific as possible.

– Examine your disposition as you prayed, noting whether prayer came easily or with resistance. Recall the easiest moments in your prayer and any moments of joy you may have experienced. Remember also if you encountered any difficulty opening yourself to God or if you felt any sadness as you prayed. Ask God to help you understand why these feelings surfaced.

– Bring to mind any moments when you added personal elements (e.g., familiar places or people from your life) or connected your prayers to other scriptures or spiritual writings. Ask yourself how

these additions helped or hindered you as you prayed. Again, if you do not know why this happened, ask God to help you understand.

- Recall imaginative contemplation of Matthew 13:1-9,18-23. Then, review your prayer in the same way as your earlier reflection your meditation on sin.
- Review your imaginative contemplation of Matthew 13:24-30 in the same manner as the previous prayers.
- Reflect on your imaginative contemplation of Matthew 13:24-30,36-43 before reviewing it in the same manner as the previous prayers.
- Revisit the ebb and flow of sensory impressions and feelings that marked your application of the senses. Isolate the most memorable moments and sensory impressions from your prayer and reflect on how God used these moments to give you a particular gift.

[3] Finally, ponder the times when images or feelings from the readings of this day or week surfaced outside these prayer periods. Consider those moments or events in which God's presence or guidance was especially strong as well as any moments when you were struggling. Think about the most memorable aspects of these experiences, asking God to explain their significance.

[4] Take a moment to allow the words, thoughts, and feelings of these prayers to linger on your mind and in your heart. Finally, conclude by allowing these desires to fade from your consciousness as you offer this traditional Irish prayer:

> *O God, I believe in you; strengthen my belief.*
> *I trust in you; confirm my trust.*
> *I love you; double my love.*
> *I repent that I angered you,*
> *Increase my repentance.*
> *Fill you my heart with awe without despair;*
> *With hope, without over-confidence;*
> *With piety without infatuation;*
> *And with joy without excess.*
> *My God, consent to guide me by your wisdom;*
> *To constrain me by your right;*
> *To comfort me by your mercy;*
> *And to protect me by your power. Amen.*

[5] After finishing these prayers, summarize your reflections on the gifts or graces you received during the prayers of this last day or week and record these thoughts in your retreat journal.

5. The Contemplation of Hell

5.1a Loving Jesus, Hear Me Calling
a sinner's plea for mercy and assistance

Take a moment to quiet your spirit, becoming completely present to this time and place. Allow all other thoughts and concerns to fall away as you come into the presence of God. Then, when you are ready, begin.

Loving Jesus, hear me calling,
Me, a sinner, poor and weak;
    Lo, I stretch mine arms to clasp you,
    And your tender solace seek,
Lest mine enemies against me
    Rise, their deeds of woe to wreak.

They that seek my soul in envy,
That would lead me from your throne,
    Be the wicked will their ruin,
    In destruction let them groan;
But, my Saviour, hear my pleading,
    Raise me, leave me not alone.

A Hymn, sung or heard (optional)

At the first sound of the trumpet's blast
The heavens shall be overcast.
    Each poor feeble soul must rise,
    And each cold body likewise.

Then some shall be whiter
Than the snow of December,
    And some shall be blacker
    Than the smith's burnt ember.

Then Christ shall stand, when all are sent,
    Delivering His Judgment.

Christ shall speak unto all assembled
"Listen to me, all you Good and Blest,
Come hither and stand upon

My right hand until I bring you to My Father's rest."

> Then Christ shall speak unto all again,
> "Depart from me, all you Bad and Curst,
> You are given to yonder foul black devils
> To work henceforth on you their worst."

Read or recite Psalm 139.

Holy Lord,
Under my thoughts may I God-thoughts find.
Half of my sins escape my mind.
> For what I said, or did not say,
> Pardon me, O Lord, I pray.

Read Jeramiah 18: 1-11, aloud or quietly.

O Lord, Jesus the Christ,
If I were in Heaven my harp I would sound
With apostles and angels and saints all around,
> Praising and thanking the Son who is crowned,
> May the poor race of Eve for that heaven be bound!

Holy Lord,
Help this foolish sinner,
I always go astray,
> I rise up in the morning
> But pray not with the day.
God I has long forsaken –
Forgotten how to pray,
> Where shall I go when Death shall come
> And I leave the world in disarray.

O Holy Lord,
> God with the Father and the Spirit,
For me is many a snare designed,
To fill my mind with doubts and fears;
> Far from the land of holy saints,
> I dwell within my vale of tears.
Let faith, let hope, let love –

Traits far above the cold world's way –
    With patience, humility, and awe,
    Become my guides from day to day.

I acknowledge, the evil I have done.
From the day of my birth till the day of my death,
    Through the sight of my eyes,
Through the hearing of my ears,
    Through the sayings of my mouth,
Through the thoughts of my heart,
    Through the touch of my hands,
Through the course of my way,
    Through all I said and did not,
Through all I promised and fulfilled not,
    Through all the laws and holy commandments I broke.
I ask even now absolution of you,
    For fear I may have never asked it as was right,
    And that I might not live to ask it again,

O Holy Lord, my King in Heaven,
May you not let my soul stray from you,
May you keep me in a good state,
    May you turn me toward what is good to do,
    May you protect me from dangers, small and great.
May you fill my eyes with tears of repentance,
    So I may avoid the sinner's awful sentence.
May the Grace of the God for ever be with me,
    And whatever my needs, may the Triune God give me.

Select one of the following options for the Lord's Prayer.

Option A

O Jesus Christ,
Lord of heaven and earth,
Help me pray as you yourself taught:
    "Our Father in heaven,
    hallowed be your name.
    Your kingdom come.
    Your will be done,

on earth as it is in heaven.
Give us this day our daily bread.
And forgive us our debts,
as we also have forgiven our debtors.
And do not bring us to the time of trial,
but rescue us from the evil one."
(Matthew 6:9-13)
From the foes of my land,
from the foes of my faith,
From the foes who would us dissever,
> O Lord, preserve me, in life and in death,
> With the Sign of the Cross for ever.
> *For the kingdom, the power, and the glory*
> *are yours now and for ever. Amen.*

Please proceed with "I beseech you, O Lord...," found after Option B.

Option B

O Jesus Christ,
Lord of heaven and earth,
Help me pray as you yourself taught:
> *Our Father in heaven,*
> *hallowed be your name,*
> *your kingdom come,*
> *your will be done,*
> *on earth as in heaven.*
> *Give us today our daily bread.*
> *Forgive us our sins*
> *as we forgive those who sin against us.*
> *Lead us not into temptation*
> *but deliver us from evil.*

From the foes of my land,
from the foes of my faith,
From the foes who would us dissever,
> O Lord, preserve me, in life and in death,
> With the Sign of the Cross for ever.
> *For the kingdom, the power, and the glory*
> *are yours now and for ever. Amen.*

I beseech you, O Lord.
God in Heaven, unsurpassed in power and might;
    Be behind me, Be on my left,
    Be before me, Be on my right!
Against each danger, you are my help;
In distress, upon you I call.
    In dark times, may you sustain me
    And lift me up again when I fall.
Lord over heaven and of earth,
You know my offenses.
    Yet, listening to my pleadings,
    You guide me away from sinful pretenses.
Lord of all creation and the many creatures,
You bestow on me many earthly treasures.
    Revealing love in each life and season,
    You share with me heavenly pleasures.
May you arouse me
In moments both of joy and of strife;
    Most holy Lord, bring me new life!

A Hymn, sung or heard (optional)

O Jesus Christ,
    Lord of heaven and earth,
    You are my riches, my store, my provision,
My star through the years
When troubles rend me,
    Through times of strife and tears,
    Sweet Jesus, defend me.

Be your cross my royal symbol,
Be its holy sign my guard;
    While against the foe, unwearied,
    I shall still keep watch and ward;
Till the powers of darkness, conquered,
    Shall adore your throne, O Lord.

Son of God, the everliving,
Tender Saviour, hear and heed,

> See me, Lord of angels, weeping,
>> Crying out to you in need;
> Grant me mercy, grant forgiveness,
>> Virtue grant in word and deed.

End this time of prayer by taking some time to bring to mind the various ways God shields you from harm or guides you through the world's tumult. Then, when you are ready, conclude by saying:

O Holy Lord, King in Heaven,
I place myself at the edge of your grace,
    On the floor of your house myself I place,
And to banish the sin of my heart away,
    I lower my knee to you this day.
Through life's torrents of pain may you bring me whole,
    And, O Lord Jesus Christ, preserve also my soul. Amen.

5.1b   Preparation for Prayer

Consideration of the Readings

After reciting or prayerfully reading the prayer sequence for this day or week:
- Read the parable of the potter and the clay in Jeremiah 18:1-11. Again, pay careful attention to any phrases or images that seem particularly meaningful to you. Then, record these highlights in your workbook so you will remember them during this day or week of prayer.
- Read the parable of the unfruitful vineyard in Isaiah 5:1-6, noting any phrases or images that seem particularly meaningful to you and record these highlights in your workbook.
- Read about Jesus telling the parable of the wedding banquet in Matthew 22:1-14. Again, note each person's appearance and actions during the episode as well as the key elements of the story and its setting. Then, record any aspects of this story that speak strongly to you.

Note: You also should consider any aspect of the prayer sequence from this day or week that seemed particularly significant to you.

Contemplation of Your Needs

When you are ready, allow any distractions to fade from your consciousness as you become aware of your desire to live in God's goodness. Feel yourself yearning to properly use the many gifts God has given you, to experience God's continuing care, and to be open to the immense love God shows for you, then:
- Read "Failge Tries to Kill Patrick" (found on page 319). Allow yourself to linger on any thoughts, phrases or images that seem particularly meaningful or significant to your earlier preparations or prayer.
- Pray for your desires in the coming day or week. Ask that the divine presence all around you may be revealed so all your intentions and actions may be directed purely to the service and praise of God. Ask also for the courage to consider the prospect of complete separation from God in hell.

- Conclude by praying to feel intense sorrow (and even tears) for your sins.

Then, record any significant thoughts, emotions, or reactions from these moments in your workbook.

After this, put your notes aside. Without straining your memory, consider in turn each of the readings for the coming day or week and allow them to take shape in your imagination. Prayerfully ponder how each reading affects you emotionally without overtly thinking about their content, asking God to illuminate the spiritual gifts offered in each reading – quieting your mind and creating a receptive space in yourself to see or hear the response.

Finally, conclude by allowing these desires to fade from your consciousness as you offer this traditional Irish prayer:

> O God, I believe in you; strengthen my belief.
> I trust in you; confirm my trust.
> I love you; double my love.
> I repent that I angered you,
> Increase my repentance.
> Fill you my heart with awe without despair;
> With hope, without over-confidence;
> With piety without infatuation;
> And with joy without excess.
> My God, consent to guide me by your wisdom;
> To constrain me by your right;
> To comfort me by your mercy;
> And to protect me by your power. Amen.

Allow these words to linger on your mind and in your heart for a few moments and then, while they are still fresh in your memory, write the most important thoughts, feelings, and desires from this preparatory time in your workbook.

5.2 A Meditation on Jeremiah 18:1-11

In this meditation on Jeremiah 18:1-11, you will see and hear Saint Patrick telling a crowd the parable of the potter and the clay.

[1]   Begin by reading the biblical selection and reviewing your notes on it from your earlier preparations.

[2]   Then, focus on this specific time and place as you allow all other concerns to fall away before considering the people and place of this moment of prayer.

- Allow an image of Patrick to emerge in your imagination, noting his physical characteristics and mannerisms. Look at what he is wearing or carrying. Make a note of whether he is sitting, standing, or walking. Ponder this mental image, allowing any other observations about Patrick to form in your mind.

- Note how many people are with Patrick, making a mental note of their appearance and demeanor. Look at Patrick's disciples, observing where they are standing and how they behave toward Patrick. Look at the crowd, noting their attitude and actions toward Patrick. Observe whether the people are sitting, standing, or walking. Take a moment to ponder this mental image, allowing other impressions of these people to form. Become familiar with the men and women you will encounter during your prayer as well as their behavior.

- Allow yourself to become aware of the location of this moment of prayer. Observe whether it is inside or outside, paying attention to its physical characteristics and the arrangement of the people in it. Look around the place and notice more details about it – if it is in dim or bright light, if it is still and silent or filled with noise, if it has an unusual smell or not, etc. Become familiar with the location of your upcoming prayer.

- Take a moment to remain in this place with these people before allowing these images to fade from your consciousness.

[3]   Become aware of your desires during this moment of prayer. Remember your desire to experience the divine presence all around you and to trust in God's plan for you, asking that all your intentions and actions may be directed purely to the service and praise of God. Reassert your desire for God's gift of courage to consider the prospect of complete separation from God in hell. Finally, recall your desire to feel intense sorrow (and even tears) for your sins.

As these desires fill your consciousness, let all other concerns fall aside as you focus on this time and place of prayer.

[4]   Allow the image of Saint Patrick and the crowd to reemerge in your imagination.

* Watch as the group assembles around Patrick. Listen to the sounds of this moment and become comfortable as you prepare to hear Patrick speak. Feel the anticipation of the people around you and share in that enthusiasm.

* As you hear Patrick begin to calm the crowd, ask God to help you enter this moment – either by joining these events or by listening quietly to them. Focus your attention on Saint Patrick, noting his physical appearance and his demeanor.

* Then, watch and listen as Patrick tells the parable of the potter and the clay. You may want to quietly read the passage while remaining prayerfully aware of your mental image of Patrick or you may choose to stay completely within the imagined realm of your prayer. Whichever you choose, know that God will offer you the words from the biblical passage that you need to hear – even if only in fragments.

* Hear Patrick explain the parable. Listen to him as he explains the meaning and significance of God's promise expressed in this story.

– Again, look around as Patrick speaks and see the reactions of his disciples and the people in the crowd. Become aware of their feelings and how they behave toward Patrick and one another.

– Remember that Saint Patrick is speaking to men and women striving to remain faithful to God's desires and promises while struggling with their sinfulness. Remember that he also is speaking to you.

* After Patrick finishes speaking, allow his image and this place to fade from your imagination as you become aware of the phrases and images from this moment which touched you most deeply. Recall the emotions and memories – including any sounds or smells – evoked during your prayer. Allow these seminal aspects of your meditation to linger on your mind and in your heart, noting any special feelings evoked by them.

[5]   When you are ready, become aware of God's presence with you in this moment and have an open and informal conversation about this prayer period and how the passage from Jeremiah expresses your own needs or desires – giving space for God to respond or to highlight different aspects from the biblical selection and your experiences during this meditation. Then, gradually allow your thoughts to recede

as you focus on God's broader presence in your life and in the world around you.

[6]   Conclude by allowing these desires to fade from your consciousness as you offer this traditional Irish prayer:

> *Confirm me in your love divine,*
> *Smooth for my feet life's rugged way;*
> *My will with yours entwine,*
> *Lest evil lead my steps astray.*
> *Be with me still as guard and guide,*
> *Keep me in holy sanctity,*
> *Let my firm faith on you abide,*
> *From fraud and error hold me free. Amen.*

[7]   Afterward, take 10-15 minutes in a quiet space to reflect on the most significant moments from this time of prayer and record your reflections in your retreat journal.

5.3 A Meditation on Isaiah 5:1-6

In this meditation on Isaiah 5:1-6, you will see and hear Saint Patrick telling a crowd the parable of the unfruitful vineyard.

[1]   Begin by reading the biblical selection and reviewing your notes on it from your earlier preparations.

[2]   Then, focus on this specific time and place as you allow all other concerns to fall away before considering the people and place of this moment of prayer.

- Allow an image of Patrick to emerge in your imagination, noting his physical characteristics and mannerisms. Look at what he is wearing or carrying. Make a note of whether he is sitting, standing, or walking. Ponder this mental image, allowing any other observations about Patrick to form in your mind.

- Note how many people are with Patrick, making a mental note of their appearance and demeanor. Look at Patrick's disciples, observing where they are standing and how they behave toward Patrick. Look at the crowd, noting their attitude and behavior toward Patrick. Observe whether the people are sitting, standing, or walking. Take a moment to ponder this mental image, allowing other impressions of these people to form. Become familiar with the men and women you will encounter during your prayer as well as their behavior.

- Allow yourself to become aware of the location of this moment of prayer. Observe whether it is inside or outside, paying attention to its physical characteristics and the arrangement of the people in it. Look around the place and notice more details about it – if it is in dim or bright light, if it is still and silent or filled with noise, if it has an unusual smell or not, etc. Become familiar with the location of your upcoming prayer.

- Take a moment to remain in this place with these people before allowing these images to fade from your consciousness.

[3]   Become aware of your desires during this moment of prayer. Remember your desire to experience the divine presence all around you and to trust in God's plan for you, asking that all your intentions and actions may be directed purely to the service and praise of God. Reassert your desire for God's gift of courage to consider the prospect of complete separation from God in hell. Finally, recall your desire to feel intense sorrow (and even tears) for your sins.

As these desires fill your consciousness, let all other concerns fall aside as you focus on this time and place of prayer.

[4]   Allow the image of Saint Patrick and the crowd to reemerge in your imagination.

- Watch as the group assembles around Patrick. Listen to the sounds of this moment and become comfortable as you prepare to hear Patrick speak. Feel the anticipation of the people around you and share in that enthusiasm.

- As you hear Saint Patrick begin to calm the crowd, ask God to help you enter this moment – either by joining these events or by listening quietly to them. Focus your attention on Saint Patrick, noting his physical appearance and his demeanor.

- Then, watch and listen as Patrick tells the parable of the unfruitful vineyard. You may want to quietly read the passage while remaining prayerfully aware of your mental image of Patrick or you may choose to stay completely within the imagined realm of your prayer. Whichever you choose, know that God will offer you the words from the biblical passage that you need to hear – even if only in fragments.

- Hear Patrick explain the parable. Listen to him as he explains the meaning and significance of God's promise expressed in this story.

– Again, look around as Patrick speaks and see the reactions of his disciples and the people in the crowd. Become aware of their feelings and how they behave toward Patrick and one another.

– Remember that Saint Patrick is speaking to men and women striving to remain faithful to God's desires and promises while struggling with their sinfulness. Remember that he also is speaking to you.

- After Patrick finishes speaking, allow his image and this place to fade from your imagination as you become aware of the phrases and images from this moment which touched you most deeply. Recall the emotions and memories – including any sounds or smells – evoked during your prayer. Allow these seminal aspects of your meditation to linger on your mind and in your heart, noting any special feelings evoked by them.

[5]   When you are ready, become aware of God's presence with you in this moment and have an open and informal conversation about this prayer period and how the passage from Isaiah expresses your own needs or desires – giving space for God to respond or to highlight different aspects from the biblical selection and your experiences

during this meditation. Then, gradually allow your thoughts to recede as you focus on God's broader presence in your life and in the world around you.

[6]   Conclude by allowing these desires to fade from your consciousness as you offer this traditional Irish prayer:

> *Confirm me in your love divine,*
> *Smooth for my feet life's rugged way;*
> *My will with yours entwine,*
> *Lest evil lead my steps astray.*
> *Be with me still as guard and guide,*
> *Keep me in holy sanctity,*
> *Let my firm faith on you abide,*
> *From fraud and error hold me free. Amen.*

[7]   Afterward, take 10-15 minutes in a quiet space to reflect on the most significant moments from this time of prayer and record your reflections in your retreat journal.

5.4 A Contemplation of Matthew 22:1-14

In this contemplation of Matthew 22:1-14, you will see and hear Jesus telling a crowd the parable of the wedding banquet.

[1] Begin by reading the biblical selection and reviewing your notes on it from your earlier preparations.

[2] Then, focus on this specific time and place as you allow all other concerns to fall away before considering the people and place of this moment of prayer.

• Allow an image of Jesus to emerge in your imagination, noting his physical characteristics and mannerisms. Look at what he is wearing or carrying. Make a note of whether he is sitting, standing, or walking. Ponder this mental image, allowing any other observations about Jesus to form in your mind.

• Note how many people are with Jesus, making a mental note of their appearance and demeanor. Look at Jesus' disciples, observing where they are standing and how they behave toward Jesus. Look at the crowd, noting their attitude and behavior toward Jesus. Observe whether the people are sitting, standing, or walking. Take a moment to ponder this mental image, allowing other impressions of these men and women to form. Become familiar with the men and women you will encounter during your prayer as well as their behavior.

• Allow yourself to become aware of the location of this moment of prayer. Observe whether it is inside or outside, paying attention to its physical characteristics and the arrangement of the people in it. Look around the place and notice more details about it – if it is in dim or bright light, if it is still and silent or filled with noise, if it has an unusual smell or not, etc. Become familiar with the location of your upcoming prayer.

• Take a moment to remain in this place with these people before allowing these images to fade from your consciousness.

[3] Become aware of your desires during this moment of prayer. Remember your desire to experience the divine presence all around you and to trust in God's plan for you, asking that all your intentions and actions may be directed purely to the service and praise of God. Reassert your desire for God's gift of courage to consider the prospect of complete separation from God in hell. Finally, recall your desire to feel intense sorrow (and even tears) for your sins.

As these desires fill your consciousness, let all other concerns fall aside as you focus on this time and place of prayer.

[4]   Allow the image of Jesus and the crowd to reemerge in your imagination.

• Watch as the group assembles around Jesus. Listen to the sounds of this moment and become comfortable as you prepare to hear Jesus speak. Feel the anticipation of the people around you and share in that enthusiasm.

• As you hear Jesus begin to calm the crowd, ask God to help you share in this experience – either by joining these events or by listening quietly to them. Focus your attention on Jesus, noting his physical appearance and his demeanor.

• Then, watch and listen as Jesus tells the parable. You may want to quietly read the passage while remaining prayerfully aware of your mental image of Jesus or you may choose to stay completely within the imagined realm of your prayer. Whichever you choose, know that God will offer you the words from the biblical passage that you need to hear – even if only in fragments.

• Hear Jesus explain the parable. Listen to him as he explains the meaning and significance of God's promise expressed in this story.

– Again, look around as Jesus speaks and see the reactions of his disciples and the people in the crowd. Become aware of their feelings and how they behave toward Jesus and one another.

– Remember that Jesus is speaking to men and women striving to remain faithful to God's desires and promises while struggling with their sinfulness. Remember that he also is speaking to you.

• After Jesus finishes speaking, allow his image and this place to fade from your imagination as you become aware of the phrases and images from this moment which touched you most deeply. Recall the emotions and memories – including any sounds or smells – evoked during your prayer. Allow these seminal aspects of your meditation to linger on your mind and in your heart, noting any special feelings evoked by them.

[5]   When you are ready, become aware of Jesus' presence with you in this moment and have an open and informal conversation about this prayer period and how the passage from Matthew's gospel expresses your own needs or desires – giving space for Jesus to respond or to highlight different aspects from the biblical account and your experiences during this contemplation. Then, gradually allow your

thoughts to recede as you focus on God's broader presence in your life and in the world around you.

[6] Conclude by allowing these desires to fade from your consciousness as you offer this traditional Irish prayer:

> *Confirm me in your love divine,*
> *Smooth for my feet life's rugged way;*
> *My will with yours entwine,*
> *Lest evil lead my steps astray.*
> *Be with me still as guard and guide,*
> *Keep me in holy sanctity,*
> *Let my firm faith on you abide,*
> *From fraud and error hold me free. Amen.*

[7] Afterward, take 10-15 minutes in a quiet space to reflect on the most significant moments from this time of prayer and record your reflections in your retreat journal.

5.5 A Repeated Contemplation of Matthew 22:1-14

In this repeated contemplation of Matthew 22:1-14, you again will see and hear Jesus telling a crowd the parable of the wedding banquet.

[1] Begin by re-reading the biblical selection and reviewing your notes on it from your earlier preparations.

[2] Then, focus on this specific time and place as you allow all other concerns to fall away before considering the people and place of this moment of prayer.

- Allow an image of Jesus to emerge in your imagination, noting his physical characteristics and mannerisms. Look at what he is wearing or carrying. Make a note of whether he is sitting, standing, or walking. Ponder this mental image, allowing any other observations about Jesus to form in your mind.

- Note how many people are with Jesus, making a mental note of their appearance and demeanor. Look at Jesus' disciples, observing where they are standing and how they behave toward Jesus. Look at the crowd, noting their attitude and behavior toward Jesus. Observe whether the people are sitting, standing, or walking. Take a moment to ponder this mental image, allowing other impressions of these people to form. Become familiar with the men and women you will encounter during your prayer as well as their behavior.

- Allow yourself to become aware of the location of this moment of prayer. Observe whether it is inside or outside, paying attention to its physical characteristics and the arrangement of the people in it. Look around the place and notice more details about it – if it is in dim or bright light, if it is still and silent or filled with noise, if it has an unusual smell or not, etc. Become familiar with the location of your upcoming prayer.

- Take a moment to remain in this place with these people before allowing these images to fade from your consciousness.

[3] Become aware of your desires during this moment of prayer. Remember your desire to experience the divine presence all around you and to trust in God's plan for you, asking that all your intentions and actions may be directed purely to the service and praise of God. Reassert your desire for God's gift of courage to consider the prospect of complete separation from God in hell. Finally, recall your desire to feel intense sorrow (and even tears) for your sins.

As these desires fill your consciousness, let all other concerns fall aside as you focus on this time and place of prayer.

[4]   Allow the image of Jesus and the crowd to reemerge in your imagination.

- Watch as the group assembles around Jesus. Listen to the sounds of this moment and become comfortable as you prepare to hear Jesus speak. Feel the anticipation of the people around you and share in that enthusiasm.
- As you hear Jesus begin to calm the crowd, ask God to help you share in their prayer – either by joining them or by listening quietly to them. Focus your attention on Jesus, noting his physical appearance and his demeanor.
- Then, watch and listen as Jesus tells the parable. You may want to quietly read the passage while remaining prayerfully aware of your mental image of Jesus or you may choose to stay completely within the imagined realm of your prayer. Whichever you choose, know that God will offer you the words from the biblical passage that you need to hear – even if only in fragments.
- Hear Jesus explain the parable. Listen to him as he explains the meaning and significance of God's promise expressed in this story.
  – Again, look around as Jesus speaks and see the reactions of his disciples and the people in the crowd. Become aware of their feelings and how they behave toward Jesus and one another.
  – Remember that Jesus is speaking to men and women striving to remain faithful to God's desires and promises while struggling with their sinfulness. Remember that he also is speaking to you.
- After Jesus finishes speaking, allow his image and this place to fade from your imagination as you become aware of the phrases and images from this moment which touched you most deeply. Recall the emotions and memories – including any sounds or smells – evoked during your prayer. Allow these seminal aspects of your meditation to linger on your mind and in your heart, noting any special feelings evoked by them.

[5]   When you are ready, become aware of Jesus' presence with you in this moment and have an open and informal conversation about this prayer period and how the passage from Matthew's gospel expresses your own needs or desires – giving space for Jesus to respond or to highlight different aspects from the biblical account and your experiences during this contemplation. Then, gradually allow your

thoughts to recede as you focus on God's broader presence in your life and in the world around you.

[6]   Conclude by allowing these desires to fade from your consciousness as you offer this traditional Irish prayer:

> *Confirm me in your love divine,*
> *Smooth for my feet life's rugged way;*
> *My will with yours entwine,*
> *Lest evil lead my steps astray.*
> *Be with me still as guard and guide,*
> *Keep me in holy sanctity,*
> *Let my firm faith on you abide,*
> *From fraud and error hold me free. Amen.*

[7]   Afterward, take 10-15 minutes in a quiet space to reflect on the most significant moments from this time of prayer and record your reflections in your retreat journal.

5.6 An Application of the Senses

[1]   Become aware of your prayerful desires during this day or week. Bring to mind your desire that the divine presence all around you may be revealed so all your intentions and actions may be directed purely to the service and praise of God. Focus on your desire to consider the prospect of complete separation from God in hell. Finally, reaffirm your desire to feel intense sorrow (and even tears) for your sins.
[2]   When you are ready, call to mind the various prayers of the preceding day or days. Allow the images and words of these prayers to linger and then slowly fade from your consciousness.

- Remember your meditation on Jeremiah 18:1-11. Consider the images and feelings evoked in you during your prayer, feeling God's presence in these memories and becoming aware of the specific sensations associated with each image.
- Recall your meditation on Isaiah 5:1-6, considering it in the same way as your memories of the Jeremiah 18.
- Review your imaginative contemplations of Matthew 22:1-14 in the same manner as the previous prayers.

Make a mental note of which senses are most active. You may see an image or a color, hear a sound or a phrase, or smell a scent or a fragrance. You may even taste a flavor or feel a sensation on your skin.
[3]   Then, relax and allow these various memories and experiences to quietly enter and leave your consciousness without being controlled. Linger on the sensory images and memories being evoked in you – noticing any images or colors, any sounds or phrases, any scents or fragrances, any flavors or physical sensations associated with each prayer.
[4]   When you are ready, become completely still and clear your mind of all thoughts and concerns. Allow an image of a special personal space to form in your imagination. Then, watch as God enters that place and forms a small image or object for you that expresses the thought or awareness that you most need to carry with you into your life.

Reverently pick up the object or image, a reflection of the most important gift you have been given during this time of prayer. Look at it carefully and become aware of the divine presence contained within it. Take a moment to register what it looks like and how it feels in your hand. Then, feel the joy and confidence that comes from touching the presence of God as you accept this gift, offering a short prayer of gratitude while you relax into the pleasure of this moment.

[5]   Then, conclude by allowing these images to fade from your consciousness as you offer this traditional Irish prayer:

Confirm me in your love divine,
Smooth for my feet life's rugged way;
My will with yours entwine,
Lest evil lead my steps astray.
Be with me still as guard and guide,
Keep me in holy sanctity,
Let my firm faith on you abide,
From fraud and error hold me free. Amen.

[6]   While your experiences are still fresh in your mind, record the most significant impressions or sensations from this time of prayer in your retreat journal.

5.7 Review of Prayer

[1] Remember your desires during the preceding day or week of prayer. Become aware of our desire to experience the divine presence all around you and to trust in God's plan for you so that all your intentions and actions may be directed purely to the service and praise of God. Recall your desire to consider courageously the prospect of complete separation from God in hell. Finally, reaffirm your desire to feel intense sorrow (and even tears) for your sins.

After bringing these thoughts and desires into your consciousness, ask God once again to fulfill these desires in your own life and in your interactions with others.

[2] Then, take a moment to allow the words, thoughts, and feelings from your prayers during the last day or week to linger before asking God to reveal the fulfillment of your deepest desires in these various memories.

• Think about the prayer sequence at the beginning of this day or week. Make a mental note of any words, insights or images that remain particularly significant or meaningful to you.

• Ponder the story, "Failge Tries to Kill Patrick". Note any words, insights, or images from it that remain particularly significant or meaningful to you.

• Remember your meditation on Jeremiah 18:1-11.

– Consider the most powerful images, phrases, or feelings from your prayer. Ask yourself what gifts God gave to you through these moments, perhaps offering you new insights or perhaps affirming an important aspect of your faith. Ask yourself how God may be calling you to change through these moments, being as specific as possible.

– Examine your disposition as you prayed, noting whether prayer came easily or with resistance. Recall the easiest moments in your prayer and any moments of joy you may have experienced. Remember also if you encountered any difficulty opening yourself to God or if you felt any sadness as you prayed. Ask God to help you understand why these feelings surfaced.

– Bring to mind any moments when you added personal elements (e.g., familiar places or people from your life) or connected your prayers to other scriptures or spiritual writings. Ask yourself how these additions helped or hindered you as you prayed. Again, if you do not know why this happened, ask God to help you understand.

- Recall your meditation on Isaiah 5:1-6. Then, review your prayer in the same way as your earlier reflection on Jeremiah 18.
- Review your imaginative contemplations of Matthew 22:1-14 in the same manner as the previous prayers.
- Reflect on the ebb and flow of sensory impressions and feelings that marked your application of the senses. Isolate the most memorable moments and sensory impressions from your prayer and reflect on how God used these moments to give you a particular gift.

[3] Finally, ponder the times when images or feelings from the readings of this day or week surfaced outside these prayer periods. Consider those moments or events in which God's presence or guidance was especially strong as well as any moments when you were struggling. Think about the most memorable aspects of these experiences, asking God to explain their significance.

[4] Take a moment to allow the words, thoughts, and feelings of these prayers to linger on your mind and in your heart. Finally, conclude by allowing these desires to fade from your consciousness as you offer this traditional Irish prayer:

> *O God, I believe in you; strengthen my belief.*
> *I trust in you; confirm my trust.*
> *I love you; double my love.*
> *I repent that I angered you,*
> *Increase my repentance.*
> *Fill you my heart with awe without despair;*
> *With hope, without over-confidence;*
> *With piety without infatuation;*
> *And with joy without excess.*
> *My God, consent to guide me by your wisdom;*
> *To constrain me by your right;*
> *To comfort me by your mercy;*
> *And to protect me by your power. Amen.*

[5] After finishing these prayers, summarize your reflections on the gifts or graces you received during the prayers of this last day or week and record these thoughts in your retreat journal.

6. Sin and Sorrow

6.1a   I Am Not Worthy, O God
a prayer of humble contrition

Take a moment to quiet your spirit, becoming completely present to this time and place. Allow all other thoughts and concerns to fall away as you come into the presence of God. Then, when you are ready, begin.

I am not worthy, O God, mine eyes
To turn unto your starry skies;
    But bowed in sin, with moans and sighs,
    I beg you, hear me.

My duty I have left undone,
Nor sought I crime or shame to shun,
    My feet in sinful paths have run,
    Sweet Christ, be near me.

A Hymn, sung or heard (optional)

My God, give me strength
So that I may make expiation for my misdeeds,
    So that I may win victory over my temptations,
    So that I may right my strong evil-inclinations,
And so that I may practise the virtues
    That are suitable to my state of life.

Fill my heart with affection for your goodness,
With hatred of my faults, with love for my neighbours,
    And with contempt for the world.
    That I may remember, O God,
To be submissive to my superiors,
To be at one with my inferiors,
    Faithful to my friends
    And charitable to my enemies.

Aid me to gain a victory
Over fleshly desires by piety,
    Over covetousness by alms-giving,
    Over passion by mildness,

And over hypocrisy by earnestness.

Read or recite Psalm 32.

Holy Triune God,
    Father, Son and Spirit
Under my thoughts may I God-thoughts find.
Half of my sins escape my mind.
    For what I said, or did not say,
    Pardon me, O Lord, I pray.

Read Matthew 25: 31-46, aloud or quietly.

O Holy God,
    Father, Son and Spirit
If I were in Heaven my harp I would sound
With apostles and angels and saints all around,
    Praising and thanking the Son who is crowned,
    May the poor race of Eve for that heaven be bound!

Holy Triune God,
Weakly I go from the load within,
Deeply repenting with woe my sin.
    I acknowledge faith in my God all my days
    With love from my heart and with hope always,

From the foot of your cross I call to you
Jesus, Lord, bow down to me.
    For I stand in the faith of my God to-day,
    Put love in my heart and hope away.

O Holy God,
    Father, Son and Spirit
For me is many a snare designed,
To fill my mind with doubts and fears;
    Far from the land of holy saints,
    I dwell within my vale of tears.
Let faith, let hope, let love –
Traits far above the cold world's way –
    With patience, humility, and awe,

    Become my guides from day to day.

I acknowledge, the evil I have done.
From the day of my birth till the day of my death,
    Through the sight of my eyes,
Through the hearing of my ears,
    Through the sayings of my mouth,
Through the thoughts of my heart,
    Through the touch of my hands,
Through the course of my way,
    Through all I said and did not,
Through all I promised and fulfilled not,
    Through all the laws and holy commandments I broke.
I ask even now absolution of you,
In the sweet name of Jesus Christ,
    For fear I may have never asked it as was right,
    And that I might not live to ask it again,

O Divine Majesty,
    Father, Son and Spirit
May you not let my soul stray from you,
May you keep me in a good state,
    May you turn me toward what is good to do,
    May you protect me from dangers, small and great.
May you fill my eyes with tears of repentance,
    So I may avoid the sinner's awful sentence.
May the Grace of the God for ever be with me,
    And whatever my needs, may the Triune God give me.

Select one of the following options for the Lord's Prayer.

Option A

O God,
Father, Son and Spirit,
help me pray as Jesus himself taught:
    "Our Father in heaven,
    hallowed be your name.
    Your kingdom come.
    Your will be done,

> on earth as it is in heaven.
> Give us this day our daily bread.
> And forgive us our debts,
> as we also have forgiven our debtors.
> And do not bring us to the time of trial,
> but rescue us from the evil one."
> (Matthew 6:9-13)

From the foes of my land,
from the foes of my faith,
From the foes who would us dissever,
> O Trinity preserve me, in life, in death,
> With the Sign of the Cross for ever.
> *For the kingdom, the power, and the glory*
> *are yours now and for ever. Amen.*

Please proceed with "I beseech the wonderful and blessed Trinity,…," found after Option B.

Option B

O God,
Father, Son and Spirit,
help me pray as Jesus himself taught:
> *Our Father in heaven,*
> *hallowed be your name,*
> *your kingdom come,*
> *your will be done,*
> *on earth as in heaven.*
> *Give us today our daily bread.*
> *Forgive us our sins*
> *as we forgive those who sin against us.*
> *Lead us not into temptation*
> *but deliver us from evil.*

From the foes of my land,
from the foes of my faith,
From the foes who would us dissever,
> O Trinity preserve me, in life, in death,
> With the Sign of the Cross for ever.
> *For the kingdom, the power, and the glory*
> *are yours now and for ever. Amen.*

I beseech the wonderful and blessed Trinity,
God in Heaven, unsurpassed in power and might;
    Be behind me, Be on my left,
    Be before me, Be on my right!
Against each danger, God is my help;
In distress, upon the Divine Majesty I call.
    In dark times, may my God sustain me
    And lift me up again when I fall.
Lord over heaven and of earth,
The Triune God knows my offenses.
    Yet, listening to my pleadings,
    Guides me away from sinful pretenses.
Lord of all creation and the many creatures,
My God bestows on me many earthly treasures.
    Revealing love in each life and season,
    My God shares with me heavenly pleasures.
May the Holy Trinity arouse me
In moments both of joy and of strife;
    God the Father, with Mary's mighty Son,
    And the noble Spirit, bring me new life!

A Hymn, sung or heard (optional)

O Divine Majesty,
Three in one Godhead, without division.
    You are my riches, my store, my provision,
My star through the years
When troubles rend me,
    Through times of strife and tears,
    O God, defend me.

Fill my soul with grief sincere,
With sorrow deep for my offence;
    Let the tear moisten my pillow;
    Hear me and grant me defense.

For all my many crimes, O God,
Toward the pains of hell I sadly plod;
    But you know my repentance,

And spare the painful sentence.

End this time of prayer by taking some time to bring to mind the various ways God shields you from harm or guides you through the world's tumult. Then, when you are ready, conclude by saying:

O Holy Triune God,
Father, Son and Spirit,
I place myself at the edge of your grace,
    On the floor of your house myself I place,
And to banish the sin of my heart away,
    I lower my knee to you this day.
Through life's torrents of pain may you bring me whole,
    And, O Blessed Trinity, preserve also my soul. Amen.

6.1b Preparation for Prayer

Consideration of the Readings

After reciting or prayerfully reading the prayer sequence for this day or week:
- Read Matthew 25:31-46. Make a mental note of Jesus' appearance and actions during the episode, the people listening to him, and the key elements of Jesus' message. Again, consider any aspects of this story that speak strongly to you before recording these observations in your workbook.
- Read Ephesians 4:17-24. Again, pay careful attention to any phrases or images that seem particularly meaningful to you. Then, record these highlights in your workbook so you will remember them during this day or week of prayer.
- Read Colossians 1:15-20, noting any phrases or images that seem particularly meaningful to you and record these highlights in your workbook.

<u>Note:</u> *You also should consider any aspect of the prayer sequence from this day or week that seemed particularly significant to you.*

Contemplation of Your Needs

When you are ready, allow any distractions to fade from your consciousness as you become aware of your desire to live in God's goodness. Feel yourself yearning to properly use the many gifts God has given you, to experience God's continuing care, and to be open to the immense love God shows for you, then:
- Read "The Conversion of Dichu" (found on page 319). Allow yourself to linger on any thoughts, phrases or images that seem particularly meaningful or significant to your earlier preparations or prayer.
- Pray for your desires in the coming day or week. Ask that the divine presence all around you may be revealed so all your intentions and actions may be directed purely to the service and praise of God. Ask also for the courage to contemplate your own sinfulness and to experience deep regret and remorse for your rebellion against God.

- Conclude by bringing this sorrow before God and repenting your sins.

Then, record any significant thoughts, emotions, or reactions from these moments in your workbook.

After this, put your notes aside. Without straining your memory, consider in turn each of the readings for the coming day or week and allow them to take shape in your imagination. Prayerfully ponder how each reading affects you emotionally without overtly thinking about their content, asking God to illuminate the spiritual gifts offered in each reading – quieting your mind and creating a receptive space in yourself to see or hear the response.

Finally, conclude by allowing these desires to fade from your consciousness as you offer this traditional Irish prayer:

O God, I believe in you; strengthen my belief.
I trust in you; confirm my trust.
I love you; double my love.
I repent that I angered you,
Increase my repentance.
Fill you my heart with awe without despair;
With hope, without over-confidence;
With piety without infatuation;
And with joy without excess.
My God, consent to guide me by your wisdom;
To constrain me by your right;
To comfort me by your mercy;
And to protect me by your power. Amen.

Allow these words to linger on your mind and in your heart for a few moments and then, while they are still fresh in your memory, write the most important thoughts, feelings, and desires from this preparatory time in your workbook.

6.2 A Meditation on Matthew 25:31-46

In this meditation on Matthew 25:31-46, you will see and hear Saint Patrick preaching to a crowd about trusting in Jesus' redemptive mission.

[1] Begin by reading the biblical selection and reviewing your notes on it.

[2] Then, focus on this specific time and place as you allow all other concerns to fall away before considering the people and place of this moment of prayer.

- Allow an image of Saint Patrick to emerge in your imagination, noting his physical characteristics and mannerisms. Look at what he is wearing or carrying. Make a note of whether he is sitting, standing, or walking. Ponder this mental image, allowing any other observations about Patrick to form in your mind.

- Note how many people are with Patrick, making a mental note of their appearance and demeanor. Look at Patrick's disciples, observing where they are standing and how they behave toward Saint Patrick. Look at the crowd, noting their attitude and behavior toward Patrick. Observe whether the people are sitting, standing, or walking. Take a moment to ponder this mental image, allowing other impressions of these people to form. Become familiar with the men and women you will encounter during your prayer as well as their behavior.

- Allow yourself to become aware of the location of this moment of prayer. Observe whether it is inside or outside, paying attention to its physical characteristics and the arrangement of the people in it. Look around the place and notice more details about it – if it is in dim or bright light, if it is still and silent or filled with noise, if it has an unusual smell or not, etc. Become familiar with the location of your upcoming prayer.

- Take a moment to remain in this place with these people before allowing these images to fade from your consciousness.

[3] Become aware of your desires during this moment of prayer. Remember your desire to experience the divine presence all around you and to trust in God's plan for you, asking that all your intentions and actions may be directed purely to the service and praise of God. Reassert your desire for God's gift of courage to contemplate your own sinfulness and to experience deep regret and remorse for your rebellion

against God. Finally, recall your desire to repent your sins and bring your sorrow before God.

As these desires fill your consciousness, let all other concerns fall aside as you focus on this time and place of prayer.

[4]   Allow the image of Saint Patrick and the crowd to reemerge in your imagination.

- Watch as the group assembles around Patrick. Listen to the sounds of this moment and become comfortable as you prepare to hear Patrick speak. Feel the anticipation of the people around you and share in that enthusiasm.

- As you hear Patrick begin to calm the crowd, ask God to help you share in this experience – either by joining these events or by listening quietly to them. Focus your attention on Saint Patrick, noting his physical appearance and his demeanor.

- Then, watch and listen as Patrick presents Matthew's gospel. You may want to quietly read the passage while remaining prayerfully aware of your mental image of Patrick or you may choose to stay completely within the imagined realm of your prayer. Whichever you choose, know that God will offer you the words from the biblical passage that you need to hear – even if only in fragments.

- Hear Patrick explain the passage. Listen to him as he explains the meaning and significance of God's promise expressed in Matthew's words.

– Again, look around as Patrick speaks and see the reactions of his disciples and the people in the crowd. Become aware of their feelings and how they behave toward Patrick and one another.

– Remember that Saint Patrick is speaking to men and women yearning to be forgiven their sins. Remember that he also is speaking to you.

- After Saint Patrick finishes speaking, allow his image and this place to fade from your imagination as you become aware of the phrases and images from this moment which touched you most deeply. Recall the emotions and memories – including any sounds or smells – evoked during your prayer. Allow these seminal aspects of your meditation to linger on your mind and in your heart, noting any special feelings evoked by them.

[5]   Then, become aware of God's presence with you in this moment and have an open and informal conversation about this prayer period and how the passage from Matthew's gospel expresses your own needs or desires – giving space for God to respond or to highlight

different aspects from the biblical selection and your experiences during this meditation. Then, gradually allow your thoughts to recede as you focus on God's broader presence in your life and in the world around you.

[6] Conclude by allowing these desires to fade from your consciousness as you offer this traditional Irish prayer:

> *Confirm me in your love divine,*
> *Smooth for my feet life's rugged way;*
> *My will with yours entwine,*
> *Lest evil lead my steps astray.*
> *Be with me still as guard and guide,*
> *Keep me in holy sanctity,*
> *Let my firm faith on you abide,*
> *From fraud and error hold me free. Amen.*

[7] Afterward, take 10-15 minutes in a quiet space to reflect on the most significant moments from this time of prayer and record your reflections in your retreat journal.

6.3 A Meditation on Ephesians 4:17-24

In this meditation on Ephesians 4:17-24, you will see and hear Saint Patrick reminding his disciples that they need to be transformed by Christ's redemptive love.

[1] Begin by reading the biblical selection and reviewing your notes on it.

[2] Then, focus on this specific time and place as you allow all other concerns to fall away before considering the people and place of this moment of prayer.

- Allow an image of Patrick to emerge in your imagination, noting his physical characteristics and mannerisms. Look at what he is wearing or carrying. Make a note of whether he is sitting, standing, or walking. Ponder this mental image, allowing any other observations about Patrick to form in your mind.

- Observe the people around Saint Patrick. Note how many people are with Patrick, becoming aware of their appearance and demeanor. Observe whether they are sitting, standing, or walking. Take a moment to ponder this mental image, allowing other impressions of these people to form. Become familiar with the men and women you will encounter during your prayer as well as their behavior.

- Allow yourself to become aware of the location of this moment of prayer. Observe whether it is inside or outside, paying attention to its physical characteristics and the arrangement of the people in it. Look around the place and notice more details about it – if it is in dim or bright light, if it is still and silent or filled with noise, if it has an unusual smell or not, etc. Become familiar with the location of your upcoming prayer.

- Take a moment to remain in this place with these people before allowing these images to fade from your consciousness.

[3] Become aware of your desires during this moment of prayer. Remember your desire to experience the divine presence all around you and to trust in God's plan for you, asking that all your intentions and actions may be directed purely to the service and praise of God. Reassert your desire for God's gift of courage to contemplate your own sinfulness and to experience deep regret and remorse for your rebellion against God. Finally, recall your desire to repent your sins and bring your sorrow before God.

As these desires fill your consciousness, let all other concerns fall aside as you focus on this time and place of prayer.

[4]   Allow the image of Saint Patrick and the crowd to reemerge in your imagination.

• Watch as the group assembles around Patrick. Listen to the sounds of this moment and become comfortable as you prepare to hear Patrick speak. Feel the anticipation of the people around you and share in that enthusiasm.

• As you hear Patrick gathers his disciples around him, ask God to help you share in this experience – either by joining these events or by listening quietly to them. Focus your attention on Saint Patrick, noting his physical appearance and his demeanor.

• Then, watch and listen as Patrick recites the words of Paul's letter to the Ephesians. You may want to quietly read the passage while remaining prayerfully aware of your mental image of Patrick or you may choose to stay completely within the imagined realm of your prayer. Whichever you choose, know that God will offer you the words from the biblical passage that you need to hear – even if only in fragments.

• Hear Patrick explain the passage. Listen to him as he explains the meaning and significance of God's promise expressed in Paul's words.

– Again, look around as Patrick speaks and see the reactions of his disciples. Become aware of their feelings and how they behave toward Patrick and one another.

– Remember that Saint Patrick is speaking to men and women yearning to be forgiven their sins and live as witnesses to God's love. Remember that he also is speaking to you.

• After Saint Patrick finishes speaking, allow his image and this place to fade from your imagination as you become aware of the phrases and images from this moment which touched you most deeply. Recall the emotions and memories – including any sounds or smells – evoked during your prayer. Allow these seminal aspects of your meditation to linger on your mind and in your heart, noting any special feelings evoked by them.

[5]   Then, become aware of God's presence with you in this moment and have an open and informal conversation about this prayer period and how the passage from Paul's epistle expresses your own needs or desires – giving space for God to respond or to highlight different aspects from the biblical selection and your experiences

during this meditation. Then, gradually allow your thoughts to recede as you focus on God's broader presence in your life and in the world around you.

[6]   Conclude by allowing these desires to fade from your consciousness as you offer this traditional Irish prayer:

Confirm me in your love divine,
Smooth for my feet life's rugged way;
My will with yours entwine,
Lest evil lead my steps astray.
Be with me still as guard and guide,
Keep me in holy sanctity,
Let my firm faith on you abide,
From fraud and error hold me free. Amen.

[7]   Afterward, take 10-15 minutes in a quiet space to reflect on the most significant moments from this time of prayer and record your reflections in your retreat journal.

6.4 A Meditation on Colossians 1:15-20

In this meditation on Colossians 1:15-20, you will see and hear Saint Patrick preaching to a crowd about trusting in Jesus Christ's redemptive power.

[1] Begin by reading the biblical selection and reviewing your notes on it.

[2] Then, focus on this specific time and place as you allow all other concerns to fall away before considering the people and place of this moment of prayer.

- Allow an image of Patrick to emerge in your imagination, noting his physical characteristics and mannerisms. Look at what he is wearing or carrying. Make a note of whether he is sitting, standing, or walking. Ponder this mental image, allowing any other observations about Patrick to form in your mind.

- Note how many people are with Jesus, making a mental note of their appearance and demeanor. Look at Patrick's disciples, observing where they are standing and how they behave toward Patrick. Look at the crowd, noting their attitude and behavior toward Patrick. Observe whether the people are sitting, standing, or walking. Take a moment to ponder this mental image, allowing other impressions of these people to form. Become familiar with the men and women you will encounter during your prayer as well as their behavior.

- Allow yourself to become aware of the location of this moment of prayer. Observe whether it is inside or outside, paying attention to its physical characteristics and the arrangement of the people in it. Look around the place and notice more details about it – if it is in dim or bright light, if it is still and silent or filled with noise, if it has an unusual smell or not, etc. Become familiar with the location of your upcoming prayer.

- Take a moment to remain in this place with these people before allowing these images to fade from your consciousness.

[3] Become aware of your desires during this moment of prayer. Remember your desire to experience the divine presence all around you and to trust in God's plan for you, asking that all your intentions and actions may be directed purely to the service and praise of God. Reassert your desire for God's gift of courage to contemplate your own sinfulness and to experience deep regret and remorse for your rebellion

against God. Finally, recall your desire to repent your sins and bring your sorrow before God.

As these desires fill your consciousness, let all other concerns fall aside as you focus on this time and place of prayer.

[4]   Allow the image of Saint Patrick and the crowd to reemerge in your imagination.

- Watch as the group assembles around Patrick. Listen to the sounds of this moment and become comfortable as you prepare to hear Patrick speak. Feel the anticipation of the people around you and share in that enthusiasm.

- As you hear Saint Patrick begin to calm the crowd, ask God to help you enter this moment – either by joining these events or by listening quietly to them. Focus your attention on Saint Patrick, noting his physical appearance and his demeanor.

- Then, watch and listen as Patrick speaks the words of Paul's letter to the Colossians. You may want to quietly read the passage while remaining prayerfully aware of your mental image of Patrick or you may choose to stay completely within the imagined realm of your prayer. Whichever you choose, know that God will offer you the words from the biblical passage that you need to hear – even if only in fragments.

- Hear Patrick explain the passage. Listen to him as he explains the meaning and significance of God's promise expressed in Paul's words.

– Again, look around as Patrick speaks and see the reactions of his disciples and the people in the crowd. Become aware of their feelings and how they behave toward Patrick and one another.

– Remember that Saint Patrick is speaking to men and women yearning to be forgiven their sins and live as witnesses to God's love. Remember that he also is speaking to you.

- After Saint Patrick finishes speaking, allow his image and this place to fade from your imagination as you become aware of the phrases and images from this moment which touched you most deeply. Recall the emotions and memories – including any sounds or smells – evoked during your prayer. Allow these seminal aspects of your meditation to linger on your mind and in your heart, noting any special feelings evoked by them.

[5]   Then, become aware of God's presence with you in this moment and have an open and informal conversation about this prayer period and how the passage from Paul's epistle expresses your own

needs or desires – giving space for God to respond or to highlight different aspects from the biblical selection and your experiences during this meditation. Then, gradually allow your thoughts to recede as you focus on God's broader presence in your life and in the world around you.

[6] Conclude by allowing these desires to fade from your consciousness as you offer this traditional Irish prayer:

> *Confirm me in your love divine,*
> *Smooth for my feet life's rugged way;*
> *My will with yours entwine,*
> *Lest evil lead my steps astray.*
> *Be with me still as guard and guide,*
> *Keep me in holy sanctity,*
> *Let my firm faith on you abide,*
> *From fraud and error hold me free. Amen.*

[7] Afterward, take 10-15 minutes in a quiet space to reflect on the most significant moments from this time of prayer and record your reflections in your retreat journal.

6.5 A Repeated Meditation on Ephesians 4:17-24

In this repeated meditation on Ephesians 4:17-24, you again will see and hear Saint Patrick reminding his disciples that they need to be transformed by Christ's redemptive love.

[1]   Begin by re-reading the biblical selection and reviewing your notes on it.

[2]   Then, focus on this specific time and place as you allow all other concerns to fall away before considering the people and place of this moment of prayer.

- Allow an image of Patrick to emerge in your imagination, noting his physical characteristics and mannerisms. Look at what he is wearing or carrying. Make a note of whether he is sitting, standing, or walking. Ponder this mental image, allowing any other observations about Patrick to form in your mind.

- Observe the people around Saint Patrick. Note how many people are with Patrick, becoming aware of their appearance and demeanor. Observe whether they are sitting, standing, or walking. Take a moment to ponder this mental image, allowing other impressions of these people to form. Become familiar with the men and women you will encounter during your prayer as well as their behavior.

- Allow yourself to become aware of the location of this moment of prayer. Observe whether it is inside or outside, paying attention to its physical characteristics and the arrangement of the people in it. Look around the place and notice more details about it – if it is in dim or bright light, if it is still and silent or filled with noise, if it has an unusual smell or not, etc. Become familiar with the location of your upcoming prayer.

- Take a moment to remain in this place with these people before allowing these images to fade from your consciousness.

[3]   Become aware of your desires during this moment of prayer. Remember your desire to experience the divine presence all around you and to trust in God's plan for you, asking that all your intentions and actions may be directed purely to the service and praise of God. Reassert your desire for God's gift of courage to contemplate your own sinfulness and to experience deep regret and remorse for your rebellion against God. Finally, recall your desire to repent your sins and bring your sorrow before God.

As these desires fill your consciousness, let all other concerns fall aside as you focus on this time and place of prayer.

[4] Allow the image of Saint Patrick and the crowd to reemerge in your imagination.

• Watch as the group assembles around Patrick. Listen to the sounds of this moment and become comfortable as you prepare to hear Patrick speak. Feel the anticipation of the people around you and share in that enthusiasm.

• As you hear Patrick gathers his disciples around him, ask God to help you enter this moment – either by joining these events or by listening quietly to them. Focus your attention on Saint Patrick, noting his physical appearance and his demeanor.

• Then, watch and listen as Patrick recites the words of Paul's letter to the Ephesians. You may want to quietly read the passage while remaining prayerfully aware of your mental image of Patrick or you may choose to stay completely within the imagined realm of your prayer. Whichever you choose, know that God will offer you the words from the biblical passage that you need to hear – even if only in fragments.

• Hear Patrick explain the passage. Listen to him as he explains the meaning and significance of God's promise expressed in Paul's words.

– Again, look around as Patrick speaks and see the reactions of his disciples. Become aware of their feelings and how they behave toward Patrick and one another.

– Remember that Saint Patrick is speaking to men and women yearning to be forgiven their sins and live as witnesses to God's love. Remember that he also is speaking to you.

• After Saint Patrick finishes speaking, allow his image and this place to fade from your imagination as you become aware of the phrases and images from this moment which touched you most deeply. Recall the emotions and memories – including any sounds or smells – evoked during your prayer. Allow these seminal aspects of your meditation to linger on your mind and in your heart, noting any special feelings evoked by them.

[5] The, become aware of God's presence with you in this moment and have an open and informal conversation about this prayer period and how the passage from Paul's epistle expresses your own needs or desires – giving space for God to respond or to highlight different aspects from the biblical selection and your experiences during this

meditation. Then, gradually allow your thoughts to recede as you focus on God's broader presence in your life and in the world around you.

[6]   Conclude by allowing these desires to fade from your consciousness as you offer this traditional Irish prayer:

> *Confirm me in your love divine,*
> *Smooth for my feet life's rugged way;*
> *My will with yours entwine,*
> *Lest evil lead my steps astray.*
> *Be with me still as guard and guide,*
> *Keep me in holy sanctity,*
> *Let my firm faith on you abide,*
> *From fraud and error hold me free. Amen.*

[7]   Afterward, take 10-15 minutes in a quiet space to reflect on the most significant moments from this time of prayer and record your reflections in your retreat journal.

6.6 An Application of the Senses

[1]   Become aware of your prayerful desires during this day or week. Bring to mind your desire that the divine presence all around you may be revealed so all your intentions and actions may be directed purely to the service and praise of God. Focus on your desire to contemplate your own sinfulness and experience deep regret and remorse for your rebellion against God. Finally, reaffirm your desire to bring this sorrow before God and to repent your sins.

[2]   When you are ready, call to mind the various prayers of the preceding day or days. Allow the images and words of these prayers to linger and then slowly fade from your consciousness.

- Remember your meditation on Matthew 25:31-46. Consider the images and feelings evoked in you during your prayer, feeling God's presence in these memories and becoming aware of the specific sensations associated with each image.
- Recall your meditations on Ephesians 4:17-24, considering it in the same way as your memories of the Matthew 25.
- Review your meditation on Colossians 1:15-20 in the same manner as the previous prayers.

Make a mental note of which senses are most active. You may see an image or a color, hear a sound or a phrase, or smell a scent or a fragrance. You may even taste a flavor or feel a sensation on your skin.

[3]   Then, relax and allow these various memories and experiences to quietly enter and leave your consciousness without being controlled. Linger on the sensory images and memories being evoked in you – noticing any images or colors, any sounds or phrases, any scents or fragrances, any flavors or physical sensations associated with each prayer.

[4]   When you are ready, become completely still and clear your mind of all thoughts and concerns. Allow an image of a special personal space to form in your imagination. Then, watch as God enters that place and forms a small image or object for you that expresses the thought or awareness that you most need to carry with you into your life.

Reverently pick up the object or image, a reflection of the most important gift you have been given during this time of prayer. Look at it carefully and become aware of the divine presence contained within it. Take a moment to register what it looks like and how it feels in your hand. Then, feel the joy and confidence that comes from touching the presence of God as you accept this gift, offering a short prayer of gratitude while you relax into the pleasure of this moment.

[5]   Then, conclude by allowing these images to fade from your consciousness as you offer this traditional Irish prayer:

> *Confirm me in your love divine,*
> *Smooth for my feet life's rugged way;*
> *My will with yours entwine,*
> *Lest evil lead my steps astray.*
> *Be with me still as guard and guide,*
> *Keep me in holy sanctity,*
> *Let my firm faith on you abide,*
> *From fraud and error hold me free. Amen.*

[6]   While your experiences are still fresh in your mind, record the most significant impressions or sensations from this time of prayer in your journal.

6.7 Review of Prayer

[1]   Remember your desires during the preceding day or week of prayer. Become aware of our desire to experience the divine presence all around you and to trust in God's plan for you so that all your intentions and actions may be directed purely to the service and praise of God. Recall your desire to contemplate your own sinfulness and to experience deep regret and remorse for your rebellion against God. Finally, reaffirm your desire to bring this sorrow before God while repenting your sins.

[2]   Then, take a moment to allow the words, thoughts, and feelings from your prayers during the last day or week to linger before asking God to reveal the fulfillment of your deepest desires in these various memories.

• Think about the prayer sequence at the beginning of this day or week. Make a mental note of any words, insights or images that remain particularly significant or meaningful to you.

• Ponder the story, "The Conversion of Dichu". Note any words, insights, or images from it that remain particularly significant or meaningful to you.

• Remember your meditation on Matthew 25:31-46.

– Consider the most powerful images, phrases, or feelings from your prayer. Ask yourself what gifts God gave to you through these moments, perhaps offering you new insights or perhaps affirming an important aspect of your faith. Ask yourself how God may be calling you to change through these moments, being as specific as possible.

– Examine your disposition as you prayed, noting whether prayer came easily or with resistance. Recall the easiest moments in your prayer and any moments of joy you may have experienced. Remember also if you encountered any difficulty opening yourself to God or if you felt any sadness as you prayed. Ask God to help you understand why these feelings surfaced.

– Bring to mind any moments when you added personal elements (e.g., familiar places or people from your life) or connected your prayers to other scriptures or spiritual writings. Ask yourself how these additions helped or hindered you as you prayed. Again, if you do not know why this happened, ask God to help you understand.

• Recall your meditations on Ephesians 4:17-24. Then, review your prayer in the same way as your earlier reflection on Matthew 25.

- Review your meditation on Colossians 1:15-20 in the same manner as the previous prayers.
- Reflect on the ebb and flow of sensory impressions and feelings that marked your application of the senses. Isolate the most memorable moments and sensory impressions from your prayer and reflect on how God used these moments to give you a particular gift.

[3] Finally, ponder the times when images or feelings from the readings of this day or week surfaced outside these prayer periods. Consider those moments or events in which God's presence or guidance was especially strong as well as any moments when you were struggling. Think about the most memorable aspects of these experiences, asking God to explain their significance.

[4] Take a moment to allow the words, thoughts, and feelings of these prayers to linger on your mind and in your heart. Finally, conclude by allowing these desires to fade from your consciousness as you offer this traditional Irish prayer:

O God, I believe in you; strengthen my belief.
I trust in you; confirm my trust.
I love you; double my love.
I repent that I angered you,
Increase my repentance.
Fill you my heart with awe without despair;
With hope, without over-confidence;
With piety without infatuation;
And with joy without excess.
My God, consent to guide me by your wisdom;
To constrain me by your right;
To comfort me by your mercy;
And to protect me by your power. Amen.

[5] After finishing these prayers, summarize your reflections on the gifts or graces you received during the prayers of this last day or week and record these thoughts in your journal.

7. The Gift of God's Love and Forgiveness

7.1a Redeemer, Sole-Begotten Son, You Are My Hope
a redeemed sinner's plea for divine aid

Take a moment to quiet your spirit, becoming completely present to this time and place. Allow all other thoughts and concerns to fall away as you come into the presence of God. Then, when you are ready, begin.

Redeemer, sole-begotten Son,
With Father and Spirit, three in one,
    You are my hope; as ages run
    Be yours all glory.

If in the balance you should weigh
My crimes, there were nor hope nor stay,
    But Lord, your clemency I pray,
    To grace restore me.

A Hymn, sung or heard (optional)

The hope of my soul is in your promise,
My homage receive of me, though late:
    Your mercy is greater than my defiance,
    So I before you lie myself prostrate.

Yours is my life and Yours my death,
God of all breath, my pride is o'er!
    One glance from you were all my wealth,
    My hope, my health, for evermore!

O you who makes the dead to live,
Who didst forgive the Thief his scorn,
    Hear now, as then, a sinner's sigh,
    The bitter cry of me forlorn.

O pierced in foot and hand and side,
crucified for hearts that burn,
    I reach to you, oh reach to me,
    I ne'er again from you shall turn.

O King of kings, O King of worlds,
O King who was, and is to be,
    Forgive, O King, with Father and Spirit my sins,
    Receive our prayer, and comfort me.

Read or recite Psalm 138.

Holy Lord,
Under my thoughts may I God-thoughts find.
Half of my sins escape my mind.
    For what I said, or did not say,
    Pardon me, O Lord, I pray.

Read John 10: 1-18, aloud or quietly.

O Lord, Jesus the Christ,
If I were in Heaven my harp I would sound
With apostles and angels and saints all around,
    Praising and thanking the Son who is crowned,
    May the poor race of Eve for that heaven be bound!

Holy Lord,
Heaven may I gain,
In the well of the grace of confession
    My words, my deeds,
    And my omissions.

Help for me, friends for me, help and God's graces,
Help I am asking in all bad places,
    Jesus – with Father and Spirit – I pray
    Drive each evil thought away,

Be with me 'til break of day,
In my sleep and on my way.
    When the hour of hours shall sound
    Jesus be within me found.

O Holy Lord,
    God with the Father and the Spirit,
For me is many a snare designed,

To fill my mind with doubts and fears;
    Far from the land of holy saints,
    I dwell within my vale of tears.
Let faith, let hope, let love –
Traits far above the cold world's way –
    With patience, humility, and awe,
    Become my guides from day to day.

I acknowledge, the evil I have done.
From the day of my birth till the day of my death,
    Through the sight of my eyes,
Through the hearing of my ears,
    Through the sayings of my mouth,
Through the thoughts of my heart,
    Through the touch of my hands,
Through the course of my way,
    Through all I said and did not,
Through all I promised and fulfilled not,
    Through all the laws and holy commandments I broke.
I ask even now absolution of you,
    For fear I may have never asked it as was right,
    And that I might not live to ask it again,

O Holy Lord, my King in Heaven,
May you not let my soul stray from you,
May you keep me in a good state,
    May you turn me toward what is good to do,
    May you protect me from dangers, small and great.
May you fill my eyes with tears of repentance,
    So I may avoid the sinner's awful sentence.
May the Grace of the God for ever be with me,
    And whatever my needs, may the Triune God give me.

Select one of the following options for the Lord's Prayer.

Option A

O Jesus Christ,
Lord of heaven and earth,
Help me pray as you yourself taught:

"Our Father in heaven,
hallowed be your name.
Your kingdom come.
Your will be done,
on earth as it is in heaven.
Give us this day our daily bread.
And forgive us our debts,
as we also have forgiven our debtors.
And do not bring us to the time of trial,
but rescue us from the evil one."
(Matthew 6:9-13)
From the foes of my land,
from the foes of my faith,
From the foes who would us dissever,
    O Lord, preserve me, in life and in death,
    With the Sign of the Cross for ever.
    For the kingdom, the power, and the glory
    are yours now and for ever. Amen.

Please proceed with "I beseech you, O Lord…," found after Option B.

Option B

O Jesus Christ,
Lord of heaven and earth,
Help me pray as you yourself taught:
    Our Father in heaven,
    hallowed be your name,
    your kingdom come,
    your will be done,
    on earth as in heaven.
    Give us today our daily bread.
    Forgive us our sins
    as we forgive those who sin against us.
    Lead us not into temptation
    but deliver us from evil.
From the foes of my land,
from the foes of my faith,
From the foes who would us dissever,

O Lord, preserve me, in life and in death,
With the Sign of the Cross for ever.
For the kingdom, the power, and the glory
are yours now and for ever. Amen.

I beseech you, O Lord.
God in Heaven, unsurpassed in power and might;
    Be behind me, Be on my left,
    Be before me, Be on my right!
Against each danger, you are my help;
In distress, upon you I call.
    In dark times, may you sustain me
    And lift me up again when I fall.
Lord over heaven and of earth,
You know my offenses.
    Yet, listening to my pleadings,
    You guide me away from sinful pretenses.
Lord of all creation and the many creatures,
You bestow on me many earthly treasures.
    Revealing love in each life and season,
    You share with me heavenly pleasures.
May you arouse me
In moments both of joy and of strife;
    Most holy Lord, bring me new life!

A Hymn, sung or heard (optional)

O Jesus Christ,
    Lord of heaven and earth,
    You are my riches, my store, my provision,
My star through the years
When troubles rend me,
    Through times of strife and tears,
    Sweet Jesus, defend me.

Creator of the heavenly light,
you gave the stars their certain way,
    Fixing the moon to shine at night,
    The fiery sun to glow by day.

Lord, let me flee each evil thing
Whereto the wicked will declines,
>   Let all my words and actions bring
>   My soul to where your glory shines.

End this time of prayer by taking some time to bring to mind the various ways God shields you from harm or guides you through the world's tumult. Then, when you are ready, conclude by saying:

O Holy Lord, King in Heaven,
I place myself at the edge of your grace,
>   On the floor of your house myself I place,
And to banish the sin of my heart away,
>   I lower my knee to you this day.
Through life's torrents of pain may you bring me whole,
>   And, O Lord Jesus Christ, preserve also my soul. Amen.

7.1b Preparation for Prayer

<u>Consideration of the Readings</u>

After reciting or prayerfully reading the prayer sequence for this day or week:
- Read about Jesus being the good shepherd in John 10:1-18. Again, consider any aspects of this selection that speak strongly to you before recording these observations in your workbook.
- Read about Jesus telling the parable of the lost sheep in Luke 15:1-10. Again, note each person's appearance and actions during the episode as well as the key elements of the story and its setting. Then, record any aspects of this story that speak strongly to you.
- Read Ephesians 2:1-10. Again, pay careful attention to any phrases or images that seem particularly meaningful to you. Then, record these highlights in your workbook so you will remember them during this day or week of prayer.

<u>Note:</u> *You also should consider any aspect of the prayer sequence from this day or week that seemed particularly significant to you.*

<u>Contemplation of Your Needs</u>

When you are ready, allow any distractions to fade from your consciousness as you become aware of your desire to live in God's goodness. Feel yourself yearning to properly use the many gifts God has given you, to experience God's continuing care, and to be open to the immense love God shows for you, then:
- Read "Patrick's Wedding Night" (found on page 320). Allow yourself to linger on any thoughts, phrases or images that seem particularly meaningful or significant to your earlier preparations or prayer.
- Pray for your desires in the coming day or week. Ask that the divine presence all around you may be revealed so all your intentions and actions may be directed purely to the service and praise of God. Ask also to experience the joy of forgiveness – to know the full depth and breadth of God's love and forgiveness – and to receive this forgiveness with gratitude.

- Conclude by praying for God's gifts of strength and faithfulness as you strive to preserve yourself in sanctity.

Then, record any significant thoughts, emotions, or reactions from these moments in your workbook.

After this, put your notes aside. Without straining your memory, consider in turn each of the readings for the coming day or week and allow them to take shape in your imagination. Prayerfully ponder how each reading affects you emotionally without overtly thinking about their content, asking God to illuminate the spiritual gifts offered in each reading.

Finally, conclude by offering this prayer:
O God, I believe in you; strengthen my belief.
I trust in you; confirm my trust.
I love you; double my love.
I repent that I angered you,
Increase my repentance.
Fill you my heart with awe without despair;
With hope, without over-confidence;
With piety without infatuation;
And with joy without excess.
My God, consent to guide me by your wisdom;
To constrain me by your right;
To comfort me by your mercy;
And to protect me by your power. Amen.

Allow these words to linger on your mind and in your heart for a few moments and then write the most important thoughts, feelings, and desires in your workbook.

7.2   A Contemplation of John 10:1-18

In this contemplation of John 10:1-18, you will see and hear Jesus preaching to a crowd about being the good shepherd.

[1]   Begin by reading the biblical selection and reviewing your notes on it.

[2]   Then, focus on this specific time and place as you allow all other concerns to fall away before considering the people and place in this moment of prayer.

• Allow an image of Jesus to emerge in your imagination, noting his physical characteristics and mannerisms. Look at what he is wearing or carrying. Make a note of whether he is sitting, standing, or walking. Ponder this mental image, allowing any other observations about Jesus to form in your mind.

• Observe the people around Jesus, becoming aware of their appearance and demeanor. Observe whether they are sitting, standing, or walking. Take a moment to ponder this mental image, allowing other impressions of these people to form.

• Allow yourself to become aware of the location of this moment of prayer. Observe its physical characteristics and the arrangement of the people in it. Look around the place and notice more details about it – if it is in dim or bright light, if it is still and silent or filled with noise, if it has an unusual smell or not, etc.

• Take a moment to remain in this place with these people before allowing these images to fade from your consciousness.

[3]   Become aware of your desires during this moment of prayer. Remember your desire to experience the divine presence all around you and to trust in God's plan for you, asking that all your intentions and actions may be directed purely to the service and praise of God. Reassert your desire to experience the joy of forgiveness – to know the full depth and breadth of God's love and forgiveness – and to receive this forgiveness with gratitude. Finally, recall your desire God's gifts of strength and faithfulness as you strive to preserve yourself in sanctity.

As these desires fill your consciousness, let all other concerns fall aside as you focus on this time and place of prayer.

[4]   Allow the image of Jesus and the crowd to reemerge in your imagination.

• Watch as the group assembles around Jesus. Listen to the sounds of this moment and become comfortable as you prepare to hear

Jesus speak. Feel the anticipation of the people around you and share in that enthusiasm.

- As you hear Jesus calm the crowd, ask God to help you enter this moment – either by joining these events or by listening quietly to them. Focus your attention on Jesus, noting his physical appearance and his demeanor.

- Then, watch and listen as Jesus speaks to the crowd about being the good shepherd. You may want to quietly read the passage in John's gospel while remaining prayerfully aware of your mental image or you may choose to stay completely within the imagined realm of your prayer. Whichever you choose, know that God will offer you the words from the biblical passage that you need to hear – even if only in fragments.

- Watch and listen to him as he explains the meaning and significance of God's promise expressed in John's gospel.

– Again, look around as Jesus speaks and see the reactions of his disciples and the people in the crowd. Become aware of their feelings and how they behave toward Jesus and one another.

– Remember that Jesus is speaking to men and women anxiously expecting God to radically transform their lives. Remember he also is speaking to you.

- After Jesus finishes speaking, allow his image and this place to fade from your imagination as you become aware of the phrases and images from this moment which touched you most deeply. Recall the emotions and memories – including any sounds or smells – evoked during your prayer. Allow these seminal aspects of your meditation to linger on your mind and in your heart, noting any special feelings evoked by them.

[5]   Then, become aware of Jesus' presence with you in this moment and have an open and informal conversation about this prayer period and how the passage from John's gospel expresses your own needs or desires – giving space for Jesus to respond or to highlight different aspects from the biblical account and your experiences during this contemplation. Then, gradually allow your thoughts to recede as you focus on God's broader presence in your life and in the world around you.

[6]   Conclude by offering this prayer:

Confirm me in your love divine,
Smooth for my feet life's rugged way;
My will with yours entwine,

Lest evil lead my steps astray.
Be with me still as guard and guide,
Keep me in holy sanctity,
Let my firm faith on you abide,
From fraud and error hold me free. Amen.

[7] Afterward, take 10-15 minutes in a quiet space to reflect on the most significant moments from your prayer and record your reflections in your journal.

7.3   A Contemplation of Luke 15:1-10

In this contemplation of Luke 15:1-10, you will see and hear Jesus telling the parable of the lost sheep.

[1]   Begin by reading the biblical selection and reviewing your notes on it.

[2]   Then, focus on this specific time and place as you allow all other concerns to fall away before considering the people and place in this moment of prayer.

- Allow an image of Jesus to emerge in your imagination, noting his physical characteristics and mannerisms. Look at what he is wearing or carrying. Make a note of whether he is sitting, standing, or walking. Ponder this mental image, allowing any other observations about Jesus to form in your mind.

- Observe the people around Jesus, becoming aware of their appearance and demeanor. Observe whether they are sitting, standing, or walking. Take a moment to ponder this mental image, allowing other impressions of these people to form.

- Allow yourself to become aware of the location of this moment of prayer. Observe its physical characteristics and the arrangement of the people in it. Look around the place and notice more details about it – if it is in dim or bright light, if it is still and silent or filled with noise, if it has an unusual smell or not, etc.

- Take a moment to remain in this place with these people before allowing these images to fade from your consciousness.

[3]   Become aware of your desires during this moment of prayer. Remember your desire to experience the divine presence all around you and to trust in God's plan for you, asking that all your intentions and actions may be directed purely to the service and praise of God. Reassert your desire to experience the joy of forgiveness – to know the full depth and breadth of God's love and forgiveness – and to receive this forgiveness with gratitude. Finally, recall your desire God's gifts of strength and faithfulness as you strive to preserve yourself in sanctity.

As these desires fill your consciousness, let all other concerns fall aside as you focus on this time and place of prayer.

[4]   Allow the image of Jesus and the crowd to reemerge in your imagination.

- Watch as the group assembles around Jesus. Listen to the sounds of this moment and become comfortable as you prepare to hear

Jesus speak. Feel the anticipation of the people around you and share in that enthusiasm.

- Ask God to help you share in this experience – either by joining these events or by listening quietly to them. Focus your attention on Jesus, noting his physical appearance and his demeanor.
- Then, watch and listen as Jesus tell the parables of the lost sheep and the lost coin. You may want to quietly read the passage while remaining prayerfully aware of your mental image or you may choose to stay completely within the imagined realm of your prayer. Whichever you choose, know that God will offer you the words from the biblical passage that you need to hear – even if only in fragments.
- Hear Jesus explain the parables. Listen to him as he explains the meaning and significance of God's promise expressed in these stories.

– Again, look around as Jesus speaks and see the reactions of his disciples and the people in the crowd. Become aware of their feelings and how they behave toward Jesus and one another.

– Remember that Jesus is speaking to men and women anxiously expecting God to radically transform their lives. Remember he also is speaking to you.

- After Jesus finishes speaking, allow his image and this place to fade from your imagination as you become aware of the phrases and images from this moment which touched you most deeply. Recall the emotions and memories – including any sounds or smells – evoked during your prayer. Allow these seminal aspects of your meditation to linger on your mind and in your heart, noting any special feelings evoked by them.

[5] Then, become aware of Jesus' presence with you in this moment and have an open and informal conversation about this prayer period and how the passage from Luke's gospel expresses your own needs or desires – giving space for Jesus to respond or to highlight different aspects from the biblical account and your experiences during this contemplation. Then, gradually allow your thoughts to recede as you focus on God's broader presence in your life and in the world around you.

[6] Conclude by offering this prayer:

> *Confirm me in your love divine,*
> *Smooth for my feet life's rugged way;*
> *My will with yours entwine,*
> *Lest evil lead my steps astray.*

Be with me still as guard and guide,
Keep me in holy sanctity,
Let my firm faith on you abide,
From fraud and error hold me free. Amen.

[7]   Afterward, take 10-15 minutes in a quiet space to reflect on the most significant moments from your prayer and record your reflections in your journal.

7.4   A Meditation on Ephesians 2:1-10

In this meditation on Ephesians 2:1-10, you will see and hear Saint Patrick teaching his disciples to trust in their redemption in Christ.

[1]   Begin by reading the biblical selection and reviewing your notes on it.

[2]   Then, focus on this specific time and place as you allow all other concerns to fall away before considering the people and place in this moment of prayer.

- Allow an image of Patrick to emerge in your imagination, noting his physical characteristics and mannerisms. Look at what he is wearing or carrying. Make a note of whether he is sitting, standing, or walking. Ponder this mental image, allowing any other observations about Patrick to form in your mind.

- Observe the people around Saint Patrick, becoming aware of their appearance and demeanor. Observe whether they are sitting, standing, or walking. Take a moment to ponder this mental image, allowing other impressions of these people to form.

- Allow yourself to become aware of the location of this moment of prayer. Observe its physical characteristics and the arrangement of the people in it. Look around the place and notice more details about it – if it is in dim or bright light, if it is still and silent or filled with noise, if it has an unusual smell or not, etc.

- Take a moment to remain in this place with these people before allowing these images to fade from your consciousness.

[3]   Become aware of your desires during this moment of prayer. Remember your desire to experience the divine presence all around you and to trust in God's plan for you, asking that all your intentions and actions may be directed purely to the service and praise of God. Reassert your desire to experience the joy of forgiveness – to know the full depth and breadth of God's love and forgiveness – and to receive this forgiveness with gratitude. Finally, recall your desire God's gifts of strength and faithfulness as you strive to preserve yourself in sanctity.

As these desires fill your consciousness, let all other concerns fall aside as you focus on this time and place of prayer.

[4]   Allow the image of Saint Patrick and his disciples to reemerge in your imagination.

- Watch as the group assembles around Patrick. Listen to the sounds of this moment and become comfortable as you prepare to hear Patrick speak. Feel the anticipation of the people around you and share in that enthusiasm.
- As you hear Patrick invite his companions to pray, ask God to help you share in this experience – either by joining these events or by listening quietly to them. Focus your attention on Saint Patrick, noting his physical appearance and his demeanor.
- Then, watch and listen as Patrick speaks the words of Paul's letter to the Ephesians. You may want to quietly read the passage while remaining prayerfully aware of your mental image or you may choose to stay completely within the imagined realm of your prayer. Whichever you choose, know that God will offer you the words from the biblical passage that you need to hear – even if only in fragments.
- Hear Patrick explain the passage. Listen to him as he explains the meaning and significance of Christ's mission expressed in Paul's epistle.

– Again, look around as Patrick speaks and see the reactions of his disciples. Become aware of their feelings and how they behave toward Patrick and one another.

– Remember that Saint Patrick is speaking to men and women anxiously expecting God to radically transform their lives. Remember he also is speaking to you.

- After Patrick finishes speaking, allow his image and this place to fade from your imagination as you become aware of the phrases and images from this moment which touched you most deeply. Recall the emotions and memories – including any sounds or smells – evoked during your prayer. Allow these seminal aspects of your meditation to linger on your mind and in your heart, noting any special feelings evoked by them.

[5] Then, become aware of God's presence with you in this moment and have an open and informal conversation about this prayer period and how the passage from Paul's epistle expresses your own needs or desires – giving space for God to respond or to highlight different aspects from the biblical selection and your experiences during this meditation. Then, gradually allow your thoughts to recede as you focus on God's broader presence in your life and in the world around you.

[6] Conclude by offering this prayer:

Confirm me in your love divine,

Smooth for my feet life's rugged way;
My will with yours entwine,
Lest evil lead my steps astray.
Be with me still as guard and guide,
Keep me in holy sanctity,
Let my firm faith on you abide,
From fraud and error hold me free. Amen.

[7] Afterward, take 10-15 minutes in a quiet space to reflect on the most significant moments from your prayer and record your reflections in your journal.

7.5   A Repeated Contemplation of Luke 15:1-10

In this repeated contemplation of Luke 15:1-10, you again will see and hear Jesus telling the parable of the lost sheep.

[1]   Begin by re-reading the biblical selection and reviewing your notes on it.

[2]   Then, focus on this specific time and place as you allow all other concerns to fall away before considering the people and place in this moment of prayer.

• Allow an image of Jesus to emerge in your imagination, noting his physical characteristics and mannerisms. Look at what he is wearing or carrying. Make a note of whether he is sitting, standing, or walking. Ponder this mental image, allowing any other observations about Jesus to form in your mind.

• Observe the people around Jesus, becoming aware of their appearance and demeanor. Observe whether they are sitting, standing, or walking. Take a moment to ponder this mental image, allowing other impressions of these people to form.

• Allow yourself to become aware of the location of this moment of prayer. Observe its physical characteristics and the arrangement of the people in it. Look around the place and notice more details about it – if it is in dim or bright light, if it is still and silent or filled with noise, if it has an unusual smell or not, etc.

• Take a moment to remain in this place with these people before allowing these images to fade from your consciousness.

[3]   Become aware of your desires during this moment of prayer. Remember your desire to experience the divine presence all around you and to trust in God's plan for you, asking that all your intentions and actions may be directed purely to the service and praise of God. Reassert your desire to experience the joy of forgiveness – to know the full depth and breadth of God's love and forgiveness – and to receive this forgiveness with gratitude. Finally, recall your desire God's gifts of strength and faithfulness as you strive to preserve yourself in sanctity.

As these desires fill your consciousness, let all other concerns fall aside as you focus on this time and place of prayer.

[4]   Allow the image of Jesus and the crowd to reemerge in your imagination.

• Watch as the group assembles around Jesus. Listen to the sounds of this moment and become comfortable as you prepare to hear

Jesus speak. Feel the anticipation of the people around you and share in that enthusiasm.

- Ask God to help you share in this experience – either by joining these events or by listening quietly to them. Focus your attention on Jesus, noting his physical appearance and his demeanor.
- Then, watch and listen as Jesus tell the parables of the lost sheep and the lost coin. You may want to quietly read the passage while remaining prayerfully aware of your mental image or you may choose to stay completely within the imagined realm of your prayer. Whichever you choose, know that God will offer you the words from the biblical passage that you need to hear – even if only in fragments.
- Hear Jesus explain the parables. Listen to him as he explains the meaning and significance of God's promise expressed in these stories.

– Again, look around as Jesus speaks and see the reactions of his disciples and the people in the crowd. Become aware of their feelings and how they behave toward Jesus and one another.

– Remember that Jesus is speaking to men and women anxiously expecting God to radically transform their lives. Remember he also is speaking to you.

- After Jesus finishes speaking, allow his image and this place to fade from your imagination as you become aware of the phrases and images from this moment which touched you most deeply. Recall the emotions and memories – including any sounds or smells – evoked during your prayer. Allow these seminal aspects of your meditation to linger on your mind and in your heart, noting any special feelings evoked by them.

[5] Then, become aware of Jesus' presence with you in this moment and have an open and informal conversation about this prayer period and how the passage from Luke's gospel expresses your own needs or desires – giving space for Jesus to respond or to highlight different aspects from the biblical account and your experiences during this contemplation. Then, gradually allow your thoughts to recede as you focus on God's broader presence in your life and in the world around you.

[6] Conclude by offering this prayer:
Confirm me in your love divine,
Smooth for my feet life's rugged way;
My will with yours entwine,
Lest evil lead my steps astray.

Be with me still as guard and guide,
Keep me in holy sanctity,
Let my firm faith on you abide,
From fraud and error hold me free. Amen.

[7] Afterward, take 10-15 minutes in a quiet space to reflect on the most significant moments from your prayer and record your reflections in your journal.

7.6   An Application of the Senses

[1]   Become aware of your prayerful desires during this day or week. Bring to mind your desire that the divine presence all around you may be revealed so all your intentions and actions may be directed purely to the service and praise of God. Focus on your desire to experience the joy of forgiveness – to know the full depth and breadth of God's love and forgiveness – and to receive this forgiveness with gratitude. Finally, reaffirm your desire for God's gifts of strength and faithfulness as you strive to preserve yourself in sanctity.

[2]   Call to mind the various prayers of the preceding day or days. Allow the images and words of these prayers to linger and then slowly fade from your consciousness.

- Remember your imaginative contemplation of John 10:1-18. Consider the images and feelings evoked in you during your prayer, feeling God's presence in these memories and becoming aware of the specific sensations associated with each image.
- Recall your imaginative contemplations of Luke 15:1-10, considering it in the same way as your memories of John 10.
- Review your meditation on Ephesians 2:1-10 in the same manner as the previous prayers.

Make a mental note of which senses are most active. You may see an image or a color, hear a sound or a phrase, or smell a scent or a fragrance. You may even taste a flavor or feel a sensation on your skin.

[3]   Then, relax and allow these various memories and experiences to quietly enter and leave your consciousness. Linger on the sensory images and memories being evoked in you – noticing any images or colors, any sounds or phrases, any scents or fragrances, any flavors or physical sensations associated with each prayer.

[4]   When you are ready, become completely still and clear your mind of all thoughts and concerns. Allow an image of a special personal space to form in your imagination. Then, watch as God enters that place and forms a small image or object for you that expresses the thought or awareness that you most need to carry with you into your life.

Reverently pick up the object or image, a reflection of the most important gift you have been given during this time of prayer. Look at it carefully and become aware of the divine presence contained within it. Register what it looks like and how it feels in your hand. Then, feel the joy and confidence that comes from touching the presence of God as you accept this gift, offering a short prayer of gratitude while you relax into the pleasure of this moment.

[5]   Then, conclude by offering this prayer:

> *Confirm me in your love divine,*
> *Smooth for my feet life's rugged way;*
> *My will with yours entwine,*
> *Lest evil lead my steps astray.*
> *Be with me still as guard and guide,*
> *Keep me in holy sanctity,*
> *Let my firm faith on you abide,*
> *From fraud and error hold me free. Amen.*

[6]   While your experiences are still fresh in your mind, record the most significant impressions or sensations from this time of prayer in your journal.

7.7 Review of Prayer

[1]   Remember your desires during the preceding day or week of prayer. Become aware of our desire to experience the divine presence all around you and to trust in God's plan for you so that all your intentions and actions may be directed purely to the service and praise of God. Recall your desire to experience the joy of forgiveness – to know the full depth and breadth of God's love and forgiveness – and to receive this forgiveness with gratitude. Finally, reaffirm your need for God's gifts of strength and faithfulness as you strive to preserve yourself in sanctity.

After bringing these thoughts and desires into your consciousness, ask God once again to fulfill these desires in your own life and in your interactions with others.

[2]   Then, take a moment to allow the words, thoughts, and feelings from your prayers during the last day or week to linger before asking God to reveal the fulfillment of your deepest desires in these various memories.

• Think about the prayer sequence at the beginning of this day or week. Make a mental note of any words, insights or images that remain particularly significant or meaningful to you.

• Ponder the story, "Patrick's Wedding Night". Note any words, insights, or images from it that remain particularly significant or meaningful to you.

• Remember your imaginative contemplation of John 10:1-18.

– Consider the most powerful images, phrases, or feelings from your prayer. Ask yourself what gifts God gave to you through these moments, perhaps offering you new insights or perhaps affirming an important aspect of your faith. Ask yourself how God may be calling you to change through these moments, being as specific as possible.

– Examine your disposition as you prayed. Recall the easiest moments in your prayer and any moments of joy you may have experienced. Remember also if you encountered any difficulty opening yourself to God or if you felt any sadness as you prayed. Ask God to help you understand why these feelings surfaced.

– Bring to mind any moments when you added personal elements (e.g., familiar places or people from your life) or connected your prayers to other scriptures or spiritual writings. Ask yourself how these additions helped or hindered you as you prayed. Again, if you do not know why this happened, ask God to help you understand.

- Recall your imaginative contemplations of Luke 15:1-10. Then, review your prayer in the same way as your earlier reflection on John 10.
- Review your meditation on Ephesians 2:1-10 in the same manner as the previous prayers.
- Reflect on the ebb and flow of sensory impressions and feelings that marked your application of the senses. Isolate the most memorable moments and sensory impressions from your prayer and reflect on how God used these moments to give you a particular gift.

[3] Finally, ponder the times when images or feelings from the readings of this day or week surfaced outside these prayer periods. Think about the most memorable aspects of these experiences, asking God to explain their significance.

[4] Take a moment to allow the words, thoughts, and feelings of these prayers to linger on your mind and in your heart. Finally, conclude by offering this prayer:

> *O God, I believe in you; strengthen my belief.*
> *I trust in you; confirm my trust.*
> *I love you; double my love.*
> *I repent that I angered you,*
> *Increase my repentance.*
> *Fill you my heart with awe without despair;*
> *With hope, without over-confidence;*
> *With piety without infatuation;*
> *And with joy without excess.*
> *My God, consent to guide me by your wisdom;*
> *To constrain me by your right;*
> *To comfort me by your mercy;*
> *And to protect me by your power. Amen.*

[5] After finishing these prayers, summarize your reflections on the gifts or graces you received during the prayers of this last day or week and record these thoughts in your journal.

8. Trusting in God's Love and Forgiveness

8.1a   Let My Tongue Be Free From Blame
a loved sinner's prayer for continued aid

Take a moment to quiet your spirit, becoming completely present to this time and place. Allow all other thoughts and concerns to fall away as you come into the presence of God. Then, when you are ready, begin.

Holy God, let my tongue be free from blame,
Nor utter words of guilt or strife;
    Lift up my eyes from deeds of shame,
    And all the vanities of life.

My heart be purged and purified
That nought of evil shall remain;
    From worldly vice and fleshly pride
    My soul by temperance restrain.

A Hymn, sung or heard (optional)

May the grace of the Holy Ghost be gained by me,
And true Faith be kept unstained by me,
    While I follow the path of the saints, endeavouring
    To walk in the temple of Christ unwavering.

Bridling the tongue so prone to mutiny,
Shunning drunkenness, shunning gluttony,
    Never to evil again inclining me,
    Seeking repentance made in time by me.

Never forsaking the rule of abstinence,
Plucking away the evil plants in me,
    Always forgiving earthly enmities,
    Purging clean my guilty conscience.

The goods of other men never envying,
Never wantonly making enemies,
    Fighting the foe of the soul for victory,
    Living for ever a life of sanctity.

As my own, my friend's fame, cherishing,
God's commandments obey in everything,
    Oaths of anger for ever abandoning,
    Besmirching no one, no one blackening.

Read or recite Psalm 145.

Holy Triune God,
    Father, Son and Spirit
Under my thoughts may I God-thoughts find.
Half of my sins escape my mind.
    For what I said, or did not say,
    Pardon me, O Lord, I pray.

Read John 8: 2-11, aloud or quietly.

O Holy God,
    Father, Son and Spirit
If I were in Heaven my harp I would sound
With apostles and angels and saints all around,
    Praising and thanking the Son who is crowned,
    May the poor race of Eve for that heaven be bound!

Holy Triune God,
May speak I the praise of the truth, not slumbering,
The end of the whole, each day remembering,
    Helping the poor and those in wretchedness,
    Musing on Christ and on His blessedness.

Striving to reach the heaven's holiness.
Paying all debts in peace and lowliness,
    Blessings of God and of men still nerving me,
    Help of apostles and saints preserving me.

O Holy God,
    Father, Son and Spirit
For me is many a snare designed,
To fill my mind with doubts and fears;
    Far from the land of holy saints,
    I dwell within my vale of tears.

Let faith, let hope, let love –
Traits far above the cold world's way –
  With patience, humility, and awe,
  Become my guides from day to day.

I acknowledge, the evil I have done.
From the day of my birth till the day of my death,
  Through the sight of my eyes,
Through the hearing of my ears,
  Through the sayings of my mouth,
Through the thoughts of my heart,
  Through the touch of my hands,
Through the course of my way,
  Through all I said and did not,
Through all I promised and fulfilled not,
  Through all the laws and holy commandments I broke.
I ask even now absolution of you,
In the sweet name of Jesus Christ,
  For fear I may have never asked it as was right,
  And that I might not live to ask it again,

O Divine Majesty,
  Father, Son and Spirit
May you not let my soul stray from you,
May you keep me in a good state,
  May you turn me toward what is good to do,
  May you protect me from dangers, small and great.
May you fill my eyes with tears of repentance,
  So I may avoid the sinner's awful sentence.
May the Grace of the God for ever be with me,
  And whatever my needs, may the Triune God give me.

Select one of the following options for the Lord's Prayer.

Option A

O God,
Father, Son and Spirit,
help me pray as Jesus himself taught:
  "*Our Father in heaven,*

> *hallowed be your name.*
> *Your kingdom come.*
> *Your will be done,*
> *on earth as it is in heaven.*
> *Give us this day our daily bread.*
> *And forgive us our debts,*
> *as we also have forgiven our debtors.*
> *And do not bring us to the time of trial,*
> *but rescue us from the evil one."*
> *(Matthew 6:9-13)*

From the foes of my land,
from the foes of my faith,
From the foes who would us dissever,
> O Trinity preserve me, in life, in death,
> With the Sign of the Cross for ever.
> *For the kingdom, the power, and the glory*
> *are yours now and for ever. Amen.*

Please proceed with "I beseech the wonderful and blessed Trinity,...," found after Option B.

Option B

O God,
Father, Son and Spirit,
help me pray as Jesus himself taught:
> *Our Father in heaven,*
> *hallowed be your name,*
> *your kingdom come,*
> *your will be done,*
> *on earth as in heaven.*
> *Give us today our daily bread.*
> *Forgive us our sins*
> *as we forgive those who sin against us.*
> *Lead us not into temptation*
> *but deliver us from evil.*

From the foes of my land,
from the foes of my faith,
From the foes who would us dissever,
> O Trinity preserve me, in life, in death,

With the Sign of the Cross for ever.
For the kingdom, the power, and the glory
are yours now and for ever. Amen.

I beseech the wonderful and blessed Trinity,
God in Heaven, unsurpassed in power and might;
    Be behind me, Be on my left,
    Be before me, Be on my right!
Against each danger, God is my help;
In distress, upon the Divine Majesty I call.
    In dark times, may my God sustain me
    And lift me up again when I fall.
Lord over heaven and of earth,
The Triune God knows my offenses.
    Yet, listening to my pleadings,
    Guides me away from sinful pretenses.
Lord of all creation and the many creatures,
My God bestows on me many earthly treasures.
    Revealing love in each life and season,
    My God shares with me heavenly pleasures.
May the Holy Trinity arouse me
In moments both of joy and of strife;
    God the Father, with Mary's mighty Son,
    And the noble Spirit, bring me new life!

A Hymn, sung or heard (optional)

O Divine Majesty,
Three in one Godhead, without division.
    You are my riches, my store, my provision,
My star through the years
When troubles rend me,
    Through times of strife and tears,
    O God, defend me.

So help me, O God, no evil do,
'Til fades in dusk the sunset flame,
That I unstained may come to you
And sing the glories of your name.

Eternal Triune Deity, your word
Made all the spheres that roll above,
    You are the everlasting Lord,
    The fount of everlasting love.

End this time of prayer by taking some time to bring to mind the various ways God shields you from harm or guides you through the world's tumult. Then, when you are ready, conclude by saying:

O Holy Triune God,
Father, Son and Spirit,
I place myself at the edge of your grace,
    On the floor of your house myself I place,
And to banish the sin of my heart away,
    I lower my knee to you this day.
Through life's torrents of pain may you bring me whole,
    And, O Blessed Trinity, preserve also my soul. Amen.

8.1b   Preparation for Prayer

Consideration of the Readings

After reciting or prayerfully reading the prayer sequence for this day or week:
- Read about Jesus and the woman caught in adultery in John 8:2-11. Make a mental note of Jesus' appearance and actions during the episode, the people listening to him, and the key elements of Jesus' message. Again, consider any aspects of this story that speak strongly to you before recording these observations in your workbook.
- Read about Jesus preaching in Luke 6:17-38. Again, note each person's appearance and actions during the episode as well as the key elements of the story and its setting. Then, record any aspects of this story that speak strongly to you.
- Read John 6:32-58, noting Jesus' appearance and actions during the episode as well as the people listening to him and the key elements of Jesus' message. Again, consider any aspects of this story that speak strongly to you before recording these observations in your workbook.

<u>Note:</u> *You also should consider any aspect of the prayer sequence from this day or week that seemed particularly significant to you.*

Contemplation of Your Needs

When you are ready, allow any distractions to fade from your consciousness as you become aware of your desire to live in God's goodness. Feel yourself yearning to properly use the many gifts God has given you, to experience God's continuing care, and to be open to the immense love God shows for you, then:
- Read "Patrick Converts Daire" (found on page 320). Allow yourself to linger on any thoughts, phrases or images that seem particularly meaningful or significant to your earlier preparations or prayer.
- Pray for your desires in the coming day or week. Ask that the divine presence all around you may be revealed so all your intentions and actions may be directed purely to the service and praise of God.

Ask also to recognize the transformative power of God's forgiveness in your life as well as the special role of Christ in your becoming a child of God.
 • Conclude by praying to receive that you truly may experience the joyful lightness of Christ's yoke as you accept becoming a "loved sinner".
Then, record any significant thoughts, emotions, or reactions from these moments in your workbook.

After this, put your notes aside. Without straining your memory, consider in turn each of the readings for the coming day or week and allow them to take shape in your imagination. Prayerfully ponder how each reading affects you emotionally without overtly thinking about their content, asking God to illuminate the spiritual gifts offered in each reading.

Finally, conclude by offering this prayer:
O God, I believe in you; strengthen my belief.
I trust in you; confirm my trust.
I love you; double my love.
I repent that I angered you,
Increase my repentance.
Fill you my heart with awe without despair;
With hope, without over-confidence;
With piety without infatuation;
And with joy without excess.
My God, consent to guide me by your wisdom;
To constrain me by your right;
To comfort me by your mercy;
And to protect me by your power. Amen.

Allow these words to linger on your mind and in your heart for a few moments and then write the most important thoughts, feelings, and desires in your workbook.

8.2　A Contemplation of John 8:2-11

In this contemplation of John 8:2-11, you will see and hear Jesus' forgiveness of a sinner.

[1]　Begin by reading the biblical selection and reviewing your notes on it.

[2]　Then, focus on this specific time and place as you allow all other concerns to fall away before considering the people and place in this moment of prayer.

- Allow an image of Jesus to emerge in your imagination, noting his physical characteristics and mannerisms. Look at what he is wearing or carrying. Make a note of whether he is sitting, standing, or walking. Ponder this mental image, allowing any other observations about Jesus to form in your mind.

- See the people around Jesus, becoming aware of their appearance and demeanor. Notice one woman standing alone, making a mental note about her appearance and demeanor. Observe whether they are sitting, standing, or walking. Take a moment to ponder this mental image, allowing other impressions of these people to form.

- Allow yourself to become aware of the location of this moment of prayer. Observe its physical characteristics and the arrangement of the people in it. Look around the place and notice more details about it – if it is in dim or bright light, if it is still and silent or filled with noise, if it has an unusual smell or not, etc.

- Take a moment to remain in this place with these people before allowing these images to fade from your consciousness.

[3]　Become aware of your desires during this moment of prayer. Remember your desire to experience the divine presence all around you and to trust in God's plan for you, asking that all your intentions and actions may be directed purely to the service and praise of God. Reassert your desire to recognize the transformative power of God's forgiveness in your life as well as the special role of Christ in your becoming a child of God. Finally, recall your desire experience the joyful lightness of Christ's yoke as you accept becoming a "loved sinner".

As these desires fill your consciousness, let all other concerns fall aside as you focus on this time and place of prayer.

[4]　Allow the image of Jesus and the crowd to reemerge in your imagination.

- Watch as the group assembles around Jesus. Listen to the sounds of this moment and become comfortable as you prepare to hear Jesus speak. Feel the anticipation of the people around you and share in that enthusiasm.
- Ask God to help you enter this moment – either by joining them or by listening quietly to them. Focus your attention on Jesus, noting his physical appearance and his demeanor.
- Then, watch and listen as Jesus forgives the woman. You may want to quietly read the passage while remaining prayerfully aware of your mental image or you may choose to stay completely within the imagined realm of your prayer. Whichever you choose, know that God will offer you the words from the biblical passage that you need to hear – even if only in fragments.
- Hear Jesus explain his actions to the woman. Listen to the sound of his voice and the love it expresses.
  – Again, look around as Jesus speaks and see the reactions of his disciples and the people in the crowd. Become aware of their feelings and how they behave toward Jesus and one another.
  – Remember that Jesus is speaking to men and women experiencing the miracle of Jesus Christ's presence in their lives. Remember he also is speaking to you.
- After Jesus finishes speaking, allow his image and this place to fade from your imagination as you become aware of the phrases and images from this moment which touched you most deeply. Recall the emotions and memories – including any sounds or smells – evoked during your prayer. Allow these seminal aspects of your meditation to linger on your mind and in your heart, noting any special feelings evoked by them.

[5] Then, become aware of Jesus' presence with you in this moment and have an open and informal conversation about this prayer period and how the passage from John's gospel expresses your own needs or desires – giving space for Jesus to respond or to highlight different aspects from the biblical account and your experiences during this contemplation. Then, gradually allow your thoughts to recede as you focus on God's broader presence in your life and in the world around you.

[6] Conclude by offering this prayer:

> *Confirm me in your love divine,*
> *Smooth for my feet life's rugged way;*
> *My will with yours entwine,*

> *Lest evil lead my steps astray.*
> *Be with me still as guard and guide,*
> *Keep me in holy sanctity,*
> *Let my firm faith on you abide,*
> *From fraud and error hold me free. Amen.*

[7]   Afterward, take 10-15 minutes in a quiet space to reflect on the most significant moments from your prayer and record your reflections in your journal.

8.3　A Contemplation of Luke 6:17-38

In this contemplation of Luke 6:17-38, you will see and hear Jesus preaching to a crowd about the call to a reformed life.

[1]　Begin by reading the biblical selection and reviewing your notes on it.

[2]　Then, focus on this specific time and place as you allow all other concerns to fall away before considering the people and place in this moment of prayer.

- Allow an image of Jesus to emerge in your imagination, noting his physical characteristics and mannerisms. Look at what he is wearing or carrying. Make a note of whether he is sitting, standing, or walking. Ponder this mental image, allowing any other observations about Jesus to form in your mind.

- Observe the people around Jesus, becoming aware of their appearance and demeanor. Observe whether they are sitting, standing, or walking. Take a moment to ponder this mental image, allowing other impressions of these people to form.

- Allow yourself to become aware of the location of this moment of prayer. Observe its physical characteristics and the arrangement of the people in it. Look around the place and notice more details about it – if it is in dim or bright light, if it is still and silent or filled with noise, if it has an unusual smell or not, etc.

- Take a moment to remain in this place with these people before allowing these images to fade from your consciousness.

[3]　Become aware of your desires during this moment of prayer. Remember your desire to experience the divine presence all around you and to trust in God's plan for you, asking that all your intentions and actions may be directed purely to the service and praise of God. Reassert your desire to recognize the transformative power of God's forgiveness in your life as well as the special role of Christ in your becoming a child of God. Finally, recall your desire experience the joyful lightness of Christ's yoke as you accept becoming a "loved sinner".

As these desires fill your consciousness, let all other concerns fall aside as you focus on this time and place of prayer.

[4]　Allow the image of Jesus and the crowd to reemerge in your imagination.

- Watch as the group assembles around Jesus. Listen to the sounds of this moment and become comfortable as you prepare to hear Jesus speak. Feel the anticipation of the people around you and share in that enthusiasm.
- As you hear Jesus calm the crowd, ask God to help you enter this moment – either by joining these events or by listening quietly to them. Focus your attention on Jesus, noting his physical appearance and his demeanor.
- Then, watch and listen as Jesus speaks to the crowd, presenting the blessings and woes of Luke's gospel. You may want to quietly read the passage while remaining prayerfully aware of your mental image or you may choose to stay completely within the imagined realm of your prayer. Whichever you choose, know that God will offer you the words from the biblical passage that you need to hear – even if only in fragments.
- Listen and watch as Jesus explains how both the blessings and the woes express God's love.
– Again, look around as Jesus speaks and see the reactions of his disciples and the people in the crowd. Become aware of their feelings and how they behave toward Jesus and one another.
– Remember that Jesus is speaking to men and women experiencing the miracle of Jesus Christ's presence in their lives. Remember he also is speaking to you.
- After Jesus finishes speaking, allow his image and this place to fade from your imagination as you become aware of the phrases and images from this moment which touched you most deeply. Recall the emotions and memories – including any sounds or smells – evoked during your prayer. Allow these seminal aspects of your meditation to linger on your mind and in your heart, noting any special feelings evoked by them.

[5] Then, become aware of Jesus' presence with you in this moment and have an open and informal conversation about this prayer period and how the passage from Luke's gospel expresses your own needs or desires – giving space for Jesus to respond or to highlight different aspects from the biblical account and your experiences during this contemplation. Then, gradually allow your thoughts to recede as you focus on God's broader presence in your life and in the world around you.

[6] Conclude by offering this prayer:

Confirm me in your love divine,

Smooth for my feet life's rugged way;
My will with yours entwine,
Lest evil lead my steps astray.
Be with me still as guard and guide,
Keep me in holy sanctity,
Let my firm faith on you abide,
From fraud and error hold me free. Amen.

[7]   Afterward, take 10-15 minutes in a quiet space to reflect on the most significant moments from your prayer and record your reflections in your journal.

8.4 A Contemplation of John 6:32-58

In this contemplation of John 6:32-58, you will see and hear Jesus explain to a crowd that he is the bread of life.

[1] Begin by reading the biblical selection and reviewing your notes on it.

[2] Then, focus on this specific time and place as you allow all other concerns to fall away before considering the people and place in this moment of prayer.

- Allow an image of Jesus to emerge in your imagination, noting his physical characteristics and mannerisms. Look at what he is wearing or carrying. Make a note of whether he is sitting, standing, or walking. Ponder this mental image, allowing any other observations about Jesus to form in your mind.

- Observe the people around Jesus, becoming aware of their appearance and demeanor. Observe whether they are sitting, standing, or walking. Take a moment to ponder this mental image, allowing other impressions of these people to form.

- Allow yourself to become aware of the location of this moment of prayer. Observe its physical characteristics and the arrangement of the people in it. Look around the place and notice more details about it – if it is in dim or bright light, if it is still and silent or filled with noise, if it has an unusual smell or not, etc.

- Take a moment to remain in this place with these people before allowing these images to fade from your consciousness.

[3] Become aware of your desires during this moment of prayer. Remember your desire to experience the divine presence all around you and to trust in God's plan for you, asking that all your intentions and actions may be directed purely to the service and praise of God. Reassert your desire to recognize the transformative power of God's forgiveness in your life as well as the special role of Christ in your becoming a child of God. Finally, recall your desire experience the joyful lightness of Christ's yoke as you accept becoming a "loved sinner".

As these desires fill your consciousness, let all other concerns fall aside as you focus on this time and place of prayer.

[4] Allow the image of Jesus and his disciples to reemerge in your imagination.

- Watch as the group assembles around Jesus. Listen to the sounds of this moment and become comfortable as you prepare to hear Jesus speak. Feel the anticipation of the people around you and share in that enthusiasm.
- As you hear Jesus calm the crowd, ask God to help you share in this experience – either by joining these events or by listening quietly to them. Focus your attention on Jesus, noting his physical appearance and his demeanor.
- Then, watch and listen as Jesus speaks to the crowd, he is the bread of life. You may want to quietly read the passage John's gospel while remaining prayerfully aware of your mental image or you may choose to stay completely within the imagined realm of your prayer. Whichever you choose, know that God will offer you the words from the biblical passage that you need to hear – even if only in fragments.
- Listen and watch as Jesus explains how nourishes all men and women as the divine bread of heaven.
- Again, look around as Jesus speaks and see the reactions of his disciples. Become aware of their feelings and how they behave toward Jesus and one another.
- Remember that Jesus is speaking to men and women experiencing the miracle of Jesus' Christ's presence in their lives. Remember he also is speaking to you.
- After Jesus finishes speaking, allow his image and this place to fade from your imagination as you become aware of the phrases and images from this moment which touched you most deeply. Recall the emotions and memories – including any sounds or smells – evoked during your prayer. Allow these seminal aspects of your meditation to linger on your mind and in your heart, noting any special feelings evoked by them.

[5]   Then, become aware of Jesus' presence with you in this moment and have an open and informal conversation about this prayer period and how the passage from John's gospel expresses your own needs or desires – giving space for Jesus to respond or to highlight different aspects from the biblical account and your experiences during this contemplation. Then, gradually allow your thoughts to recede as you focus on God's broader presence in your life and in the world around you.

[6]   Conclude by offering this prayer:

Confirm me in your love divine,
Smooth for my feet life's rugged way;

My will with yours entwine,
Lest evil lead my steps astray.
Be with me still as guard and guide,
Keep me in holy sanctity,
Let my firm faith on you abide,
From fraud and error hold me free. Amen.

[7]   Afterward, take 10-15 minutes in a quiet space to reflect on the most significant moments from your prayer and record your reflections in your journal.

8.5 A Repeated Contemplation of Luke 6:17-38

In this repeated contemplation of Luke 6:17-38, you again will see and hear Jesus preaching to a crowd about the call to a reformed life.

[1] Begin by re-reading the biblical selection and reviewing your notes on it.

[2] Then, focus on this specific time and place as you allow all other concerns to fall away before considering the people and place in this moment of prayer.

- Allow an image of Jesus to emerge in your imagination, noting his physical characteristics and mannerisms. Look at what he is wearing or carrying. Make a note of whether he is sitting, standing, or walking. Ponder this mental image, allowing any other observations about Jesus to form in your mind.

- Observe the people around Jesus, becoming aware of their appearance and demeanor. Observe whether they are sitting, standing, or walking. Take a moment to ponder this mental image, allowing other impressions of these people to form.

- Allow yourself to become aware of the location of this moment of prayer. Observe its physical characteristics and the arrangement of the people in it. Look around the place and notice more details about it – if it is in dim or bright light, if it is still and silent or filled with noise, if it has an unusual smell or not, etc.

- Take a moment to remain in this place with these people before allowing these images to fade from your consciousness.

[3] Become aware of your desires during this moment of prayer. Remember your desire to experience the divine presence all around you and to trust in God's plan for you, asking that all your intentions and actions may be directed purely to the service and praise of God. Reassert your desire to recognize the transformative power of God's forgiveness in your life as well as the special role of Christ in your becoming a child of God. Finally, recall your desire experience the joyful lightness of Christ's yoke as you accept becoming a "loved sinner".

As these desires fill your consciousness, let all other concerns fall aside as you focus on this time and place of prayer.

[4] Allow the image of Jesus and the crowd to reemerge in your imagination.

- Watch as the group assembles around Jesus. Listen to the sounds of this moment and become comfortable as you prepare to hear Jesus speak. Feel the anticipation of the people around you and share in that enthusiasm.
- As you hear Jesus calm the crowd, ask God to help you enter this moment – either by joining these events or by listening quietly to them. Focus your attention on Jesus, noting his physical appearance and his demeanor.
- Then, watch and listen as Jesus speaks to the crowd, presenting the blessings and woes of Luke's gospel. You may want to quietly read the passage while remaining prayerfully aware of your mental image or you may choose to stay completely within the imagined realm of your prayer. Whichever you choose, know that God will offer you the words from the biblical passage that you need to hear – even if only in fragments.
- Listen and watch as Jesus explains how both the blessings and the woes express God's love.
  – Again, look around as Jesus speaks and see the reactions of his disciples and the people in the crowd. Become aware of their feelings and how they behave toward Jesus and one another.
  – Remember that Jesus is speaking to men and women experiencing the miracle of Jesus Christ's presence in their lives. Remember he also is speaking to you.
- After Jesus finishes speaking, allow his image and this place to fade from your imagination as you become aware of the phrases and images from this moment which touched you most deeply. Recall the emotions and memories – including any sounds or smells – evoked during your prayer. Allow these seminal aspects of your meditation to linger on your mind and in your heart, noting any special feelings evoked by them.

[5] Then, become aware of Jesus' presence with you in this moment and have an open and informal conversation about this prayer period and how the passage from Luke's gospel expresses your own needs or desires – giving space for Jesus to respond or to highlight different aspects from the biblical account and your experiences during this contemplation. Then, gradually allow your thoughts to recede as you focus on God's broader presence in your life and in the world around you.

[6] Conclude by offering this prayer:

Confirm me in your love divine,

Smooth for my feet life's rugged way;
My will with yours entwine,
Lest evil lead my steps astray.
Be with me still as guard and guide,
Keep me in holy sanctity,
Let my firm faith on you abide,
From fraud and error hold me free. Amen.

[7]   Afterward, take 10-15 minutes in a quiet space to reflect on the most significant moments from your prayer and record your reflections in your journal.

8.6 An Application of the Senses

[1] Become aware of your prayerful desires during this day or week. Bring to mind your desire that the divine presence all around you may be revealed so all your intentions and actions may be directed purely to the service and praise of God. Focus on your desire to recognize the transformative power of God's forgiveness in your life as well as the special role of Christ in your becoming a child of God. Finally, reaffirm your desire to receive that you truly may experience the joyful lightness of Christ's yoke as you accept becoming a "loved sinner"

[2] Call to mind the various prayers of the preceding day or days. Allow the images and words of these prayers to linger and then slowly fade from your consciousness.

- Remember your imaginative contemplation of John 8:2-11. Consider the images and feelings evoked in you during your prayer, feeling God's presence in these memories and becoming aware of the specific sensations associated with each image.
- Recall your imaginative contemplations of Luke 6:17-38 considering it in the same way as your memories of John 8.
- Review your imaginative contemplation of John 6:32-58 in the same manner as the previous prayers.

Make a mental note of which senses are most active. You may see an image or a color, hear a sound or a phrase, or smell a scent or a fragrance. You may even taste a flavor or feel a sensation on your skin.

[3] Then, relax and allow these various memories and experiences to quietly enter and leave your consciousness. Linger on the sensory images and memories being evoked in you – noticing any images or colors, any sounds or phrases, any scents or fragrances, any flavors or physical sensations associated with each prayer.

[4] When you are ready, become completely still and clear your mind of all thoughts and concerns. Allow an image of a special personal space to form in your imagination. Then, watch as God enters that place and forms a small image or object for you that expresses the thought or awareness that you most need to carry with you into your life.

Reverently pick up the object or image, a reflection of the most important gift you have been given during this time of prayer. Look at it carefully and become aware of the divine presence contained within it. Register what it looks like and how it feels in your hand. Then, feel the joy and confidence that comes from touching the presence of God as you accept this gift, offering a short prayer of gratitude while you relax into the pleasure of this moment.

[5]   Then, conclude by offering this prayer:

Confirm me in your love divine,
Smooth for my feet life's rugged way;
My will with yours entwine,
Lest evil lead my steps astray.
Be with me still as guard and guide,
Keep me in holy sanctity,
Let my firm faith on you abide,
From fraud and error hold me free. Amen.

[6]   While your experiences are still fresh in your mind, record the most significant impressions or sensations from this time of prayer in your journal.

8.7 Review of Prayer

[1] Remember your desires during the preceding day or week of prayer. Become aware of our desire to experience the divine presence all around you and to trust in God's plan for you. Recall your desire to recognize the transformative power of God's forgiveness in your life as well as the special role of Christ in your becoming a child of God. Finally, reaffirm your desire to experience the joyful lightness of Christ's yoke as you accept becoming a "loved sinner".

After bringing these thoughts and desires into your consciousness, ask God once again to fulfill these desires in your own life and in your interactions with others.

[2] Then, take a moment to allow the words, thoughts, and feelings from your prayers during the last day or week to linger before asking God to reveal the fulfillment of your deepest desires in these various memories.

- Think about the prayer sequence at the beginning of this day or week. Make a mental note of any words, insights or images that remain particularly significant or meaningful to you.
- Ponder the story, "Patrick Converts Daire". Note any words, insights, or images from it that remain particularly significant or meaningful to you.
- Remember your imaginative contemplation of John 8:2-11.

– Consider the most powerful images, phrases, or feelings from your prayer. Ask yourself what gifts God gave to you through these moments, perhaps offering you new insights or perhaps affirming an important aspect of your faith. Ask yourself how God may be calling you to change through these moments, being as specific as possible.

– Examine your disposition as you prayed. Recall the easiest moments in your prayer and any moments of joy you may have experienced. Remember also if you encountered any difficulty opening yourself to God or if you felt any sadness as you prayed. Ask God to help you understand why these feelings surfaced.

– Bring to mind any moments when you added personal elements (e.g., familiar places or people from your life) or connected your prayers to other scriptures or spiritual writings. Ask yourself how these additions helped or hindered you as you prayed. Again, if you do not know why this happened, ask God to help you understand.

- Recall your imaginative contemplations of Luke 6:17-38. Then, review your prayer in the same way as your earlier reflection on John 8.
- Review your imaginative contemplation of John 6:32-58 in the same manner as the previous prayers.
- Reflect on the ebb and flow of sensory impressions and feelings that marked your application of the senses. Isolate the most memorable moments and sensory impressions from your prayer and reflect on how God used these moments to give you a particular gift.

[3] Finally, ponder the times when images or feelings from the readings of this day or week surfaced outside these prayer periods. Think about the most memorable aspects of these experiences, asking God to explain their significance.

[4] Take a moment to allow the words, thoughts, and feelings of these prayers to linger on your mind and in your heart. Finally, conclude by offering this prayer:

O God, I believe in you; strengthen my belief.
I trust in you; confirm my trust.
I love you; double my love.
I repent that I angered you,
Increase my repentance.
Fill you my heart with awe without despair;
With hope, without over-confidence;
With piety without infatuation;
And with joy without excess.
My God, consent to guide me by your wisdom;
To constrain me by your right;
To comfort me by your mercy;
And to protect me by your power. Amen.

[5] After finishing these prayers, summarize your reflections on the gifts or graces you received during the prayers of this last day or week and record these thoughts in your journal.

9. Responding to God's Love and Forgiveness

9.1a Jesus, My Love, My Saviour
a loved sinner's prayer of praise and service

Take a moment to quiet your spirit, becoming completely present to this time and place. Allow all other thoughts and concerns to fall away as you come into the presence of God. Then, when you are ready, begin.

Jesus, my love, my Saviour,
The joy of every heart,
    You bring light unto my night,
    For light itself you impart.

The night of sin is broken,
The power of hell o'erthrown,
    The heavenly door made wide once more
    By you, most Holy One.

A Hymn, sung or heard (optional)

May the grace of the Holy Ghost be gained by me,
And the true Faith be kept unstained by me,
    While I follow the path of the saints, endeavouring
    To walk in the temple of Christ unwavering.

And may I seek the eternal Trinity
Trusting in Christ and in Christ's divinity,
    Helping the poor and relieving them
    Walking with God and receiving them.

Devils that tempt me, still repelling them.
All my faults to Heaven confessing them.
    Fighting with all that wounds, with energy,
    Ceasing from lies and evil calumny.

Let me not mix with strife and devilry,
Fall I to prayer instead of revelry,
    Thanking the Lord for all his generosity
    Throwing aside my evil ways from me.

My life disorderly now amending it;
My evil will no more defending it;
    All sorts of sin avoiding carefully,
    In friendship with God rejoicing prayerful'y.

Read or recite Psalm 84.

Holy Lord,
Under my thoughts may I God-thoughts find.
Half of my sins escape my mind.
    For what I said, or did not say,
    Pardon me, O Lord, I pray.

Read Ephesians 6: 10-18, aloud or quietly.

O Lord, Jesus the Christ,
If I were in Heaven my harp I would sound
With apostles and angels and saints all around,
    Praising and thanking the Son who is crowned,
    May the poor race of Eve for that heaven be bound!

Holy Lord,
The law of God may I perform
The Commandments of God may I keep,
    The glory of the Heavens may I see,
    And the sweet music of the angels may I hear.

Word of the everlasting Father,
Seal me with faith, with love inspire:
    Confirm my hope, O Holy One,
    True God and sole-begotten Son.

O Holy Lord,
    God with the Father and the Spirit,
For me is many a snare designed,
To fill my mind with doubts and fears;
    Far from the land of holy saints,
    I dwell within my vale of tears.
Let faith, let hope, let love –
Traits far above the cold world's way –

    With patience, humility, and awe,
    Become my guides from day to day.

I acknowledge, the evil I have done.
From the day of my birth till the day of my death,
    Through the sight of my eyes,
Through the hearing of my ears,
    Through the sayings of my mouth,
Through the thoughts of my heart,
    Through the touch of my hands,
Through the course of my way,
    Through all I said and did not,
Through all I promised and fulfilled not,
    Through all the laws and holy commandments I broke.
I ask even now absolution of you,
    For fear I may have never asked it as was right,
    And that I might not live to ask it again,

O Holy Lord, my King in Heaven,
May you not let my soul stray from you,
May you keep me in a good state,
    May you turn me toward what is good to do,
    May you protect me from dangers, small and great.
May you fill my eyes with tears of repentance,
    So I may avoid the sinner's awful sentence.
May the Grace of the God for ever be with me,
    And whatever my needs, may the Triune God give me.

Select one of the following options for the Lord's Prayer.

Option A

O Jesus Christ,
Lord of heaven and earth,
Help me pray as you yourself taught:
    "Our Father in heaven,
    hallowed be your name.
    Your kingdom come.
    Your will be done,
    on earth as it is in heaven.

> *Give us this day our daily bread.*
> *And forgive us our debts,*
> *as we also have forgiven our debtors.*
> *And do not bring us to the time of trial,*
> *but rescue us from the evil one."*
> *(Matthew 6:9-13)*

From the foes of my land,
from the foes of my faith,
From the foes who would us dissever,
> O Lord, preserve me, in life and in death,
> With the Sign of the Cross for ever.
> *For the kingdom, the power, and the glory*
> *are yours now and for ever. Amen.*

Please proceed with "I beseech you, O Lord…," found after Option B.

Option B

O Jesus Christ,
Lord of heaven and earth,
Help me pray as you yourself taught:
> *Our Father in heaven,*
> *hallowed be your name,*
> *your kingdom come,*
> *your will be done,*
> *on earth as in heaven.*
> *Give us today our daily bread.*
> *Forgive us our sins*
> *as we forgive those who sin against us.*
> *Lead us not into temptation*
> *but deliver us from evil.*

From the foes of my land,
from the foes of my faith,
From the foes who would us dissever,
> O Lord, preserve me, in life and in death,
> With the Sign of the Cross for ever.
> *For the kingdom, the power, and the glory*
> *are yours now and for ever. Amen.*

I beseech you, O Lord.
God in Heaven, unsurpassed in power and might;
> Be behind me, Be on my left,
> Be before me, Be on my right!
Against each danger, you are my help;
In distress, upon you I call.
> In dark times, may you sustain me
> And lift me up again when I fall.
Lord over heaven and of earth,
You know my offenses.
> Yet, listening to my pleadings,
> You guide me away from sinful pretenses.
Lord of all creation and the many creatures,
You bestow on me many earthly treasures.
> Revealing love in each life and season,
> You share with me heavenly pleasures.
May you arouse me
In moments both of joy and of strife;
> Most holy Lord, bring me new life!

A Hymn, sung or heard (optional)

O Jesus Christ,
> Lord of heaven and earth,
> You are my riches, my store, my provision,
My star through the years
When troubles rend me,
> Through times of strife and tears,
> Sweet Jesus, defend me.

It was heavenly love impelled you
Thus to redeem our race,
> And bless my sight with the sweet light
> That shines from your face.

You to the stars ascended
Have banished fear, O Lord;
> Be yours all praise, through endless days.
> Be you my sweet reward.

End this time of prayer by taking some time to bring to mind the various ways God shields you from harm or guides you through the world's tumult. Then, when you are ready, conclude by saying:

O Holy Lord, King in Heaven,
I place myself at the edge of your grace,
    On the floor of your house myself I place,
And to banish the sin of my heart away,
    I lower my knee to you this day.
Through life's torrents of pain may you bring me whole,
    And, O Lord Jesus Christ, preserve also my soul. Amen.

9.1b Preparation for Prayer

Consideration of the Readings

After reciting or prayerfully reading the prayer sequence for this day or week:
- Read Romans 8:1-17. Again, pay careful attention to any phrases or images that seem particularly meaningful to you. Then, record these highlights in your workbook so you will remember them during this day or week of prayer.
- Read Ephesians 6:10-18, noting any phrases or images that seem particularly meaningful to you and record these highlights in your workbook.
- Read Jeremiah 29:11-14, noting any phrases or images that seem particularly meaningful to you and record these highlights in your workbook.
- Read "The Deer's Cry" (found on page 321).

Note: You also should consider any aspect of the prayer sequence from this day or week that seemed particularly significant to you.

Contemplation of Your Needs

When you are ready, allow any distractions to fade from your consciousness as you become aware of your desire to live in God's goodness. Feel yourself yearning to properly use the many gifts God has given you, to experience God's continuing care, and to be open to the immense love God shows for you, then:
- Read "The Young Patrick and the Flooded House" and "The Young Patrick and the Wolf" (both found on page 321). Allow yourself to linger on any thoughts, phrases or images that seem particularly meaningful or significant to your earlier preparations or prayer.
- Pray for your desires in the coming day or week. Ask that the divine presence all around you may be revealed so all your intentions and actions may be directed purely to the service and praise of God. Ask also to open yourself to experience the joy and empowerment that comes with placing your confidence in Christ in gratitude for the gift of God's love.

- Conclude by praying that you may linger in the joy of being a "loved sinner" and, strengthened by gratitude, may live your life fully in accord with God's desires.

Then, record any significant thoughts, emotions, or reactions from these moments in your workbook.

After this, put your notes aside. Without straining your memory, consider in turn each of the readings for the coming day or week and allow them to take shape in your imagination. Prayerfully ponder how each reading affects you emotionally without overtly thinking about their content, asking God to illuminate the spiritual gifts offered in each reading.

Finally, conclude by allowing these desires to fade from your consciousness as you offer this traditional Irish prayer collected by Douglas Hyde in *The Religious Songs of Connacht*:

> *O God, I believe in you; strengthen my belief.*
> *I trust in you; confirm my trust.*
> *I love you; double my love.*
> *I repent that I angered you,*
> *Increase my repentance.*
> *Fill you my heart with awe without despair;*
> *With hope, without over-confidence;*
> *With piety without infatuation;*
> *And with joy without excess.*
> *My God, consent to guide me by your wisdom;*
> *To constrain me by your right;*
> *To comfort me by your mercy;*
> *And to protect me by your power. Amen.*

Allow these words to linger on your mind and in your heart for a few moments and then write the most important thoughts, feelings, and desires in your workbook.

9.2   A Meditation on Romans 8:1-17

In this meditation on Romans 8:1-17, you will see and hear Saint Patrick preaching to a crowd about living a new life in Christ.

[1]   Begin by reading the biblical selection and reviewing your notes on it.

[2]   Then, focus on this specific time and place as you allow all other concerns to fall away before considering the people and place in this moment of prayer.

- Allow an image of Patrick to emerge in your imagination, noting his physical characteristics and mannerisms. Look at what he is wearing or carrying. Make a note of whether he is sitting, standing, or walking. Ponder this mental image, allowing any other observations about Patrick to form in your mind.

- Observe the people around Saint Patrick, becoming aware of their appearance and demeanor. Observe whether they are sitting, standing, or walking. Take a moment to ponder this mental image, allowing other impressions of these people to form.

- Allow yourself to become aware of the location of this moment of prayer. Observe its physical characteristics and the arrangement of the people in it. Look around the place and notice more details about it – if it is in dim or bright light, if it is still and silent or filled with noise, if it has an unusual smell or not, etc.

- Take a moment to remain in this place with these people before allowing these images to fade from your consciousness.

[3]   Become aware of your desires during this moment of prayer. Remember your desire to experience the divine presence all around you and to trust in God's plan for you, asking that all your intentions and actions may be directed purely to the service and praise of God. Reassert your desire to experience the joy and empowerment that comes with placing your confidence in Christ in gratitude for the gift of God's love. Finally, recall your desire to linger in the joy of being a "loved sinner" and, strengthened by gratitude, to live your life fully in accord with God's desires.

As these desires fill your consciousness, let all other concerns fall aside as you focus on this time and place of prayer.

[4]   Allow the image of Saint Patrick and the crowd to reemerge in your imagination.

- Watch as the group assembles around Patrick. Listen to the sounds of this moment and become comfortable as you prepare to hear Patrick speak. Feel the anticipation of the people around you and share in that enthusiasm.
- Ask God to help you enter this moment – either by joining these events or by listening quietly to them. Focus your attention on Saint Patrick, noting his physical appearance and his demeanor.
- Then, watch and listen as Patrick speaks the words of Paul's letter to the Romans. You may want to quietly read the passage while remaining prayerfully aware of your mental image or you may choose to stay completely within the imagined realm of your prayer. Whichever you choose, know that God will offer you the words from the biblical passage that you need to hear – even if only in fragments.
- Hear Patrick explain the passage. Listen to him as he explains the meaning and significance of God's promise expressed in Paul's words.

– Again, look around as Patrick speaks and see the reactions of his disciples and the people in the crowd. Become aware of their feelings and how they behave toward Patrick and one another.

– Remember that Saint Patrick is speaking to men and women experiencing the transformative presence of Jesus Christ in their lives. Remember he also is speaking to you.

- After Saint Patrick finishes speaking, allow his image and this place to fade from your imagination as you become aware of the phrases and images from this moment which touched you most deeply. Recall the emotions and memories – including any sounds or smells – evoked during your prayer. Allow these seminal aspects of your meditation to linger on your mind and in your heart, noting any special feelings evoked by them.

[5] Then, become aware of God's presence with you in this moment and have an open and informal conversation about this prayer period and how the passage from Paul's epistle expresses your own needs or desires – giving space for God to respond or to highlight different aspects from the biblical selection and your experiences during this meditation. Then, gradually allow your thoughts to recede as you focus on God's broader presence in your life and in the world around you.

[6] Conclude by offering this prayer:

Confirm me in your love divine,
Smooth for my feet life's rugged way;

My will with yours entwine,
Lest evil lead my steps astray.
Be with me still as guard and guide,
Keep me in holy sanctity,
Let my firm faith on you abide,
From fraud and error hold me free. Amen.

[7]   Afterward, take 10-15 minutes in a quiet space to reflect on the most significant moments from your prayer and record your reflections in your journal.

9.3 A Meditation on Ephesians 6:10-18

In this meditation on Ephesians 6:10-18, you will see and hear Saint Patrick teaching his disciples to remain strong in their faith.

[1] Begin by reading the biblical selection and reviewing your notes on it.

[2] Then, focus on this specific time and place as you allow all other concerns to fall away before considering the people and place in this moment of prayer.

- Allow an image of Patrick to emerge in your imagination, noting his physical characteristics and mannerisms. Look at what he is wearing or carrying. Make a note of whether he is sitting, standing, or walking. Ponder this mental image, allowing any other observations about Patrick to form in your mind.

- Observe the people around Saint Patrick, becoming aware of their appearance and demeanor. Observe whether they are sitting, standing, or walking. Take a moment to ponder this mental image, allowing other impressions of these people to form.

- Allow yourself to become aware of the location of this moment of prayer. Observe its physical characteristics and the arrangement of the people in it. Look around the place and notice more details about it – if it is in dim or bright light, if it is still and silent or filled with noise, if it has an unusual smell or not, etc.

- Take a moment to remain in this place with these people before allowing these images to fade from your consciousness.

[3] Become aware of your desires during this moment of prayer. Remember your desire to experience the divine presence all around you and to trust in God's plan for you, asking that all your intentions and actions may be directed purely to the service and praise of God. Reassert your desire to experience the joy and empowerment that comes with placing your confidence in Christ in gratitude for the gift of God's love. Finally, recall your desire to linger in the joy of being a "loved sinner" and, strengthened by gratitude, to live your life fully in accord with God's desires.

As these desires fill your consciousness, let all other concerns fall aside as you focus on this time and place of prayer.

[4] Allow the image of Saint Patrick and his disciples to reemerge in your imagination.

- Watch as the group assembles around Patrick. Listen to the sounds of this moment and become comfortable as you prepare to hear Patrick speak. Feel the anticipation of the people around you and share in that enthusiasm.
- As you hear Patrick quiet his companions, ask God to help you enter this moment – either by joining these events or by listening quietly to them. Focus your attention on Saint Patrick, noting his physical appearance and his demeanor.
- Then, watch and listen as Patrick speaks the words of Paul's letter to the Ephesians. You may want to quietly read the passage while remaining prayerfully aware of your mental image or you may choose to stay completely within the imagined realm of your prayer. Whichever you choose, know that God will offer you the words from the biblical passage that you need to hear – even if only in fragments.
- Hear Patrick explain the passage. Listen to him as he explains the meaning and significance of God's promise expressed in Paul's words.

– Again, look around as Patrick speaks and see the reactions of his disciples. Become aware of their feelings and how they behave toward Patrick and one another.

– Remember that Saint Patrick is speaking to men and women experiencing the transformative presence of Jesus Christ in their lives. Remember he also is speaking to you.

- After Saint Patrick finishes speaking, allow his image and this place to fade from your imagination as you become aware of the phrases and images from this moment which touched you most deeply. Recall the emotions and memories – including any sounds or smells – evoked during your prayer. Allow these seminal aspects of your meditation to linger on your mind and in your heart, noting any special feelings evoked by them.

[5] Then, become aware of God's presence with you in this moment and have an open and informal conversation about this prayer period and how the passage from Paul's epistle expresses your own needs or desires – giving space for God to respond or to highlight different aspects from the biblical selection and your experiences during this meditation. Then, gradually allow your thoughts to recede as you focus on God's broader presence in your life and in the world around you.

[6] Conclude by offering this prayer:

Confirm me in your love divine,

> *Smooth for my feet life's rugged way;*
> *My will with yours entwine,*
> *Lest evil lead my steps astray.*
> *Be with me still as guard and guide,*
> *Keep me in holy sanctity,*
> *Let my firm faith on you abide,*
> *From fraud and error hold me free. Amen.*

[7] Afterward, take 10-15 minutes in a quiet space to reflect on the most significant moments from your prayer and record your reflections in your journal.

9.4 A Meditation on Jeremiah 29:11-14

In this meditation on Jeremiah 29:11-14, you will see and hear Saint Patrick preaching to a crowd about trusting in God's plan for them.

[1] Begin by reading the biblical selection and reviewing your notes on it.

[2] Then, focus on this specific time and place as you allow all other concerns to fall away before considering the people and place in this moment of prayer.

- Allow an image of Patrick to emerge in your imagination, noting his physical characteristics and mannerisms. Look at what he is wearing or carrying. Make a note of whether he is sitting, standing, or walking. Ponder this mental image, allowing any other observations about Patrick to form in your mind.

- Observe the people around Saint Patrick, becoming aware of their appearance and demeanor. Observe whether they are sitting, standing, or walking. Take a moment to ponder this mental image, allowing other impressions of these people to form.

- Allow yourself to become aware of the location of this moment of prayer. Observe its physical characteristics and the arrangement of the people in it. Look around the place and notice more details about it – if it is in dim or bright light, if it is still and silent or filled with noise, if it has an unusual smell or not, etc.

- Take a moment to remain in this place with these people before allowing these images to fade from your consciousness.

[3] Become aware of your desires during this moment of prayer. Remember your desire to experience the divine presence all around you and to trust in God's plan for you, asking that all your intentions and actions may be directed purely to the service and praise of God. Reassert your desire to experience the joy and empowerment that comes with placing your confidence in Christ in gratitude for the gift of God's love. Finally, recall your desire to linger in the joy of being a "loved sinner" and, strengthened by gratitude, to live your life fully in accord with God's desires.

As these desires fill your consciousness, let all other concerns fall aside as you focus on this time and place of prayer.

[4] Allow the image of Saint Patrick and the crowd to reemerge in your imagination.

- Watch as the group assembles around Patrick. Listen to the sounds of this moment and become comfortable as you prepare to hear Patrick speak. Feel the anticipation of the people around you and share in that enthusiasm.
- Ask God to help you share in this experience – either by joining these events or by listening quietly to them. Focus your attention on Saint Patrick, noting his physical appearance and his demeanor.
- Then, watch and listen as Patrick speaks the words of Jeremiah. You may want to quietly read the passage while remaining prayerfully aware of your mental image or you may choose to stay completely within the imagined realm of your prayer. Whichever you choose, know that God will offer you the words from the biblical passage that you need to hear – even if only in fragments.
- Hear Patrick explain the passage. Listen to him as he explains the meaning and significance of God's promise expressed in Jeremiah's words.

– Again, look around as Patrick speaks and see the reactions of his disciples and the people in the crowd. Become aware of their feelings and how they behave toward Patrick and one another.

– Remember that Saint Patrick is speaking to men and women experiencing the transformative presence of Jesus Christ in their lives. Remember he also is speaking to you.

- After Saint Patrick finishes speaking, allow his image and this place to fade from your imagination as you become aware of the phrases and images from this moment which touched you most deeply. Recall the emotions and memories – including any sounds or smells – evoked during your prayer. Allow these seminal aspects of your meditation to linger on your mind and in your heart, noting any special feelings evoked by them.

[5] Then, become aware of God's presence with you in this moment and have an open and informal conversation about this prayer period and how the passage from Jeremiah expresses your own needs or desires – giving space for God to respond or to highlight different aspects from the biblical selection and your experiences during this meditation. Then, gradually allow your thoughts to recede as you focus on God's broader presence in your life and in the world around you.

[6] Conclude by offering this prayer:

Confirm me in your love divine,
Smooth for my feet life's rugged way;

My will with yours entwine,
Lest evil lead my steps astray.
Be with me still as guard and guide,
Keep me in holy sanctity,
Let my firm faith on you abide,
From fraud and error hold me free. Amen.

[7] Afterward, take 10-15 minutes in a quiet space to reflect on the most significant moments from your prayer and record your reflections in your journal.

9.5   A Meditation on "The Deer's Cry"

In this meditation, you will see and hear Saint Patrick reminding his disciples to trust in God's protective presence by praying "The Deer's Cry" with them.

[1]   Begin by reading Saint Patrick's "The Deer's Cry" (see page 321) and reviewing your notes on it.

[2]   Then, focus on this specific time and place as you allow all other concerns to fall away before considering the people and place in this moment of prayer.

• Allow an image of Patrick to emerge in your imagination, noting his physical characteristics and mannerisms. Look at what he is wearing or carrying. Make a note of whether he is sitting, standing, or walking. Ponder this mental image, allowing any other observations about Patrick to form in your mind.

• Imagine the disciples around Saint Patrick, becoming aware of their appearance and demeanor. Observe whether they are sitting, standing, or walking. Take a moment to ponder this mental image, allowing other impressions of these people to form.

• Allow yourself to become aware of the location of this moment of prayer. Observe its physical characteristics and the arrangement of the people in it. Look around the place and notice more details about it – if it is in dim or bright light, if it is still and silent or filled with noise, if it has an unusual smell or not, etc.

• Take a moment to remain in this place with these people before allowing these images to fade from your consciousness.

[3]   Become aware of your desires during this moment of prayer. Remember your desire to experience the divine presence all around you and to trust in God's plan for you, asking that all your intentions and actions may be directed purely to the service and praise of God. Reassert your desire to experience the joy and empowerment that comes with placing your confidence in Christ in gratitude for the gift of God's love. Finally, recall your desire to linger in the joy of being a "loved sinner" and, strengthened by gratitude, to live your life fully in accord with God's desires.

As these desires fill your consciousness, let all other concerns fall aside as you focus on this time and place of prayer.

[4]   Allow the image of Saint Patrick and his disciples to reemerge in your imagination.

- Watch as the group assembles around Patrick. Listen to the sounds of this moment and become comfortable as you prepare to hear Patrick speak. Feel the anticipation of the people around you and share in that enthusiasm.
- Ask God to help you share in this experience – either by joining these events or by listening quietly to them. Focus your attention on Saint Patrick, noting his physical appearance and his demeanor.
- Then, watch and listen as Patrick begins reciting "The Deer's Cry". Read the passage while remaining prayerfully aware of your mental image of being with Patrick and his disciples – allowing its words to evoke images and feelings from the days or weeks of this retreat.
- After Saint Patrick finishes praying, allow his image and this place to fade from your imagination as you become aware of the phrases and images from this moment which touched you most deeply. Recall the emotions and memories – including any sounds or smells – evoked during your prayer. Allow these seminal aspects of your meditation to linger on your mind and in your heart, noting any special feelings evoked by them.

[5] Then, become aware of God's presence with you in this moment and have an open and informal conversation about your prayer and how the words of "The Deer's Cry" express your own needs or desires – giving space for God to respond or to highlight different aspects of your experiences during this meditation. Gradually allow your thoughts to recede as you focus on God's presence in your life and in the world around you.

[6] Conclude by offering this prayer:
> *Confirm me in your love divine,*
> *Smooth for my feet life's rugged way;*
> *My will with yours entwine,*
> *Lest evil lead my steps astray.*
> *Be with me still as guard and guide,*
> *Keep me in holy sanctity,*
> *Let my firm faith on you abide,*
> *From fraud and error hold me free. Amen.*

[7] Afterward, take 10-15 minutes in a quiet space to reflect on the most significant moments from your prayer and record your reflections in your journal.

9.6 An Application of the Senses

[1]   Become aware of your prayerful desires during this day or week. Bring to mind your desire that the divine presence all around you may be revealed so all your intentions and actions may be directed purely to the service and praise of God. Focus on your desire open yourself to experience the joy and empowerment that comes with placing your confidence in Christ in gratitude for the gift of God's love. Finally, reaffirm your desire to linger in the joy of being a "loved sinner" and, strengthened by gratitude, may live your life fully in accord with God's desires.

[2]   Call to mind the various prayers of the preceding day or days. Allow the images and words of these prayers to linger and then slowly fade from your consciousness.

- Remember your meditations on Romans 8:1-17. Consider the images and feelings evoked in you during your prayer, feeling God's presence in these memories and becoming aware of the specific sensations associated with each image.
- Recall your meditation on Ephesians 6:10-18 considering it in the same way as your memories of Romans 8.
- Review your meditation on Jeremiah 29:11-14 in the same manner as the previous prayers.
- Review your meditation of "The Deer's Cry" in the same manner as the previous prayers.

Make a mental note of which senses are most active. You may see an image or a color, hear a sound or a phrase, or smell a scent or a fragrance. You may even taste a flavor or feel a sensation on your skin.

[3]   Then, relax and allow these various memories and experiences to quietly enter and leave your consciousness. Linger on the sensory images and memories being evoked in you – noticing any images or colors, any sounds or phrases, any scents or fragrances, any flavors or physical sensations associated with each prayer.

[4]   When you are ready, become completely still and clear your mind of all thoughts and concerns. Allow an image of a special personal space to form in your imagination. Then, watch as God enters that place and forms a small image or object for you that expresses the thought or awareness that you most need to carry with you into your life.

Reverently pick up the object or image, a reflection of the most important gift you have been given during this time of prayer. Look at it carefully and become aware of the divine presence contained within it. Register what it looks like and how it feels in your hand. Then, feel the joy and confidence that comes from touching the presence of God as you accept this gift, offering a short prayer of gratitude while you relax into the pleasure of this moment.

[5]   Then, conclude by offering this prayer:

> *Confirm me in your love divine,*
> *Smooth for my feet life's rugged way;*
> *My will with yours entwine,*
> *Lest evil lead my steps astray.*
> *Be with me still as guard and guide,*
> *Keep me in holy sanctity,*
> *Let my firm faith on you abide,*
> *From fraud and error hold me free. Amen.*

[6]   While your experiences are still fresh in your mind, record the most significant impressions or sensations from this time of prayer in your journal.

9.7 Review of Prayer

[1] Remember your desires during the preceding day or week of prayer. Become aware of our desire to experience the divine presence all around you and to trust in God's plan for you. Recall your desire to open yourself to experience the joy and empowerment that comes with placing your confidence in Christ in gratitude for the gift of God's love. Finally, reaffirm your desire to linger in the joy of being a "loved sinner" so, strengthened by gratitude, you may live your life fully in accord with God's desires.

After bringing these thoughts and desires into your consciousness, ask God once again to fulfill these desires in your own life and in your interactions with others.

[2] Then, take a moment to allow the words, thoughts, and feelings from your prayers during the last day or week to linger – on your mind and in your heart – before asking God to reveal the fulfillment of your deepest desires in these various memories.

• Think about the prayer sequence at the beginning of this day or week. Make a mental note of any words, insights or images that remain particularly significant or meaningful to you.

• Ponder the stories, "The Young Patrick and the Flooded House" and "The Young Patrick and the Wolf". Note any words, insights, or images from them that remain particularly significant or meaningful to you.

• Remember your meditations on Romans 8:1-17.

– Consider the most powerful images, phrases, or feelings from your prayer. Ask yourself what gifts God gave to you through these moments, perhaps offering you new insights or perhaps affirming an important aspect of your faith. Ask yourself how God may be calling you to change through these moments, being as specific as possible.

– Examine your disposition as you prayed, noting whether prayer came easily or with resistance. Recall the easiest moments in your prayer and any moments of joy you may have experienced. Remember also if you encountered any difficulty opening yourself to God or if you felt any sadness as you prayed. Ask God to help you understand why these feelings surfaced.

– Bring to mind any moments when you added personal elements (e.g., familiar places or people from your life) or connected your prayers to other scriptures or spiritual writings. Ask yourself how

these additions helped or hindered you as you prayed. Again, if you do not know why this happened, ask God to help you understand.

- Recall your meditation on Ephesians 6:10-18. Then, review your prayer in the same way as your earlier reflection on Romans 8.
- Review your meditation on Jeremiah 29:11-14 in the same manner as the previous prayers.
- Reminisce on your meditation on "The Deer's Cry" in the same manner as the previous prayers.
- Reflect on the ebb and flow of sensory impressions and feelings that marked your application of the senses. Isolate the most memorable moments and sensory impressions from your prayer and reflect on how God used these moments to give you a particular gift, perhaps offering you new insights or changing you in some way.

[3] Finally, ponder the times when images or feelings from the readings of this day or week surfaced outside these prayer periods. Consider those moments or events in which God's presence or guidance was especially strong as well as any moments when you were struggling. Think about the most memorable aspects of these experiences, asking God to explain their significance.

[4] Take a moment to allow the words, thoughts, and feelings of these prayers to linger on your mind and in your heart. Finally, conclude by allowing these desires to fade from your consciousness as you offer this prayer:

> *O God, I believe in you; strengthen my belief.*
> *I trust in you; confirm my trust.*
> *I love you; double my love.*
> *I repent that I angered you,*
> *Increase my repentance.*
> *Fill you my heart with awe without despair;*
> *With hope, without over-confidence;*
> *With piety without infatuation;*
> *And with joy without excess.*
> *My God, consent to guide me by your wisdom;*
> *To constrain me by your right;*
> *To comfort me by your mercy;*
> *And to protect me by your power. Amen.*

[5] After finishing these prayers, summarize your reflections on the gifts or graces you received during the prayers of this last day or week and record these thoughts in your journal.

The Call of the King of Heaven

The Call of the King of Heaven

At the conclusion of this period of intense prayer, you have come to recognize and embrace the love God has for you even though you are a sinner. In these preceding days or weeks, you have encountered many different expressions of God's love while also confronting the forces in and around you that would deny that love. While you may not yet be fully aware of the personal transformations you have experienced, you are now living in a world marked by God's grace – shaping you in new ways and inviting your participation in God's redemptive plan of creation. Yet, through humility and prayer, you will recognize that you cannot dwell in this new realm without continually returning to Christ for strength when serving God's desires and forgiveness when you fail in your efforts.

The ancient Celtic saints understood this idea of the "loved sinner". For them, the repentance and forgiveness of sins were part of an ongoing cycle which offered greater strength and conviction with each repeated act of penance and absolution. The recognition of a sin and its repentance before another person – as well as the completion of the appropriate penance – offered new insights into a person's temptations and weaknesses which, in turn, taught that individual new insights into recognizing and avoiding future sins. Also, because the practices of repenting sin involved a moment of spiritual communion with another person, the ancient Celtic saints cultivated a humble awareness that any truly final repentance and absolution of sin was not something that could be achieved alone. It required a soul friend, a companion for the journey.

In his *Spiritual Exercises*, Saint Ignatius recognizes this need for companionship by counter opposing two types of leaders – an earthly king in Christ the King – through his consideration of "The Kingdom". Filled with gratitude after their prayers of the previous days or weeks, individuals are asked to compare the call to a worthy cause from an admirable human leader before considering the call to serve God presented by Jesus Christ. The men and women receiving this invitation are no longer helpless creatures buffeted by the forces of sin, they have been transformed by divine love and grace into worthy co-participants in God's redemptive work. While these individuals remained weakened by their sinful tendencies, the humility and confidence evoked by God's forgiveness gives them the strength to respond to Christ's invitation.

It is worthwhile to note that the image of the king used by St. Ignatius would have been familiar to the ancient Celtic saints who often referred to Christ as the "King of Heaven". For both Ignatius and the ancient Celts, participating in the cause of a great king or leader involved a recognition that they were in some way capable of doing or achieving something the individual could not on his or her own. Still, the acceptance of another person's leadership was not simply about becoming a follower. Instead, it was a highly personal invitation to become a companion in the cause advocated or pursued by that leader – a pattern seen both in the communities that emerged around particular Celtic saints as well as in the early companions gathered around Ignatius. Service in the cause of a leader was an act of generosity, not compulsion.

A Contemplation of the Kingdom of Jesus Christ

So, through the following exercise, consider the qualities of Christ that would lead you to respond generously when Jesus calls you into his service:

>*Note:* At this point, you may want to read the text of this exercise as Ignatius presented it is in his Spiritual Exercises (see page 310). This review might offer you different perspectives on various aspects of this exercise, illuminate your reflections and open you to a broader awareness of God's activity during your prayer. However, you should feel free to ignore this suggestion if it distracts you from your prayers.

[1] Focus on this specific time and place as you allow all other concerns to fall away. As you become still, become aware of your desires during this moment of prayer. Ask of Jesus Christ that you may not be deaf to his call but that you remain alert and eager to fulfill his most holy will to the best of your ability. Ask also that you might fully

understand the qualities of Jesus the king of heaven which attract you to his service.

As these desires fill your consciousness, let all other concerns fall aside as you focus on this specific time and place of prayer.

[2]   Then, slowly and deliberately, consider the invitation of Jesus Christ to become his companion.

• In your imagination, allow yourself to see a human king, queen or other leader chosen by God. Take a moment to look at this person, making a mental note of his or her physical appearance and demeanor. Watch as this person interacts with others, commanding their respect and service. Listen to the way this leader speaks to his or her followers, presenting a powerful and noble vision worthy of your devotion and service. Watch and listen as this leader speaks directly to you, asking you to join in fulfilling these dreams and building a better world.

Linger for a time in this moment, becoming aware of all the emotions and thoughts evoked by your conversation with this great human leader. Then, allow this moment to fade from your consciousness while retaining an awareness of the feelings evoked in you by this invitation and the challenges opposed to accepting this invitation through your frail human nature.

• When you are ready, allow yourself to see Jesus Christ standing in front of you with a few of his companions. Take a moment to look at Jesus and those around him, noting their physical appearance and demeanor. Watch as Jesus interacts with his companions and witness the respect these companions have for Jesus and their joy in being his companion. Listen to Jesus as he speaks with his companions, presenting his desire to redeem humanity and creation with their assistance. Hear Jesus assure them that they are now liberated from sin and fully capable of serving in this great cause. Then, watch and listen has Jesus speaks directly to you and asks that you join him in fulfilling this redemptive and restorative mission.

Again, linger in this moment and become aware of all the emotions and thoughts evoked by this conversation with Jesus. Then, allow this moment to fade from your consciousness while retaining an awareness of the feelings evoked in you by this invitation and the sense of liberation you have been offered in this moment.

• Afterward, allow the various words and images of your prayer to flow freely in your consciousness without being controlled. Become aware of those aspects of your prayer that arouse holy desires in you, toward God and toward others (including nonhuman creatures).

Become aware of those aspects of your prayer that make you feel shame for those times you fall short of these holy aspirations.
- Gradually allow these thoughts and images to fade from your consciousness and become aware of the return of Jesus, standing or sitting with you in this moment. Then, have open and informal conversation about your experiences during this meditation. Speak about how these experiences express your own desires and fears, giving space for Jesus to explain the love that motivates the call to serve in building his kingdom. At the end of this conversation, ask Jesus to help you reform those aspects of your personality and life that impede your ability to respond to his invitation to service and companionship.
- Then, gradually allow your thoughts to recede as you focus on Jesus' continuing presence in your life and in the world around you.

[3]　Conclude by offering this prayer adapted from a Christian song collected in Daniel Joseph Donahoe's *Early Christian Hymns* (Series II):

> *Hear me, Christ, my King,*
> *Hear you the praise I bring,*
> *And lead me on;*
> *In tender mercy bend,*
> *My soul from harm defend,*
> *And let my hopes ascend*
> *Unto your throne.*
> *Upon the road of life*
> *Keep me from stain and strife*
> *In your sweet care;*
> *Extend your right hand, Lord,*
> *your gracious aid afford,*
> *Be you my watch and ward;*
> *Lord, hear my prayer. Amen.*

[4]　Afterward, take 10-15 minutes in a quiet space to reflect on the most significant moments from your prayer and record your reflections in your retreat journal.

Manifesting God's Mercy

Introduction

nurturing a holistic spirituality

After completing this retreat, you should take some time to review the gifts you received during your spiritual journey. Some of these gifts will be easy to see, allowing you to embrace them with enthusiasm and joy. Other gifts may be less obvious, requiring you to approach them cautiously and in a spirit of prayerful discernment. Finally, still other gifts will remain outside of your consciousness – perhaps creating feelings of anxiety or concern as they arouse unfamiliar feelings or impulses. In whatever manner these gifts manifest themselves, you are being transformed into an instrument of God's loving presence in the world.

Almost always, this transformation requires time and further prayer. Holy desires evoked during the intense prayers of your retreat may become difficult to sustain and realize when they are challenged by the demands of your daily life. So, you should approach the spiritual gifts of this retreat as seeds that have been planted in well-prepared soil by God. Through God's continuing activity in your life, and through your own efforts, these seeds will germinate and send their tendrils out into various aspects of your life as they seek nourishment and strength before blossoming and manifesting their purpose and beauty in the larger world around you.

Nourishing the Gifts of the Retreat

So, as you nourish the gifts you received during your retreat, you should remain aware that God's loving benevolence does not diminish. Instead, it remains constant has the seeds planted during your time of prayer come to fulfill their purpose in you and in God's greater plan of creation. For this reason, you need to maintain the spirit of generosity that you displayed during your retreat while also being careful to remain vigilant for any distractions or temptations which might undermine the nurturing activity of God in you or undercut the full potential of the gifts you have received.

With these thoughts in mind, it is important that you honor the sensitive time immediately following your retreat by avoiding the temptation to make any significant life-changing decisions. Instead, you may find it helpful to spend the first three months after your retreat in a prayerful and gentle review of your experiences of intense prayer and generosity towards God by:

- Reviewing your thoughts and feelings by making at least one examen daily, paying particular attention to those moments in your day when thoughts on the retreat surface in your consciousness.
- Repeating at least once every week a significant contemplation or meditation from your retreat. It is important these contemplations or meditations become an organic expression of your relationship with God.
- Considering once every week a specific "memento of grace" you received during the retreat – a particular moment of prayer or an insight that had a transformative effect on how you approached God and others.

Note: Do not allow these prayers to become a burden. Instead, approach them as an opportunity to quietly re-engage the seminal aspects of your retreat. So, it is important to chronicle your experiences as the gifts of your earlier prayers deepen and mature – again without making any life-choices based on them.

After this period of gentle prayer, you may begin considering aspects of your life you feel called to change (e.g., joining a prayer group, getting involved in a social ministry, etc.). Approach these spiritual leadings with the same spirit of generosity and openness that you displayed during your retreat, knowing that you are not alone in this process and that you are being transformed by the ongoing activity of God in your life to become an instrument of love.

Nurturing a Holistic Spirituality

However, as you approach these changes, remember that faith is not only a matter of personal piety. Your transformative relationship with God becomes tangible through your lifestyle choices, your interactions with other people and your demonstrated concern for God's other creatures.

In both Celtic and Ignatian spirituality, prayer creates a deepening relationship with God prayer creates a deepening relationship with God and invites each person to find his or her unique way of helping to build God's kingdom. This fosters a dynamic spiritual life in which your prayer and spiritual disciplines interact with the requirements of our "citizenship" in heaven and the impulses to share our faith with others as our love for God overflows to those around us. The ancient Celtic saints referred to this dynamic and multifaceted approach to faith as becoming "colonies of heaven".

The relationships within this understanding of spirituality may be demonstrated with the following diagram:

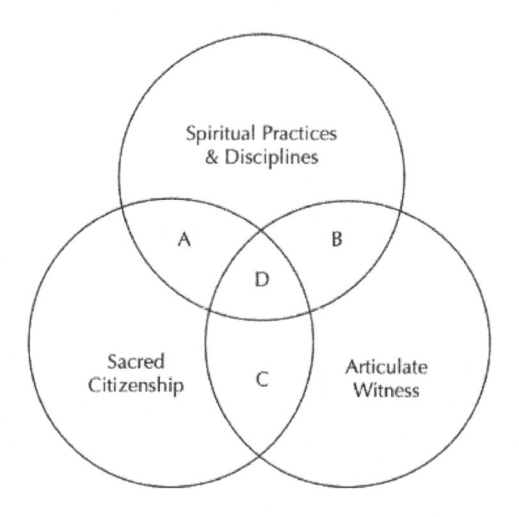

A = Ideals – seeing a vision of new possibilities
B = Language – hearing a voice of hope
C = Advocacy – speaking truth to power
D = Place of Resurrection – manifesting the Kingdom of God

In this holistic approach, the three primary aspects of a life of faith (or spirituality) – spiritual practices and disciplines, sacred citizenship (the ways in which our faith requires us to behave toward others as fellow children of God) and articulate witness (the impulse to share our experience of God's love with others) – interact to give you insight and guidance as you strive to respond to God's love with courage and consistency.

Of these three components of a spiritual life, the most important is your devotion to the spiritual practices and disciplines that nurture a mutual relationship of love between you and God. Without this loving bond, the rest of your spiritual life will quickly wither. However, both your fulfillment of the responsibilities of sacred citizenship and your ability to respond to the invitation to articulate witness helps sustain your life of prayer by making your faith tangible and by reminding you of the need you have for God's continuing support.

Ultimately, however, the interplay between these three aspects of the spiritual life offers the direction you need to find and fulfill your ultimate purpose in God's plan. When your prayer embraces the challenges of sacred citizenship, you see the possibilities of God's kingdom and embrace the ideals that allow you to act in the world with justice and compassion. Similarly, when your love for God invites you to offer witness and you bring these desires prayer, you discover the language you need to express hope to others. Finally, when you feel called to give witness to God's love as a "citizen of heaven", God provides you with the words to speak truth to power and the tools to advocate for a more just world.

With consistent prayer and discernment, these seemingly distinct but interconnected ingredients in the spiritual life converge to reveal the place or ministry that best allows you to give hope-filled witness to God's love to those around you in the world. This is the modern equivalent of what the ancient Celtic saints called the "place of resurrection". It is the place that has been prepared for you in which you will know the fullness of God's love and forgiveness – where you will live in the love and joy of God while creating a "colony of heaven".

Resources for Prayer and Reflection

The resources in this section are designed to help you cultivate this holistic approach to your spiritual life by providing materials for prayer and reflection related to each of these aspects of spirituality. This includes reflections, prayer materials and spiritual exercises intended to foster a spiritual life that also embraces sacred citizenship and articulate witness.

The materials related to spiritual practices include:

• A collection of traditional Irish prayers used in the development of the prayer sequences for this retreat and scriptural citations related to the themes of the retreat. The prayers are intended to offer more focused reflection on the concerns at the heart of the retreat while the scriptural citations are intended to expand your reflection and prayer on the themes of the retreat.

• An exercise designed to help you create your own personal penitential, a tool for assessing and correcting your sinful behavior. Penitentials served an important role in early Celtic prayer, fostering awareness of an individual's personal sins as well as offering the tools to amend sinful behaviors.

The resources related to sacred citizenship focus on the social dimensions of Saint Patrick's ministry, especially his letter to the soldiers of Coroticus. Through reflection questions on the readings concerning Saint Patrick, you will be able to begin to reflect on how your own spiritual life extends outward towards others in the service of God's creation.

Finally, the materials focusing on articulate witness explore the process of discerning those passions in your life – both material and spiritual – that you wish to share with others through some form of public witness. These reflections explore the various experiences of spiritual clarity you might experience in this process as well as offer tools to discern God's desires when you are less certain.

Spiritual Practices

Traditional Prayers

The following early Christian hymns and traditional Irish prayers were woven into the fabric of the prayer sequences introducing the themes of your retreat. Individually, they offer a treasury of spiritual insight and devotion. By using them alone or by integrating them into your existing prayers, you should draw upon these ancestral voices to enrich and extend your spiritual vocabulary.

Short Prayers

O Splendour of God's face,
Bringer of glory from above,
True light, and Fount of every grace,
Illume my day with faith and love.
Pour on my way, O Sun Divine,
your holy truth with rays serene,
And let the heavenly spirit shine
With purging fires to make me clean.

Source:
Early Christian Hymns

I cry out to you, Lord.
Both morning and night.
Come to me, guide me,
And save me from fright,
And make me repentant
And wash me with tears,
And lead me to heaven
When spent are my years.

Source:
The Religious Songs of Connacht, Volume 2

In your hands I do lay my soul.
Let it not fall out of your control,
Countenance brighter than the sun,
Shield me from pain when the race is run.

The will of God be done by me,
The law of God be kept surely,
My evil will controlled by me,
My tongue in check be held securely,
Repentance timely made by me,
Christ's passion understood contritely,
Each sinful crime be shunned by me,
And my sins be mused nightly.

Source:
The Religious Songs of Connacht, Volume 2

I call on you to save me,
From grovelling deeds of shame;
O make me yours by grace divine,
To love and bless your name.
Drive from my heart all darkness,
All evil from my mind;
Forever be my joy in you,
O Saviour of mankind.

Source:
Early Christian Hymns

Loving Jesus, hear me calling,
Me, a sinner, poor and weak ;
Lo, I stretch mine arms to clasp you,
And your tender solace seek,
Lest mine enemies against me
Rise, their deeds of woe to wreak.
They that seek my soul in envy,
That would lead me from your throne,
Be the wicked will their ruin,
In destruction let them groan ;
But, my Saviour, hear my pleading,
Raise me, leave me not alone.

Source:
Early Christian Hymns, Series 2

Help this foolish sinner,
I always go astray,
I rise up in the morning

But pray not with the day.
God I has long forsaken –
Forgotten how to pray,
Where shall I go when Death shall come
And I leave the world in disarray.

Source:
The Religious Songs of Connacht, Volume 2

Fill my soul with grief sincere,
With sorrow deep for my offence;
Let the tear moisten my pillow;
Hear me and grant me defense.
For all my many crimes, O God,
Toward the pains of hell I sadly plod;
But you know my repentance,
And spare the painful sentence.

Source:
Early Christian Hymns

Creator of the heavenly light,
you gave the stars their certain way,
Fixing the moon to shine at night,
The fiery sun to glow by day.
Lord, let me flee each evil thing
Whereto the wicked will declines,
Let all my words and actions bring
My soul to where your glory shines.

Source:
Early Christian Hymns, Series 2

Holy God, let my tongue be free from blame,
Nor utter words of guilt or strife;
Lift up my eyes from deeds of shame,
And all the vanities of life.
My heart be purged and purified
That nought of evil shall remain;
From worldly vice and fleshly pride
My soul by temperance restrain.

Source:
Early Christian Hymns

May speak I the praise of the truth, not slumbering,
The end of the whole, each day remembering,
Helping the poor and those in wretchedness,
Musing on Christ and on His blessedness.
Striving to reach the heaven's holiness.
Paying all debts in peace and lowliness,
Blessings of God and of men still nerving me,
Help of apostles and saints preserving me.

Source:
The Religious Songs of Connacht, Volume 2

Long Prayers

O God, make me wise in the things that pass near me.
Valiant in danger, patient in tribulation,
And humble in going forward through the world.
May I never forget
To put heed in my prayers,
Moderation in my ways,
Earnestness in my cares,
And perseverance in the things I set before me.
Lord, stir me up to keep a right conscience,
Give me courtesy on the out-side,
Profitable conversation, and orderly bearing.
Vouchsafe me always
To get the upper hand of my natural disposition
By inclining to your graces,
By fulfilling your commandments,
And by working out my salvation.
Show me, God, the nothingness of this world,
The majesty of the heaven of God,
The shortness of time
And the length of eternity.
Grant me to put myself into a state of fitness for death,
To be afraid of your judgment,
To shun condemnation,

And at last to gain heaven.

Source:
The Religious Songs of Connacht, Volume 2

My God, give me strength
So that I may make expiation for my misdeeds,
So that I may win victory over my temptations,
So that I may right my strong evil-inclinations,
And so that I may practise the virtues
That are suitable to my state of life.
Fill my heart with affection for your goodness,
With hatred of my faults, with love for my neighbours,
And with contempt for the world.
That I may remember, O God,
To be submissive to my superiors,
To be at one with my inferiors,
Faithful to my friends
And charitable to my enemies.
Aid me to gain a victory
Over fleshly desires by piety,
Over covetousness by alms-giving,
Over passion by mildness,
And over hypocrisy by earnestness.

Source:
The Religious Songs of Connacht, Volume 2

The hope of my soul is in your promise,
My homage receive of me, though late:
Your mercy is greater than my defiance,
So I before you lie myself prostrate.
Yours is my life and Yours my death,
God of all breath, my pride is o'er!
One glance from you were all my wealth,
My hope, my health, for evermore!
O you who makes the dead to live,
Who didst forgive the Thief his scorn,
Hear now, as then, a sinner's sigh,
The bitter cry of me forlorn.
O pierced in foot and hand and side,
crucified for hearts that burn,

I reach to you, oh reach to me,
I ne'er again from you shall turn.
O King of kings, O King of worlds,
O King who was, and is to be,
Forgive, O King, with Father and Spirit my sins,
Receive our prayer, and comfort me.

> Source:
> *The Religious Songs of Connacht,* Volume 2

May the grace of the Holy Ghost be gained by me,
And the true Faith be kept unstained by me,
While I follow the path of the saints, endeavouring
To walk in the temple of Christ unwavering.
And may I seek the eternal Trinity
Trusting in Christ and in Christ's divinity,
Helping the poor and relieving them
Walking with God and receiving them.
Devils that tempt me, still repelling them.
All my faults to Heaven confessing them.
Fighting with all that wounds, with energy,
Ceasing from lies and evil calumny.
Let me not mix with strife and devilry,
Fall I to prayer instead of revelry,
Thanking the Lord for all his generosity
Throwing aside my evil ways from me.
My life disorderly now amending it;
My evil will no more defending it;
All sorts of sin avoiding carefully,
In friendship with God rejoicing prayerful'y.

> Source:
> *The Religious Songs of Connacht,* Volume 2

Preparing a Personal Penitential

An excerpt from* Nurturing the Courage of Pilgrims, *with minor variations.

Living as "colonies of heaven", the ancient Celtic saints were especially concerned with the effects of sin on the life of faith. Repentance and penance were central to their spiritual practices since any form of sinful behavior was seen as an impediment to living as "citizens of heaven". However, they also understood that forgiveness is an essential aspect of Christ's ongoing mission of redemption. As such, they embraced both the sorrow begotten of our sin and the joy received through God's redemptive love.

This duality is expressed most clearly in the manuals used by the ancient Celtic saints to govern their practices of confessing sins and imposing penances for the forgiveness of these sins. Called penitentials, these books often prescribed specific – and sometimes quite harsh – penalties for various types of sinful behavior. Yet, the goal of these penances was not merely punishment. For the Celtic saints, the purpose of these penitential penalties was to help the repentant sinner develop habits of behavior that avoided future sinful actions.

With these thoughts in mind, it might be helpful for you to develop your own personal penitential manual.

Part One

Before preparing your penitential, it is important for you to come to an appreciation of the emotional dynamics of sin and forgiveness, an intermingling of sorrow and joy. Their experience is perhaps demonstrated most clearly in what is known as the "gift of tears". The tears of repentant sinners express the sorrow men and women feel after alienating themselves from God – and from their true nature as children of God – but these tears also become a reminder the salvific water a baptism that washed away sin.

Now, in a single session, bring these thoughts to prayer.

1. After taking the time you need to focus on the present moment, begin by reading the following anonymous poem (found in the *Celtic Spirituality* anthology in The Classics of Western Spirituality series) slowly and deliberately. Allow each word and phrase to rest gently in your consciousness and feel the emotions evoked in your reading as you allow yourself to focus entirely on your experiences in the moment. Allow yourself to pause between words and phrases to express your own prayers to God.

> Grant me tears, O Lord, to blot out my sins; may I not cease from them, O God, until I have been purified.
>
> May my heart be burned by the fire of redemption; grant me pure tears for Mary and Ita.
>
> When I contemplate my sins, grant me tears always, for great are the claims of tears on cheeks.
>
> Grant me tears when rising, grant me tears when resting, beyond your every gift all together for love with you, Mary's son.
>
> Grant me tears in bed to moisten my pillow, so that his dear ones may help to cure the soul.
>
> Grant me contrition of hard so that I may not be in disgrace; O Lord, protect me and grant me tears.
>
> For the dalliance I had with (wo)men, who did not reject me, grant me tears, O Creator, flowing in streams from my eyes.
>
> For my anger, my jealousy, and my pride, a foolish deed, in pools from my inmost parts bring forth tears.
>
> My falsehoods, my lying, and my greed, grievous the three, to banish them all from me, O Mary, grant me tears.

2. Remaining prayerful, read the following selection from *The Spiritual Exercises of Saint Ignatius*:

> True spiritual consolation may be known by the following signs. A certain interior impulse raises the soul towards the Creator, makes it love Him with an ardent love and no longer permits it to love any other

creature but for Him; sometimes gentle tears cause this love, tears that flow from repentance of past faults or the sight of the sorrows of Jesus Christ or any other motive that enlightened religion inspires; finally, all that increases faith, hope, charity; all that fills the soul with holy joy, makes it more attached to meditation on heavenly things and more careful of salvation; all that leads it to find repose and peace in the Lord – all this is true and spiritual consolation.

Spiritual Exercises, #316

3. Now, imagine Jesus standing or sitting in front of you. Read the previous passage concerning tears together and speak to one another about the meaning of the various words and phrases of the passage. Ask Jesus to help you better understand the consoling nature of tears. As always, allow Jesus to guide the conversation. At the end of your conversation, ask that you may receive tears – with both joy and sorrow – as you repent your sins.
4. Record any significant thoughts or observations from your prayers in your journal.

On a separate day, approach Luke 7:36-50 as an imaginative contemplation.
1. Either from the woman's perspective or paying specific attention to the woman of this story, see Simon the Pharisee's house and the people in it (i.e., Jesus, Simon, and the other guests). Observe the reactions of everyone, including Jesus, as she enters and begins to wash Jesus' feet. Hear Jesus tell the parable of the debtors and his explanation of the story to Simon. Watch as Jesus forgives the woman, noting her response and the reaction of the other people in the house.
2. Allow this scene to fade from your consciousness, holding onto the emotions you experienced during your contemplation of Jesus at Simon the Pharisee's house. In your imagination, see Jesus sitting or standing in front of you and bring your thoughts to him in conversation. Again, allow Jesus to guide the conversation.
3. When you are finished, record any significant thoughts or observations from your prayers in your journal.

Part Two

The path to redemptive forgiveness begins with humility and sorrow. These feelings are graces given by God that open us to accept the pain through our separation from God and the humble acceptance that this loss results from our own misguided choices. So, as you begin to prepare your personal penitential, you should begin by considering prayers of contrition that allow you to express the sorrow you experience from your sins and the humility with which you are now approaching God in the hope of forgiveness.

In a single prayer session, bring this traditional Celtic act of contrition to prayer.
1.   After taking the time you need to focus on the present moment, begin by reading the following prayer from *The Religious Songs of Connacht* slowly and deliberately. Allow each word and phrase to rest gently in your consciousness and feel the emotions evoked in your reading as you allow yourself to focus entirely on your experiences in the moment. Allow yourself to pause between words and phrases to express your own prayers to God.

>   I place myself at the edge of Thy grace,
>   On the floor of Thy House myself I place,
>   I lower my knee to my King this day,
>   Asking He banish the sin of my heart away,
>   O Jesus sore-suffering,
>   Martyr of pain,
>   Thou wast offered, an offering,
>   Slain with the slain,
>   Despised and rejected,
>   A mock among men,
>   May my soul be protected
>   From sin and from stain.
>   Each sin I have sinned
>   From the day of my fall,
>   May the One Son of Mary
>   Forgive me them all!
>   May the child who was tortured,
>   God-man without stain,

> Guide us safe through the torments
> And shoutings of pain.

2. Now, imagine Jesus standing or sitting in front of you. Say the prayer to him and ask about the meaning of the various words and phrases in the prayer. When you are finished, speak with Jesus about the specific issues of repentance and contrition. Again, allow Jesus to guide the conversation.

3. After your prayer, record any significant thoughts or observations from your prayers in your journal.

☧

On another day, in a single session, bring these thoughts Psalm 51:1-12 to prayer.

1. After taking the time you need to focus on the present moment, begin by reading Psalm 51:1-12 slowly and deliberately. Allow each word and phrase to rest gently in your consciousness and feel the emotions evoked in your reading as you allow yourself to focus entirely on your experiences in the moment. Allow yourself to pause between words and phrases to express your own prayers to God.

> Have mercy on me, O God,
>> according to your steadfast love;
> according to your abundant mercy
>> blot out my transgressions.
> Wash me thoroughly from my iniquity,
>> and cleanse me from my sin.
> For I know my transgressions,
>> and my sin is ever before me.
> Against you, you alone, have I sinned,
>> and done what is evil in your sight,
> so that you are justified in your sentence
>> and blameless when you pass judgment.
> Indeed, I was born guilty,
>> a sinner when my mother conceived me.
> You desire truth in the inward being;
>> therefore teach me wisdom in my secret heart.

> Purge me with hyssop, and I shall be clean;
>> wash me, and I shall be whiter than snow.
> Let me hear joy and gladness;
>> let the bones that you have crushed rejoice.
> Hide your face from my sins,
>> and blot out all my iniquities.
> Create in me a clean heart, O God,
>> and put a new and right spirit within me.
> Do not cast me away from your presence,
>> and do not take your holy spirit from me.
> Restore to me the joy of your salvation,
>> and sustain in me a willing spirit.

2.   Now, imagine Jesus standing or sitting in front of you. Read the psalm together and speak about the meaning of the various words and phrases of the in it. Again, speak with Jesus about the specific issues of repentance and contrition, allowing Jesus to guide the conversation.

3.   After your prayer, record any significant thoughts or observations from your prayers in your journal.

On a separate day, look at your notebook for this penitential and divide it into nine equal sections. Label the beginning of the first section "Contrition" and write the prayer from *The Religious Songs of Connacht* and the selection from Psalm 51 under that heading. If you know any other prayers of contrition – either from your own denomination or from other sources – write them in this section as well.

In the future, add different prayers of contrition to this section of your penitential as you encounter them. You may find it helpful to use different prayers at different times, both to avoid allowing your prayer to become routine and to express the different types of sorrow you experience when confessing specific sins.

Part Three

Embracing the grace of contrition gives you the courage to approach God as you confess your sins. It is important to remember God loves you and wants to forgive you, so it is also important that you be as humble and open as possible when confessing your sinful actions. God already knows all your transgressions and is waiting for you to acknowledge them before asking for forgiveness.

To better understand this, approach Luke 18:9-14 as an imaginative contemplation.
1. Listen to Jesus as he tells the parable of the pharisee and the tax collector. See Jesus with a group of people, either from a distance or close to Jesus. Note whether the group is large or small as well as if the group is inside or outside. Observe whether Jesus is speaking to his disciples or to strangers. Hear Jesus tell the parable and allow the story to unfold in your mind before watching the reaction of the group to parable.
2. Allow this scene to fade from your consciousness, holding onto the emotions you experienced during your contemplation of the parable of the pharisee and the tax collector. In your imagination, see Jesus sitting or standing in front of you and bring your thoughts to him in conversation. Again, allow Jesus to guide the conversation into the issues of sorrow, humility, and contrition.
3. When you are finished, record any significant thoughts or observations from your prayers in your journal.

On a separate day, in a single session, reflect on the following concerns as you continue to prepare your personal penitential.
1. Consider the following excerpts from the Penitential of Cummean (also found in the *Celtic Spirituality* anthology in The Classics of Western Spirituality series):
    (a) "He who steals someone else's property by any means shall restore four times as much to him who he has injured."
    (b) "He who incapacitates or maims a man with a blow in a quarrel shall meet his medical expenses and shall make good damages for the injury and shall do his work until he has recovered and shall do penance for half a year. If he does not have the resources to make restitution for these things, he shall do penance for one year."

(c) "A priest or Deacon who commits natural fornication... shall do penance for seven years. He shall ask pardon every hour and shall perform a special fast every week."

<u>Note:</u> *Observe that Cummean's penitential emphasizes both the repair of the human problems – sometimes in a manner going beyond proportional justice, such as in the case of stealing – caused by sin as well as specific actions designed to remind the person of the sin he or she committed and to foster better spiritual habits. These are essential aspects of Celtic spirituality that need to be incorporated into your own personal penitential.*

2. Reflect on the Seven Deadly Sins as they relate to your own life experience: pride, greed, envy, wrath, lust, gluttony, and sloth.
    (a) Consider the general effects of each type of sin. Consider...
        (i) **Pride**, usually regarded as the most serious of the Seven Deadly Sins, places an individual at the center of the universe. It denies the importance of all others, including God and our fellow creatures. By subverting humility and modesty, it diminishes our capacities for reverence and respectful behavior.
        (II) **Greed** emerges from a desire to possess more than we need. It makes the acquisition of material goods more important than our relationships with others, including God. It undermines our capacities for benevolence, generosity, and sacrifice.
        (iii) **Envy** begets a resentful covetousness toward the gifts of others (such as personality traits or possessions) and undermines a person's awareness of their own giftedness. This simmering dissatisfaction severs human relationships and diminishes the capacity for kindness, compassion, and joy.
        (iv) **Wrath** evokes uncontrolled feelings of anger and even hatred toward others. It seeks vengeance at the expense of justice while also undermining the human capacities for forgiveness and mercy.
        (v) **Lust** leads to the disordered love of individuals. It diminishes our capacity to recognize and love others as we objectify them. Generally regarded as the least offensive of the Seven Deadly Sins, lust diminishes our capacity for to act towards others with the purity of intention required of children of God.
        (vi) **Gluttony** involves overindulgence and waste, usually focused on food. However, it also involves any excessive desire that

deprives others of their needs. As such, gluttony is an act of selfishness that places a person's concerns, impulses, or interests above the well-being of others.

(vii) **Sloth** goes beyond laziness, leading a person to become indifferent towards his or her own life as well as those of others. Its indolence leads to passivity, apathy, and rancor. It subverts the diligence and persistence necessary to live a good life in harmony with God's desires.

(b) Consider the effects of each type of sin on you, deciding which sins tempt you the most and which tempt you the least. Remember that sinful behavior changes. You may have overcome certain temptations, only to find that other sins become more attractive. So, be attentive to your entire personal history and all the sins you have committed throughout your life (or at least as many as possible).

(c) Consider specific sinful actions that emerge from these sins and how they affect you, the people you know and the people you do not know.

(d) Consider the specific sinful actions that emerge from these sins that affect the non-human parts of creation.

Note: *Take as much time as you need for this consideration of the* Seven Deadly Sins. *You may also find it useful to return to this set of reflections in the future as you expand your penitential.*

3. In your penitential notebook, label the second through eighth sections for the Seven Deadly Sins. Either use the order I provided above or list them according to the degree of influence each sin has on you, beginning with the one that tempts you the most and ending with the least tempting. Then, divide the sections for each sin into four equal subsections and label them "Self", "Family and Friends", "Strangers" and "Creation".

4. List specific sinful actions or transgressions in your penitential, grouping them according to the specific deadly sin involved and the person or thing hurt by that sin (i.e., you, your family or friends, strangers, creation). Make the description of each sin as succinct and specific as possible (e.g., lying to a friend, envying a coworker, etc.) and attach a corresponding penance that includes:

(a) a human action intended to repair the effects of the sin (e.g., apologizing, paying for any damage, etc.).

(b) the number of times a penitential action should be repeated (e.g., each day for a week, every morning for a month, etc.).
(c) additional penances (e.g., fasting, saying special prayers, etc.) you feel will help you remember the pain of the sin.

Note: *The entry for each sin might be something like, "For hurtfully mocking a friend, apologize. Then, repent each day for the following month. Say a prayer of contrition at the beginning of each week of that month."*

5. Develop a short formula of repentance (e.g., "For the sin of [state sin], forgive this sinner.") to be used during your confession and as part of your penance afterward. Both when confessing and repenting again later as a penance, bring your sin into your consciousness by breathing in deeply. Then, release your breath slowly and say the formula with a heart-felt awareness of the sin you committed.

When using this penitential during confession, begin by allowing all other thoughts and concerns to fall away and focus on the consideration of your sins. Then, begin with an examination of consciousness as you reflect on the period since your last confession. Bring each sinful action into focus and find the corresponding send in your penitential before confessing your sin using the formula of repentance. Afterward, give yourself time to accept the forgiveness of God as your sin Is absolved.

Note: *It is important to remember that while your sin has been forgiven in the moment of your confession, the penance you enact afterward is intended to remind you of your past behavior and help you to avoid sinful actions in the future.*

Part Four

With your sins now forgiven, you return to your daily life with joy. Restored to your rightful place as a child of God, you again experience the fullness of God's love. You feel the protection and guidance that your relationship with God offers, and you should express that sense of joyful trust in prayers of gratitude and assurance.

Then, in a single session, bring Psalm 23:1-6 to prayer.

1.   After taking the time you need to focus on the present moment, begin by reading Psalm 23:1-6 slowly and deliberately. Allow each word and phrase to rest gently in your consciousness and feel the emotions evoked in your reading as you allow yourself to focus entirely on your experiences in the moment. Allow yourself to pause between words and phrases to express your own prayers to God.

> The Lord is my shepherd, I shall not want.
> > He makes me lie down in green pastures;
> he leads me beside still waters;
> > he restores my soul.
> He leads me in right paths
> > for his name's sake.
> Even though I walk through the darkest valley,
> > I fear no evil;
> for you are with me;
> > your rod and your staff –
> > they comfort me.
> You prepare a table before me
> > in the presence of my enemies;
> you anoint my head with oil;
> > my cup overflows.
> Surely goodness and mercy shall follow me
> > all the days of my life,
> and I shall dwell in the house of the Lord
> > my whole life long.

2.   Now, imagine Jesus standing or sitting in front of you. Read the psalm together and speak about the meaning of the various words and phrases of the in it. Again, speak with Jesus about your trust in God's guidance and protection, allowing Jesus to guide the conversation.
3.   After your prayer, record any significant thoughts or observations from your prayers in your journal.

On another day, in a single session, contemplate the following prayers.

1.   After taking the time you need to focus on the present moment, begin by reading the following prayers, one being an ancient prayer known as the Anima Christi (Soul of Christ) suggested by Saint Ignatius in his *Spiritual Exercises* and the other being an Irish variation collected in Douglas Hyde's *The Religious Songs of Connacht* slowly and deliberately.

Allow each word and phrase to rest gently in your consciousness and feel the emotions evoked in your reading as you allow yourself to focus entirely on your experiences in the moment. Allow yourself to pause between words and phrases to express your own prayers to God.

Anima Christi (traditional)

Soul of Christ, be my sanctification.
Body of Christ, be my salvation.
Blood of Christ, fill all my veins.
Water of Christ's side, wash out my stains.
Passion of Christ, my comfort be.
O good Jesus, listen to me.
In your wounds I fain would hide,
Never to be parted from your side,
Guard me, should the foe assail me.
Call me when my life shall fail me.
Bid me come to you above,
With your saints to sing your love,
World without end. Amen.

Edward's Testament

O Soul of Christ bless me.
O Body of Christ save me.
O Blood of Christ satisfy me.
O Water of Christ's side wash me.
O Passion of Christ strengthen me.
O Jesus of the Elements, hear me O Lord.
Make a protection for me of thy wounds.
Permit me not to be separated from thee.
Keep me from the attack of the Adversary.
I call me to thee at the time of my death.

> In hope that I may praise thee
> Along with the angels
> For ever and ever. Amen.

2. Now, imagine Jesus standing or sitting in front of you. Say the prayer to him. When you are finished, speak with Jesus about your trust in his guidance and protection, allowing Jesus to guide the conversation.
3. After your prayer, record any significant thoughts or observations from your prayers in your journal.

On a separate day, look at your notebook for this penitential. Label the final section "Joyful Trust" and write the version of the Anima Christi you prefer and Psalm 23 under that heading. If you know any other prayers of joyful trust, write them in this section as well.

In the future, add different prayers of joyful trust to this section of your penitential as you encounter them. Like the prayers of contrition, you may find it helpful to use different prayers at different times, both to avoid allowing your prayer to become routine and to express differently your joy at being forgiven and your trust in God's future guidance.

Part Five

Having prepared your personal penitential, it is time for you to confess your sins using it. Begin by allowing all your daily concerns to fall away so that you may be completely with God. Then…
1. In a slow and deliberate manner, say your prayer of contrition. Allow each word and phrase to linger in your consciousness and evoke the sorrow and humility needed to approach God.
2. Take time to carefully consider your various sins and the effect they have had on Your life and your relationship with God. Allow your sorrow to enter your consciousness as you consider each sin, recognizing the ways it harmed you as well as your relationship with God and others. Then, knowing God wants to embrace and forgive you, confess your sins and feel God's loving response to each confession.

3. Conclude your confession by offering a prayer of joyful trust, allowing each word and phrase to linger on your consciousness and invoke the joy and trust that you feel after restoring your relationship with love with God.

4. Go back into your daily life, aware of God's love and protection while offering the penances that are appropriate to the sins of your confession.

Sacred Citizenship

Patrick the Apostle – Kyrie Eleison

In this excerpt from *A Passion for Justice: Social Ethics in the Celtic Tradition* (2008), Johnston McMaster examines aspects of Saint Patrick's response to injustice in his "Letter to the Soldiers of Coroticus".

God as Liberator

In the Letter to the soldiers of Coroticus we hear the voice of pain. Many of Patrick's new converts to Christian faith have been murdered by Coroticus and his homicidal pirates or they have been taken off into captivity as slaves. Patrick's anger in the Letter is tangible. There is the strongest possible protest to Coroticus and his soldiers and there is also in Patrick's voice of pain a cry for God's help and retribution.

Such a cry is possible because of Patrick's experience of God. It is not at heart a cry for human vengeance. Motives can be mixed and ambivalent in our human fallibility and weakness. But ultimately the cry of pain is rooted in the moral sense of justice and the consciousness of God's justice. In the Hebrew Scriptures the God of Exodus is the God who sees, hears and knows the cries of people in political and economic oppression inflicted by the imperial power of Egypt. Exodus is for ancient Israel the paradigm for justice and liberation. The God of justice is the God of liberation who is engaged with human collaboration (Moses and Aaron) in bringing about freedom from all that dehumanizes and oppresses and building communities of justice, fairness and abundant life and well-being. "The cry of the slaves... is always and everywhere the cry for liberation." Patrick's voice of pain arises from his solidarity with those killed and enslaved and from his relationship with the Trinitarian God of community and justice. His profoundly intimate God-consciousness is of a God who cares and who is engaged for justice in the world and who liberates. After all at the heart of the Jesus story is a cross, symbol of injustice and violence and at the same time a window into the suffering of God in the face of violence, injustice and innocent suffering. In the Letter to the soldiers of Coroticus Patrick's voice of pain is one of hope and committed action with God for liberation. His God-shaped ethical consciousness rooted in his experience of God, becomes an ethic of liberation praxis
...

Protesting Evil

The Letter to the soldiers of Coroticus reflects a disturbing and difficult time for those living in Britain. The Roman imperial control was breaking down, soldiers were being recalled to deal with the collapse of the Empire at its heart. Angles, Saxons, Jutes and Frisians were constantly raiding Britain, while Picts and Irish made life difficult from the north and west. Raiding parties were commonplace and many were taken as prisoners of war or as slaves. Such raids also took place in Ireland and in one such raid many of Patrick's recently baptized Christians were killed or taken from Ireland into slavery, itself a brutal and dehumanizing experience. The Letter protests against Coroticus and his soldiers, and it includes a cry for God's retribution.

In the face of serious injustice, genocide and ill-treatment the cry for retribution is understandable. It is a sign that moral sensibility is alive and well. Anger in the face of injustice, even hatred for the abusers and their actions, is a just and ethical response. It is when like is returned with like, violence is met with violence and evil is returned with evil, that ethics is diminished and such actions in response become immoral. The cry for retribution is, nevertheless, the cry for justice and liberation.

Patrick protests evil in the strongest possible terms. Coroticus and his soldiers are "father-killer and the brother-killer... raging wolves". They are like "someone who hands over the 'members of Christ' to a whore house." The latter is a strong image describing a prostitute as a "she wolf" devouring parts of Christ's body. Coroticus is behaving like the apostate he is.

Patrick's language mirrors the Psalms of Lament in the Hebrew scriptures. Here to our strong cries of protest, at times savage urgency in the honesty of expression and the cry for justice and divine action. The strength of the language sometimes disturbs us, no doubt in our self-made comfort zones. The cry to "dash the heads of little ones against the rocks" (Psalm 137) may well horrify us as a literal response to the enemy and rightly so. But we may have experienced little of the community trauma and total collapse of all the institutions and symbols of meaning experienced by the southern kingdom of Judah at the hands of the Babylonian superpower. It is impossible to sing the Lord's song by the rivers of Babylon (exile). Patrick has some sense of such loss as he protests the genocide and captivity of Irish Christians.

The Letter is a decree of excommunication and at the same time a prayer to God for divine justice and liberation.

The actions of Coroticus are condemned as sacrilege. The image of the God of life has been wiped out or destroyed by someone who claims to be part of the Christian community. The basic right to life has been denied while others are dehumanized and treated as sub-human or, worse, non-entities – objects of commercial gain.

Passivity is not possible in the face of such inhumanity. Silence is not an option in view of the evil of genocide and the abuse of life and freedom. It is a particular evil when carried out by people making faith claims and, worse, legitimizing murder, "collateral damage" or personal or structural abuse of the innocent by co-opting God.

The strength of Patrick's protest and language used is obvious and an ethical imperative. Patrick is committed to justice and such a commitment leads him to protest evil. The strength of his justice commitment and compassion is also encountered in the stirring lament towards the end of the Letter for the victims of murder and those victims still alive but whom he fears he may never see again. "So with sadness and grief I cry out… And so my dearest friends, I grieve, grieve deeply, for you…". The cry for justice, the protest against evil is born in the shared pain and solidarity with life's victims.

Before proceeding to the next section, ask yourself the following questions:
1.   Does a particular part of this excerpt stand out for you? Why? Does it relate to a particular concern in your life or in your interactions with others?
2.   Does any aspect of the excerpt relate to your experiences of prayer during your retreat? If so, which?

3.   What does the excerpt tell you about Saint Patrick? How does this help you in your own spiritual life? How does this challenge your beliefs about spirituality?

4.   How does this excerpt help you understand your calling to become a "citizen of heaven"?

Saint Patrick's "Letter to the Soldiers of Coroticus"

An excerpt from *The Epistles and Hymn of Saint Patrick* (1876), edited by Thomas Olden.

After reading each of the following sections of Saint Patrick's "Letter to the Soldiers of Coroticus", ask yourself the following questions:
1. What is the most important aspect of the selection? Why?
2. Were there any parts of the selection that you found challenging?
3. Were there any parts of the selection that you found comforting?
4. How will you bring these challenging or comforting aspects of the selection before God in prayer?
5. What is the grace you will ask from God in your prayer regarding these issues?
6. How does the selection help you better understand your relationship with God and with others?
7. What does this selection say to you about your life choices in the past?
8. What does this selection say to you about your desires for the future?

In answering these questions, be specific in your responses and focus on the concrete actions you feel drawn to pursue either in the present or in the future. If a particular question provokes a significant response, record these insights in your retreat journal.

Selections from The Letter to the Soldiers of Coroticus

<u>Note:</u> *The translator of this version of Saint Patrick's letter to the soldiers of Coroticus observes, "Most of the texts quoted in the Epistle, and particularly these, differ widely from the Vulgate, and are evidently taken from one of the earlier versions; but, in some cases, perhaps the writer meant to give the substance only, and not the exact words of Scripture."*

1. Compelled to Speak out in Defense of his Flock

I, Patrick, a sinner and unlearned, declare that I was made Bishop in Ireland. I most certainly hold that it was from God I received what I am, and therefore for the love of God I dwell a pilgrim and an exile among a barbarous people. He is witness that I speak the truth. It was not my wish to use language so harsh and severe [as in this letter,] but I am compelled by a zeal for God, and the truth of Christ, who stirred me up for the love of my neighbours and sons, for whom I have given up country and parents, and am ready to give my life also if I am worthy. I have made a vow to my God to teach the people, although some may despise me. With my own hand I have written and composed these words to be delivered to the soldiers of Coroticus, I say not, to my fellow-citizens, nor to the fellow-citizens of the Roman saints, but to the fellow-citizens of demons, who, on account of their evil deeds, abide in death after the hostile rite of the barbarians; companions of the Scots and apostate Picts, desiring, as it were, to glut themselves with the blood of innocent Christians, multitudes of whom I have begotten to God and confirmed in Christ.

2. Defense of the Innocent

A cruel slaughter and massacre was committed by them [the soldiers of Coroticus] on some neophytes, while still in their white robes, the day after they had been anointed with chrism, and while it was yet visible on their foreheads. And I sent a letter by a holy Presbyter, whom I taught from his infancy, accompanied by other clergymen, to intreat that they would restore some of the booty or of the baptised captives whom they had taken, but they turned them into ridicule. Therefore I know not for whom I should rather grieve, whether for those who were slain, or those whom they took captive, or those whom Satan has so grievously ensnared, and who shall be delivered over like himself to the eternal pains of hell, for "whosoever, committeth sin is the servant of sin (John 8:44)," the child of the devil.

3. Attack on those Who Plunder and Destroy God's Work

Wherefore, let every one who fears God know, that strangers to me and to Christ my God, whose ambassador I am, are parricides and fratricides, ravening wolves, "eating up the Lord's people as they eat bread (Psalm 14:4)," as he says, "Lord, the wicked have made void thy law (Psalm 119:126)," with which Ireland had been in these latter days, most excellently and auspiciously planted and taught by God's favour. I do not usurp another's rights, but I have a share with those whom he called and appointed to preach the Gospel amidst no small persecutions, even to the end of the earth, although the enemy grudges [us our success] through the tyranny of Coroticus, who fears not God, nor his priests, whom he has chosen, and granted to them that most high and divine power, that those whom "they bind on earth are bound in heaven (Matthew 18:18)".

4. Plunder of the Poor is an Abomination

Wherefore, I earnestly beseech those who are holy and humble of heart not to be flattered by them, nor to eat or drink with them, nor to receive alms from them, until they repent with bitter tears, and make satisfaction to God , and set free those servants of God and baptized handmaids of Christ, for whom He was crucified and died. "The Most High rejects the offerings of the unjust; he who offers a sacrifice from the substance of the poor is like one who offers a son as a victim in the sight of his father (Ecclesiasticus 24:23-24)". The riches which he has gathered unjustly shall be vomited forth again; the angel of death drags him, [away,] he shall be punished by the rage of dragons; the tongue of the adder shall slay him; unquenchable fire shall consume him (Job 20:15-16,26)".

And therefore "woe to them that fill themselves with that which is not their own (Habakkuk 2:6)" or "What is a man profited, if he shall gain the whole world and lose his own soul (Matthew 16:26)".

It were too long to enter into particulars, or to enumerate one by one the testimonies from the [Divine] law against such cupidity. Avarice is a deadly crime. "Thou shalt not covet thy neighbour's goods (Exodus 20:17)". "Thou shalt not kill (Exodus 20:13)". No murderer can dwell with Christ. "Whosoever hateth his brother is reckoned a murderer (1 John 3:15)". "He who loveth not his brother abideth in death (1 John 3:4)". How much more is he guilty who has stained his hands with the blood of the sons of God, whom He has lately acquired in the very ends of the earth, through my humble exhortations.

5. The Love of God Creates New Relationships

Did I come to Ireland without the Divine will, or merely from carnal motives? Who compelled me? I am bound in the spirit not to see my kindred anymore. Do I show a true compassion for that nation which formerly took me captive? I am free-born according to the flesh, for my father was a magistrate. I have bartered my nobility for the good of others. I am not ashamed, nor do I repent of it. In short, I am delivered over in Christ to a foreign people for the unspeakable glory of the eternal life, which is in Christ Jesus our Lord, although my own friends do not acknowledge me. "A prophet has no honour in his own country (John 4:44)". Are we not of one fold– have we not one father? as the Lord says, "Whosoever is not with me is against me, and he who gathereth not with me scattereth (Matthew 12:30)". It is not fitting that "one should destroy and another build. (Ecclesiastes 34:28.)" Do I seek my own?

6. Mission, Suffering, and a Call to Repentance

Not to me, but to God be the praise, who put into my heart this anxious desire, that I should be one of the hunters and fishers whom God long since foretold should come in these last days; I am envied. What shall I do, Lord? I am greatly despised. Behold, thy sheep around me are torn and pillaged by the aforementioned robbers, by the orders of Coroticus, our enemy. Far from the love of God is he who delivers Christians into the hands of the Scots and Picts. Ravening wolves, they have devoured the Lord's flock, which was increasing rapidly in Ireland with the utmost diligence; and the sons and daughters of Scotic princes were becoming monks and virgins of Christ in greater numbers than I can tell. He who incurs thy displeasure by his oppression of the righteous, shall abide under it for ever.

7. The Judgement Against Sinners

Which of the saints would not shrink from partaking of the sports and banquets of such men. They have filled their houses with the spoils of the Christian dead. They live by rapine; they know not mercy; they drink poison; they reach the deadly food to their friends and children, like Eve who knew not that she was giving death to her husband. It is the custom of the Roman and Gallic Christians to send men of holy life, and fit for the office, to the Franks and [other] foreign people, with many thousand shillings, to redeem baptized captives. You who so often kill them, or sell them to a foreign people ignorant of God, delivering over the members of Christ, as it were, to infamy, what hope have you in God?

Whosoever consents with you, or uses words of flattery to you, God will judge, for it is written, "Not only they who do evil, but they that consent thereto are to be condemned (Romans 1:32)".

8.   Lamenting of the Enslaved

I know not what more to say or to speak, of the sons of God who are dead, slain with the sword , for it is written, "Weep with them that do weep (Romans 12:15)"; and again, "If one member suffers, all the m suffer with it (1 Corinthians 12:26)". Wherefore the Church weeps and laments her sons and daughters whom the sword of the enemy has not slain, but who have been carried away to far-off lands, where sin openly prevails and shamelessly abounds. There Christian freemen are sold and reduced to slavery, and that by the most unworthy, most infamous and apostate Picts. Therefore, I will cry aloud with sorrow and grief; O most goodly and well-beloved brethren and sons whom I have begotten in Christ without number, what shall I do for you? I am not worthy to aid the cause of God or men. The unrighteousness of the unrighteous has prevailed against us. We are become as aliens. Perhaps they do not believe that we have received one baptism, and have one God and Father (Ephesians 4:5-6). With them it is a crime that we were born in Iberia, but it is said, Have ye not one God, why do ye wrong one to another? Where fore I grieve for you; I grieve, m y well-beloved, for myself, but at the same I rejoice that I have not laboured in vain, and that my pilgrimage has not been in vain. A crime has been committed which is horrible and unspeakable. Thanks be to God, ye, O believers and baptized ones, have departed from the world to Paradise. I behold you. Ye have begun your journey to that region where there shall be "no night," nor "sorrow," nor death anymore (Revelation 21:4-5,25), but ye shall be as "calves let loose, and ye shall tread down the wicked, and they shall be as ashes under your feet (Malachi 4:3-4)".

9. Condemnation of the Unfaithful

Ye therefore shall reign with the Apostles, and Prophets, and Martyrs, and shall receive an everlasting kingdom, as He himself bears witness, saying, "They shall come from the east and from the west, and shall sit down with Abraham and Isaac and Jacob, in the kingdom of heaven (Revelation 22:15)". "Without are dogs, and sorcerers, and murderers and liars, and perjurers, whose part shall be the lake of fire eternal." For not without reason does the Apostle say, "If the righteous scarcely be saved, where shall the ungodly, and the sinner, and the transgressor of the law be found (1 Peter 4:18)"? Where shall Coroticus be with his wicked rebels against Christ? Where shall they find themselves, who distribute among their depraved followers, baptized women and captive orphans, for the sake of a wretched earthly kingdom, which passes away in a moment like a cloud, or smoke scattered by the wind? Thus shall sinners and deceivers perish from the face of the Lord, but the righteous shall feast continually with Christ, and judge the nations, and rule over unjust kings for ever and ever.

10. The Damned Have Hope... If They Repent

I bear witness before God and his holy angels, that it shall be as my ignorance has said. These are not my words, but those of God and the Apostles and Prophets, who have never lied, which I have put forth in Latin. "He who believeth shall be saved, and he who believeth not shall be damned (Mark 16:16)". God hath spoken. I earnestly entreat whatever servant of God is willing to be the bearer of this letter, that it may not be kept back from any one, but may rather be read before all the people, and in the presence of Coroticus himself.

But oh that God would inspire them, that at some time they may return unto Him, that thus even though late they may repent of their evil deeds. They have murdered the brethren of the Lord. But let them repent and release the baptized women whom they have already taken captive, that so they may be worthy to live unto God, and may be made whole here and for eternity. Peace be to the Father, and to the Son, and to the Holy Ghost. Amen.

Articulate Witness

Discerning Your Passions

Articulate witness involves sharing your faith in a manner capable of capturing the imagination of others without frightening or alienating them. It should never intimidate others. It also should avoid giving the impression that your faith in any way makes you superior or dominant. Instead, the demonstration of your faith should inspire others to approach life in a different way because of the joy and purpose you find through your faith.

Slowly and deliberately, consider the words of Psalm 96:1-13:

> O sing to the Lord a new song;
>> sing to the Lord, all the earth!
> Sing to the Lord, bless his name;
>> tell of his salvation from day to day.
> Declare his glory among the nations,
>> his marvelous works among all the peoples!
> For great is the Lord, and greatly to be praised;
>> he is to be feared above all gods.
> For all the gods of the peoples are idols;
>> but the Lord made the heavens.
> Honor and majesty are before him;
>> strength and beauty are in his sanctuary.
> Ascribe to the Lord, O families of the peoples,
>> ascribe to the Lord glory and strength!
> Ascribe to the Lord the glory due his name;
>> bring an offering, and come into his courts!
> Worship the Lord in holy array;
>> tremble before him, all the earth!
> Say among the nations, "The Lord reigns!
>> Yea, the world is established, it shall never be moved;
>> he will judge the peoples with equity."
> Let the heavens be glad, and let the earth rejoice;
>> let the sea roar, and all that fills it;
>> let the field exult, and everything in it!
> Then shall all the trees of the wood sing for joy
>> before the Lord, for he comes,
>> for he comes to judge the earth.

> He will judge the world with righteousness,
>   and the peoples with his truth.

Now, ask yourself the following questions:
1. What aspect or aspects of your experience of God make you want to sing a song?
2. What are the activities of God that you experience and wish to share with others?
3. Is it a song of celebration, consolation, or condemnation?
- Do you wish to celebrate or praise God's presence through your song so others may share your joy?
- Do you wish to console the men and women around you who are not able to experience the presence of God as you have?
- Do you wish to chastise those who in some way cheapened, denigrate, or diminish the presence and activity of God in the world?

4. Is your song an act of creative expression?
- Do you want to sing actual songs about God's presence and activity in the world, either written by you or by others?
- Do you feel drawn toward writing about the activity of God in you and in the world around you?
- What form of writing does this take – poetry, stories (including long-form such as a novel), plays or nonfiction of varying lengths?
- Do you want to present these literary works through performance and readings, either by you or by others?
- Do you want to depict God's presence and activity through the visual arts?

5. Is your song expressed through social actions?
- Do you feel drawn to some form of social engagement, such as caring for the poor or advocating some social cause?
- Do these activities take place in a religious environment or institution?
- If these activities do not occur within a religious context, how is the religious character of your social enthusiasm expressed to others?

These and other questions need to be answered before you can bring your song to the world and offer others an inspiring and articulate witness to your experience of God. So, it is very important for you to take time to understand the depth and breadth of your passion – your specific experience of God's activity in you and in the world around you – and allow your deepening appreciation of these experiences to guide you towards the most appropriate means of sharing your faith with others. In this way, you will become a living expression of God's invitation to restore creation to its proper purposes.

Part 1

In his *Spiritual Exercises*, Ignatius of Loyola refers to these life choices as making an election – choosing a path of service based solely on the desire to praise God through actions reflecting the ideals of the Principle and Foundation (found on page 309). In his considerations on these life-shaping decisions, Ignatius points out that there are three different experiences of this call to service:

- moments of intense awareness which leave you with no doubt about how you are being called;
- a progressive awareness of how you are being called involving a consideration of its history through discernment;
- an unclear inclination toward God service that is not reinforced by an immediate awareness of God's desires or a sense of its history emerging in you.

As you consider your own spiritual leadings toward some form of articulate witness, take some time to remember those times when you have experienced God in each of these distinct ways.

First, recall those times when you have experienced absolute certainty that your actions reflected the love of God (e.g., defending someone from a bully, offering a to a homeless person, comforting someone in despair, etc.) Then, considering each event separately, ask yourself the following questions:

- How did this event unfold? Specifically, what are the physical moments within this event?

- When and how did you experience the desire to act in this moment?
- What emotions did you experience before, during and after this event?
- Were you aware of God's presence during this event or afterward?
- Did your actions during this event help you understand God in a different way or strengthen your faith in some manner?

After each consideration, record the most important thoughts in your retreat workbook.

Second, recall aspects of your faith journey that evolved over time (e.g., consistency in prayer, trusting God's actions, etc.). Then, considering each of these aspects of your spiritual life separately, ask yourself the following questions:
- How did their experience with God develop over time? Specifically, what is the history of your relationship with God in these matters?
- How did you come to certainty that you were making the correct choices in this matter?
- Were there particular emotions or insights that helped guide you regarding this particular concern?
- How did your choices regarding this matter strengthen your relationship with (and awareness of) God in your life?

Again, after each consideration, record the most important thoughts in your retreat workbook.

Third, recall moments in your faith history that began as vague desires and the effects of the choices related to them. These moments should include both decisions that strengthened your relationship with God and those which ultimately undermined that relationship. Then, considering these various moments within your relationship with God separately, ask yourself the following questions:
- How did their experience in your faith life develop over time? Specifically, how did you become aware that your actions were having a positive or negative effect on your relationship with God?
- How was the positive or negative character of your choices in this matter ultimately revealed to you?

- What were the emotions or insights that helped guide you to strengthen your choices (if they were positive) or to amend them (if they were negative)?
- How did this moment in your faith history deepen or weaken your relationship with God?
- How do you know that this situation has been completely resolved in a loving and positive manner by God?

Again, after each consideration, record the most important thoughts in your retreat workbook.

When you have completed these reviews, you should put them aside for at least a week before continuing your consideration of the passions at the heart of your call to some form of articulate witness.

Note: *This is a moment of trust as you choose to take time to allow thoughts and emotions of this section to mature. God's presence in these choices will not be diminished by putting your reflections aside for short period of time. However, if the passions at the heart of your call to articulate witness strengthen during this quiet time, proceed to the next section and address them using the guidelines for following the spiritual leadings accompanied the sense of certitude.*

Part 2

After allowing the reflections of the previous section to deepen and mature, consider the two types of passion involved in your call to articulate witness: the subject about which you feel passionately (e.g., social justice, the environment, reconciliation, hospice work, etc.) and the manner in which you wish to express your awareness of God's presence and activity in these issues or concerns (e.g., using creative expression, advocating a social cause, or working in social improvement projects, etc.).

Treat each type of passion separately and address each according to the degree of certitude you experience concerning them following the guidelines suggested below:

1.   If you feel complete certainty about the God-given nature of your passion, either by the immediate intensity of your experience of God in this leading or by confirming it through consideration of its history, you should still take time to confirm this awareness so it will help strengthen you as you move forward. With this in mind...

• Separate the different aspects of your passion and review each of these using the "Rules for Discernment" Saint Ignatius proposed as being most useful after completing the first "week" of his *Spiritual Exercises* (found on page 312). Be careful not to over-think your initial response(s) during this review. Simply acknowledge whether a particular aspect of your passion energizes you in God's service or leaves you feeling deflated. Then, take these emotional responses prayer and ask God to clarify them.

<u>Note:</u> *Even though you feel certainty about the spiritual leadings, they remain fragile and need to be treated gently. Allow God to nurture and strengthen these desires in you so that you will be able to share them in a more public (and potentially hostile) setting in the future.*

• Take time to imagine the various ways you might express your passions to others, whether publicly or through some form of more indirect communication. Again, review the feelings evoked during these imaginative exercises and register the various ways these emotions lead you during your prayers. As with the earlier review using the "Rules for Discernment", be careful to treat these leadings gently.

• When you feel ready, speak to other people about the issue or concern about which you feel passionately and how you wish to express your feelings and insights to others. At first, these conversations should be limited to people who are neutral regarding your concerns (such as a spiritual director) since your ideas may remain fragile and open to the influence of others during the process of deepening in you.

• After gaining clarity in your thoughts and confidence in the God-given nature of your passions, you may begin sharing your thoughts and feelings with friends and family who (out of love and concern for you) may be resistant to your desires). However, in this moment, you should not be prepared to "win over" the other person since they may not be able to see beyond their concern for you. Be patient and take these conversations to prayer in order to separate valuable criticism from negativity.

2.   If you do not have certainty about the God-given nature of your passion, but you retain an awareness of God's presence within these desires, you should carefully review each aspect of this leading.

- Review your earlier notes concerning the passions you are experiencing, both in terms of their subject and the actions involved in your response. Separate and distinguish the various dimensions of your passion(s) and reflect on the implications of each (e.g., the benefits and challenges it presents to you, the time and energy it will require, etc.). Also, think about the uniqueness of what you desire and how your actions might be necessary for the benefit of others.

- Consider each of aspect of your passions using the "Rules for Discernment" Saint Ignatius proposed as being most useful after completing the first "week" of his *Spiritual Exercises* (found on page 312). Be careful not to over-think your initial response(s) during this review. Simply acknowledge whether a particular aspect of your passion energizes you in God's service or leaves you feeling deflated. Then, take these emotional responses prayer and ask God to clarify them.

- Reread the "Principle and Foundation" in *The Spiritual Exercises of Saint Ignatius* (found on page 309) and compare your desires to the ideals articulated by Saint Ignatius. Bring these thoughts to God in prayer, asking that you may be guided only by these desires and not by any other motivations than the love and service of God. Then, in conversation with God, ask that you may remain neutral regarding your passions (both in terms of their benefits and their costs) so that the only concern you have is that your actions reflect the desires of God. Conclude your prayer by asking that God guide you toward a deeper appreciation of the nature of your passion and the actions they should evoke.

- Then, take the time you need to review your earlier notes concerning your passions once again. Begin each consideration by requesting that God allow you to better understand how your passions reflect God's own desires for you and the world around you. Then, after asking that God reveal the advantages and disadvantages each choice offers, examine in turn your passions separately and record your thoughts in your retreat workbook.

- After this prayerful and thoughtful review, decide if you are experiencing a strong and undeniable meeting from God concerning your passions. If so, present your feelings and the actions you desire to pursue before God and ask that you be led only by the desire to love and serve God through your choices.

<u>Note:</u> *If you have not received a strong and undeniable leading from God concerning your passions, present the desires in your heart to God and ask that you may be led to always act in God's service has these passions take form and substance in the future.*

Part 3

With certainty about the nature of your passions, take your insights and concerns to prayer. Imagine yourself sitting with Jesus in a comfortable space and tell him about your most intimate experiences of God and how you feel they lead to some form of public witness. Listen as Jesus asks you questions about these matters and make a mental note about your reactions to Jesus' questions and observations. Then, explain both your willingness and your reluctance to share these experiences with others in some way. Again, listen to Jesus' response before asking for his continued support as you move forward.

Afterward, take some time to answer the following questions:
- What aspects of your passions excite you and leave you without any doubt about their need to be shared with other people?
- What emotions make you reluctant to share your passions with others?
- What are you willing to sacrifice as God asks you to share your passions and deepest spiritual experiences with others?
- How will you recognize God's presence in the responses (both positive and negative) you receive when sharing your passions and concerns with others?

Part 4

After confirming the God-given nature of your passions and addressing your reservations about acting on these passions, you should explore the various ways to express them to others.
- If your calling is to write, then begin writing and sharing your work with others.
- If your call is to social ministry or advocacy, join an organization that allows you to deepen in your appreciation of your passions while acting on them.

However, it is very important that you never stop the process of discerning the effects of your actions on you and those around you.

Over time, your passions will deepen and clarify. They will lead you to concrete actions that you will be able to recognize and evaluate using the tools Saint Ignatius presents in his *Spiritual Exercises*. Still, while these resources will always be helpful, it is your direct relationship with God in prayer that will nurture and sustain the process of transforming passions into concrete expressions of articulate witness. So, you may find it helpful to return to the prayerful process of discerning your passions presented in this section.

Also, in the other books of this series, there will be sections addressing other aspects of cultivating your unique forms of articulate witness (specifically the issues of defining your style of expression and the discovery of your unique voice speaking on behalf of God). However, if you choose not to use these resources, remain assured that the seeds planted through the exercises of this section will allow God to nurture and strengthen your passions into articulate expressions of God's love and presence in the world.

Textual Resources

From Saint Ignatius' *Spiritual Exercises*

Excerpts from *The Spiritual Exercises of Saint Ignatius of Loyola*, edited by Charles Seager.

<u>The Principle and Foundation (23)</u>

23. Man was created for this end, that he might praise and reverence the Lord his God, and, serving Him, at length be saved. But the other things which are placed on the earth were created for man's sake, that they might assist him in pursuing the end of his creation: whence it follows, that they are to be used or abstained from in proportion as they profit or hinder him in pursuing that end. Wherefore we ought to be indifferent towards all created things (in so far as they are subject to the liberty of our will, and not prohibited), so that (to the best of our power) we seek not health more than sickness, nor prefer riches to poverty, honour to contempt, a long life to a short one. But it is fitting, out of all, to choose and desire those things only which lead to the end.

<u>A Meditation on Personal Sin (55-61)</u>

55. **A meditation concerning sins; comprehending, after the preparatory prayer and two preludes, five articles or points, with a colloquy at the end [asking that we seek] intense grief concerning sins, with abundant weeping.**

56. Let the first point be, a certain inquest by which the sins of one's whole life are recalled into the memory, the person going through, step by step, and examining the several years and spaces of time. In which thing we are assisted by a threefold summing up, by considering, that is to say, the places where we have lived, the various modes of intercourse we have had with others, and the different kinds of offices or occupations in which we have been engaged.

57. The second is, to weigh the sins themselves, how great is the foulness and wickedness of each on account of its own nature, even though it had not been prohibited.

58. The third is, to consider myself, who or of what kind I am, adding comparisons which may bring me to a greater contempt of myself; as if I reflect how little I am when compared with all men; then what the whole multitude of mortals is, as compared with the Angels and all the Blessed: after these things I must consider what, in fact, all creation is in comparison with God the Creator Himself: what, now,

can I, one mere human being, be? Lastly, let me look at the corruption of my whole self, the wickedness of my soul, and the pollution of my body; and account myself to be a kind of ulcer or boil, from which so great and foul a flood of sins, so great a pestilence of vices, has flowed down.

59. The fourth is, to consider what God is, Whom I have thus offended, collecting the perfections which are God s peculiar attributes and comparing them with my opposite vices and defects; comparing, that is to say, His supreme power, wisdom, goodness, and justice, with my extreme weakness, ignorance, wickedness, and iniquity.

60. The fifth, to break forth into exclamation, from a vehement commotion of the feelings, admiring greatly how all creatures (going over them severally) have borne with me so long, and even to this time preserved me alive; how the angels, bearing the sword of the divine justice, have patiently borne with me, guarded me, and even assisted me with their prayers; how the saints have interceded for me; how the sky, the sun, the moon, and the other heavenly bodies, the elements, and all kinds of animals and productions of the earth, in place of the vengeance due, have served me; how, lastly, the earth has not opened and swallowed me up, unbarring a thousand hells, in which I might suffer everlasting punishments.

61. Lastly, this meditation must be concluded by a colloquy, in which I extol the infinite mercy of God, giving thanks to the best of my power, that He has preserved my life up to this day; whence proposing for the future the amendment of myself, I shall say once *Pater noster* [Our Father/The Lord's Prayer].

A Contemplation of the Kingdom of Jesus Christ (91-98)

91. **A contemplation of the kingdom of Jesus Christ, from the likeness of an earthly king calling out his subjects to war...**

The first prelude for the construction of the place will now be, to imagine that we see the synagogues, villages, and towns, through which Christ passed preaching; and so concerning other places.

The second, relating to the obtaining of grace, will here be, to ask of God that we may not be deaf when Christ calls us; but be ready to follow and obey.

92. Let the first point be, to place before my eyes a human king, chosen of God, whom all Christian princes and people are bound to reverence and obey.

93.   The second, to imagine that I hear that king speaking to all his subjects: I propose to subject to my power all the countries of the unbelievers. Whosoever, therefore, chooses to follow me, let him be prepared to use no other food, clothing, or other things, than what he sees me use.

He must also persevere in the same labours, watchings, arid other difficulties with me, that each may partake of the victory and felicity in proportion as he shall have been a companion of the labours and troubles;

94.   The third is, to consider what his faithful subjects ought to answer this most loving and liberal king, and how promptly to offer themselves prepared for all his will. And, on the other hand, if any one did not hearken, of how great reproach he would be worthy among all men, and how worthless a soldier he would have to be accounted.

95.   The second part of this exercise, consists in drawing a comparison between the said king and our Lord Jesus Christ, concerning these three points:

First, we shall thus apply the example: if that earthly king, with his warlike calling forth, is worthy to receive attention and obedience, how much more worthy is Christ, the Eternal King, and conspicuous to the whole world, Who invites each to Himself in these words: "This is My most just will, to claim to Myself the dominion of the whole world, to conquer all My enemies, and so to enter into My Father's glory. Whoever then desires to come thither with Me, he must needs labour with Me; for the reward will be according to the labour."

96.   The second, we shall reason, that there will be no one of a sound mind, who will not most eagerly offer and dedicate himself entire to the service of Christ.

97.   Thirdly, it must be judged, that they who shall think good to be altogether subjected to the obedience of Him, will offer, not merely themselves for the endurance of labours, but also some greater and more illustrious offerings, conquering the rebellion of the flesh, of the senses, and of the love of self and the world whence each; will answer to the following effect:

98.   "Behold, Supreme King and Lord of all things, I, though most unworthy, yet, relying on Thy grace and help, offer myself altogether to Thee, and submit to Thy will all that is mine; testifying before Thine infinite goodness, as also in the sight of Thy glorious Virgin Mother, and of the whole court of heaven, that this is my mind, this my desire, this my most certain determination, that (so it turn to the greater

advancement of Thy praise and my obedience) I may follow Thee as closely as possible, and imitate Thee in bearing all injuries and adversities with the true poverty, both of spirit, and also of goods; if (I say) it please Thy most holy Majesty to choose and receive me to such a state of life."

Rules for the Discernment of Spirits, Week 1 (313-327)

313. Some rules for the discerning of the motions of the soul which different spirits excite, in order that the good ones alone may be admitted, and the evil ones driven away. It must be observed, that they suit more especially the Exercises of the First Week.

314. The first rule is, that to those who easily sin mortally, and add sin to sin, our enemy is wont usually to present the allurements of the flesh and senses, that he may keep them full of sins, and ever increase the amount. But the good spirit, on the contrary, pricks continually their conscience, and by the office of remorse and reason deters them from sinning.

315. The second, that to others, who take anxious pains to purify themselves from their faults and sins, and advance daily more and more in the desire of obeying God, the malignant spirit suggests feelings of molestation, scruples, sadnesses, false reasonings, and other such disturbances, by which to impede that advance. Of the good spirit, on the other hand, it is the property and custom to add courage and strength to those who act rightly, to console them, to call forth the tears of devotion, to enlighten the mind, and give tranquillity, removing all obstacles, in order that they may the more easily and cheerfully by good works ever advance farther.

316. The third, that spiritual consolation, properly so called, is then known to be present, when, by a certain internal motion, the soul burns up with the love of her Creator, and can no longer love any creature except for His sake. Also when there are shed tears stirring up that love, whether they flow from grief concerning sins, or from meditation on the Passion of Christ, or from any other cause whatsoever, which is rightly ordered to the worship and honour of God. Lastly, any increase of faith, hope, and charity, may be called a consolation: also every joy which is wont to stir up the soul to the meditation of heavenly things, to the desire of salvation, to the possession of rest and peace with the Lord.

317. The fourth, that, on the other hand, we should call by the name of spiritual desolation, any darkening of the mind, disturbance therein,

instigation to the lowest or earthly things; together with every disquietude and agitation, or temptation, which moves to distrust concerning salvation, and expels hope and charity; whence the soul feels that she is saddened, grows lukewarm, becomes torpid, and almost despairs of the mercy of God her Creator Himself. For as desolation is the opposite to consolation, so also the thoughts which spring from either are altogether contrary to those which spring from the other.

318.   The fifth, that, in time of desolation, one must not deliberate on anything, or make any change concerning one's purpose of mind, or state of life, but persevere in those things which had been settled before, suppose, during the preceding day or hour of consolation. For as, whilst any one enjoys that consolation of which we have spoken, he is led, not by his own instinct, but by that of the good spirit; so when desolation presents itself to him, he is urged on by the evil spirit, by whose instigation nothing right is ever effected.

319.   The sixth, that, although a man affected with desolation ought by no means to change his former decisions, it will never the less be expedient that those things should be provided and increased which tend to oppose the impulse of desolation; such as are, to be earnest in prayer, with self-examination, and to undertake some penance.

320.   The seventh, that, as long as we are oppressed with desolation, we must consider that the Lord leaves us to ourselves for the time, for the sake of probation, in order that we may learn to resist even by our natural strength the attacks of our enemy; which we are certainly able to do, the Divine help being continually with us, although it be then not at all perceived, in consequence of the Lord's having with drawn the former fervour of charity, leaving nevertheless that grace which may suffice for performing good works and gaining eternal salvation.

321.   The eighth, that he who is under the attack of temptation will be wonderfully helped by the endeavour of maintaining patience, this being the virtue which is especially opposed to, and diametrically resists, vexations of this kind. He must also call in hope, and the thought of the consolation which will soon be at hand: if especially the force of the desolation be broken by the holy endeavours pointed out in the sixth rule.

322.   The ninth, that the chief causes of desolation are three. The first, because, on account of our lukewarmness, and want of pains-taking in spiritual practices or exercises, we are deservedly deprived of the Divine consolation. The second, in order that we may be proved, what

kind of persons we are, and how we spend ourselves for we are the service and honour of God without the present pay, as it were, of consolations and spiritual gifts. The third, in order that we may be quite sure, that it is not of our own strength to acquire or retain the fervour of devotion, the vehemence of love, the abundance of tears, or any other inward consolation; but that all these things are the gratuitous gifts of God, which if we claim to ourselves as our own, we shall incur the charge of pride and vain-glory, not without seriously endangering our salvation.

323.   The tenth, that he who is enjoying consolation must consider for the future, how he will be able to bear himself when desolation afterwards occurs; in order that even from that time he may gain spirit and strength of mind to repel its attack.

324.   The eleventh, that he who is in this same case, when consolation flows in, depress and humble himself as much as possible, thinking with himself, how weak and cowardly he will appear, when attacked by desolation, unless by the help of the Divine grace and consolation he be quickly raised. He on the other hand who is troubled by desolation, ought to think that with the grace of God he can do very much, and will easily conquer all his enemies, provided he place his hope in the strength of God, and confirm his mind.

Note: *The following rule presents an image offensive to modern readers. Still, the behavior being described remains important to understand. So, it may be helpful to connect the patterns of temptation with the actions of a bully or the tantrum of a small child being denied something they desire by an adult.*

325.   The twelfth, that our enemy resembles the nature and habit of a woman, as to weakness of strength and obstinacy of spirit. For as a woman contending with a man, if she sees him resist with an erect and firm countenance, immediately loses courage and turns her back; but if she perceives him to be timid and cowardly, rises to the utmost audacity, and attacks him fiercely; in like manner is the demon accustomed to lose altogether his spirit and strength, as often as he sees the spiritual athlete with a fearless heart and lofty forehead resist his temptations: but if he is alarmed when the first attacks are to be endured, and gives way as it were to despair, there is then no beast on the earth more infuriated than that enemy, more fierce, and more

pertinacious against man, to fulfil, to our destruction, the desire of his malignant and obstinate mind.

326. The thirteenth, that the same enemy of ours follows the plan of any most wicked lover, who, desiring to seduce the daughter of virtuous parents, or the wife of some good man, takes the utmost care that his words and counsels may be secret, and fears and dislikes nothing more than if the daughter makes them known to her father, or the wife to her husband, as knowing that in this case it is all over with his desires and attempts; in the same way, the devil studiously endeavours, that the soul which he desires to circumvent and ruin, should keep his deceitful suggestions secret; but is in the highest degree displeased, and most grievously tormented, if his at tempts be made known to any one, either hearing confession, or being a spiritual man; because he understands that, such being the case, he altogether fails in them.

327. The fourteenth, that the adversary is accustomed also to imitate some leader of war, who desiring to take and plunder a citadel which he has besieged, having first ascertained the nature and defence of the place, attacks the weaker part. For so he too goes round the soul, and searches out skilfully what virtues, moral (that is to say) or theological, she is either defended by or destitute of; and at that particular part in us which he has seen beforehand to be less strengthened and guarded than the rest, bringing up all his engines, he rushes on, and hopes to overthrow us.

From Celtic Sources

1. A Description of Saint Patrick from *Lives of Saints from The Book of Lismore*, edited by Whitley Stokes.

A true man, surely, was that man from purity of nature, like a patriarch. A true pilgrim, like Abraham. Gentle, forgiving of heart, like Moses. A praiseful psalmist, like David. A student of wisdom and knowledge, like Solomon. A chosen vessel for proclaiming righteousness, like Paul the Apostle. A man full of the grace and favour of the Holy Spirit, like John. A fair garden with plants of virtues. A vine-branch with fruitfulness. A flashing fire with the fervour of the warming and heating of the sons of Life, for kindling and illuminating charity. A lion for great strength and might. A dove for gentleness and simplicity. A serpent for cunning and prudence. A man mild, gentle, humble, tender to the sons of Life; (but) rough, ungentle to the sons of Death. A slave in labour and service to Christ.

2. Stories about Saint Patrick from *Lives of Saints from The Book of Lismore* and *Three Middle-Irish homilies on the lives of Saints Patrick, Brigit and Columba*, edited by Whitley Stokes.

The Leper and the Floating Stone

Patrick then fared forth on his road, four and twenty men were his number, and he found a ship in readiness before him on the strand of the sea of Britain. When Patrick came into the boat, a leper was asking him for a place, and there was no empty place therein. So he put out before him (to swim in the sea) the stone altar whereon he used to make offering every day. However, God wrought a great miracle here, to wit, the stone went not to the bottom, nor did it stay behind. But it swam round about the boat [with the leper on it] until it arrived in Ireland. (*Three Homilies*)

Patrick Receives the Staff of Jesus

Then he went to sea with nine in his number; and he came to the island where he saw the new house and a married pair therein. And he asked the young man who dwelt in the house, how long they had been therein. "From the time of Jesus," saith he, "and He blessed us, together with our house, and we shall be thus till Doom; and God hath enjoined thee to go and preach in the land of the Gaels, and Jesus left with us a staff to be given to thee." So Patrick took the staff of Jesus with him, and went to consult Germanus, the bishop who ordained him.

Afterward, saith the angel Victor to him, 'God hath enjoined thee to go and preach in the land of the Gael. "If I should hear," saith Patrick, "I would go." "Come," saith Victor, "to converse with Him on Mount Hermon."

Then Patrick went and complained to God of the hard-heartedness of the Gael. "I," saith God, "will be thy helper." (*Book of Lismore*)

God Protects Patrick from His Enemies

When terror seized the queen she went to Patrick and said to him, "O righteous one and O mighty one, kill not the king, for he shall submit to thee, and give thee thine own will." The king came and gave his will to Patrick by word of mouth, but gave it not from his heart; and he told Patrick to go after him to Tara that he might give him his will before the men of Ireland. That, however, was not what he had in his mind, but to kill Patrick, for he left ambushes before him on every road from that to Tara.

Thereafter went Patrick (and his train of) eight, together with Patrick's attendant, Benen, past all the ambushes, in the shape of eight deer and behind them one fawn with a white bird on its shoulder, that is, Benen with Patrick's book-satchel on his back; and thereafter he went into Tara, the doors being shut, to the middle of the palace. The king was then feasting with the kings of Ireland around him at this festival, for that was the Feast of Tara…

Patrick is then called to the king's couch that he might eat food, and Patrick refused not that. The wizard Lucatmael put a drop of poison into Patrick's cruse, and gave it into Patrick's hand: but Patrick blessed the cruse and inverted the vessel, and the poison fell thereout, and not even a little of the ale fell. And Patrick afterwards drank the ale. (*Three Homilies*)

Patrick is Betrayed for a Cauldron

Then Patrick went into the territory of Hui Neill, visiting with Sen-Chianan; but he betrayed Patrick and sold him for a cauldron of brass. He sets the cauldron on the wall of his house, and his hands then clave to the cauldron. His wife went to help him. Her hands clave to the cauldron. The whole household went to the cauldron, and all their hands clave thereto, and the cauldron clave to the wall. Then they said:

"He whom we have sold is servant of a most mighty King. Let him be called back to us." Thereafter Patrick went to them, and owing to their repentance, released their hands; and they returned the cauldron. (*Book of Lismore*)

Failge Tries to Kill Patrick

Then Failge Berraide boasted that he would kill Patrick wherever he should meet him, in revenge for the idol Cenn Cruaich, Failge's god. So his people hid from Patrick what Failge said. And one day Odran, his charioteer, said to Patrick: "Since for a long time I have been charioteering for thee, O master, O Patrick, let me to-day be in the chief seat, and do thou be charioteer." Patrick did so. Thereafter Patrick went into the district of Hui Failgi. Failge came, and gave a thrust through Odran in the form of Patrick. Not long afterwards Failge died, and his soul went into hell. Then the Devil entered Failge's body, so that it dwelt amongst men as if it were alive. Then Patrick after a long while came to Failge, and tarried outside before the fortress, and asked one of Failge's slaves where Failge was biding. "I left him in his house," saith the slave. "Tell him," saith Patrick, "to come and speak with me." Then the servant goes to fetch Failge, and found of him in the house nought save his bare bones, bloodless, fleshless. The slave comes to Patrick in grief and sorrow, and tells him how he had seen Failge. Said Patrick, "From the day when Failge slew my charioteer, in my presence, his soul went to hell for the deed he had done, and the Devil entered his body." And that is the tragical death of Failge. (*Book of Lismore*)

The Conversion of Dichu

Patrick went afterwards in his boat to Inverslany, and there came against him Dichu, who set against him a fierce hound which he had. However, Patrick made the sign of the cross of the Lord against it, and he chanted the prophetic verse, "Deliver not up, O Lord, to beasts the souls that confess to Thee", and the hound stopped in that place and was unable to stir. Then, Dichu bared his brand, and went to kill Patrick. Patrick made the sign of Christ's cross against him, so that he could not stir either foot or hand. Thereafter Dichu repented and knelt before Patrick and gave him his full will, and Dichu believed in the one God, and he and great hosts along with him were baptized, and he gave that land (whereon he was converted) to God and to Patrick. In that place Patrick built a church which is called Saball Patraic to-day, and he foretold to Dichu that it would be there until he should go to heaven. (*Three Homilies*)

Patrick's Wedding Night

Now the time of Patrick's release from bondage drew nigh, for the heathen were wont to free their slaves in the seventh year. As Miliucc [Patrick's owner] could not think how else he could detain Patrick, he bought a bondmaid and wedded her to Patrick. On the bridal-night, when they were put into a house apart, then Patrick preached to the bondmaid, and they spent the whole night in prayer. On the next morning Patrick beheld the white scar on the bondmaid's face, and he asked of her the cause of the scar. Said the bondmaid, "When I was in Nemtur in Britain, I fell, and my head struck against a stone, so that death was near me. When my brother Succet [Patrick's name in childhood] beheld the wound, he made the sign of Christ's cross over it, so that I was well at once." Patrick said this – "I myself am thy brother, and I am he that healed thee." They then gave thanks to God, and did go into the wilderness. (*Three Homilies*)

Patrick Converts Daire

Thereafter Patrick, at the angel's word, went to the Macha. There was there a certain wealthy and venerable man, named Daire. Patrick asked this man to give him a site for his church on Druim Sailech, the stead whereon Armagh stands to-day. Daire said that he would not give him the hill, but that he would give him a site in the valley, where the Ferta stands to-day. So Patrick founded his cell and stayed there for a long while. One day two horses of Daire's were brought to graze in that place. Patrick was angered thereby, and slew the horses straightway. Daire was angered at the killing of his horses, and told his men to kill the cleric. Illness and sudden colic came to Daire, so that death was nigh unto him. "Vexing the cleric is the cause of that," saith his wife. "And do ye his will," saith she.

Then they went to seek holy water from Patrick for Daire ... Saith Patrick, "Had it not been for his wife, he would not have had resurrection till Doom." Patrick blessed the water and said that it should be given to Daire and sprinkled over the horses. Thus is it done, and Daire with his horses straightway arose. Then a brazen cauldron was brought in offering to Patrick from Daire. "Deo gratias [Thanks be to God]," saith Patrick. He then asked of his household what the cleric had said. "Gratiam," say the household. "That is a bad reward for a good cauldron," saith Daire. "Let it be taken again from him," saith he then. They took back the cauldron from him. "Deo gratias" saith Patrick. His household did tell their master what Patrick had said. "That is a first word with him, the Gratiam" saith Daire – "Gratiam when giving it to him, Gratiam when taking it from him." Daire and his wife afterwards went wholly in accordance with Patrick's will, and they offered him the cauldron, and the hill for which he had previously asked, which is named Armagh to-day. (*Book of Lismore*)

The Young Patrick and the Flooded House

Once upon a time came a flood of water into the house wherein was Patrick, and quenched all the fire, and the vessels were afloat. Patrick then went to a dry place which was in the house and dipped his five fingers into the water, and the five drops which trickled from them became sparks of fire, and that fire was kindled in the house, and the water at once ceased to rise, and God's name and Saint Patrick's were magnified through that miracle. (*Three Homilies*)

The Young Patrick and the Wolf

At another time a wolf went and carried off a sheep of the flock from Patrick when he was shepherding; and his foster-mother rebuked him much for the loss of the sheep. But as Patrick was at the same place the next day, the wolf came and showed the sheep safe before him, [which thing was a marvel] for up to that time restitution from him was not usual. God's name and Patrick's were magnified therein. (*Three Homilies*)

3.   "The Deer's Cry" from *Selections from Ancient Irish Poetry*, translated by Kuno Meyer.

I arise to-day
>Through a mighty strength, the invocation of the Trinity,
>Through belief in the threeness,
>Through confession of the oneness
>Of the Creator of Creation.

I arise to-day
>Through the strength of Christ's birth with His baptism,
>Through the strength of His crucifixion with His burial,
>Through the strength of His resurrection with His ascension,

> Through the strength of His descent for the judgment of Doom.

I arise to-day
> Through the strength of the love of Cherubim,
> In obedience of angels,
> In the service of archangels,
> In hope of resurrection to meet with reward,
> In prayers of patriarchs,
> In predictions of prophets,
> In preachings of apostles,
> In faiths of confessors,
> In innocence of holy virgins,
> In deeds of righteous men.

I arise to-day
> Through the strength of heaven:
> Light of sun,
> Radiance of moon,
> Splendour of fire,
> Speed of lightning,
> Swiftness of wind,
> Depth of sea,
> Stability of earth,
> Firmness of rock.

I arise to-day
> Through God's strength to pilot me:
> God's might to uphold me,
> God's wisdom to guide me,
> God's eye to look before me,
> God's ear to hear me,
> God's word to speak for me,
> God's hand to guard me,
> God's way to lie before me,
> God's shield to protect me,
> God's host to save me
> From snares of devils,
> From temptations of vices,
> From every one who shall wish me ill,
> Afar and anear,

      Alone and in a multitude.

I summon to-day all these powers between me and those evils,
      Against every cruel merciless power that may oppose my body and soul,
      Against incantations of false prophets,
      Against black laws of pagandom,
      Against false laws of heretics,
      Against craft of idolatry,
      Against spells of women and smiths and wizards,
      Against every knowledge that corrupts man's body and soul.

Christ to shield me to-day
      Against poison, against burning,
      Against drowning, against wounding,
      So that there may come to me abundance of reward.
      Christ with me, Christ before me, Christ behind me,
      Christ in me, Christ beneath me, Christ above me,
      Christ on my right, Christ on my left,
      Christ when I lie down, Christ when I sit down, Christ when I arise,
      Christ in the heart of every man who thinks of me,
      Christ in the mouth of every one who speaks of me,
      Christ in every eye that sees me,
      Christ in every ear that hears me.

I arise to-day
      Through a mighty strength, the invocation of the Trinity,
      Through belief in the threeness,
      Through confession of the oneness
      Of the Creator of Creation.

Prayer Resources

Considerations

In this section, you will find resources designed to help you cultivate habits of prayer that will enrich your prayerful experiences during this retreat and the other retreats in this series. Some of these materials are excerpts from *A Pilgrimage to the Land of the Saints* (sometimes with minor revisions) or present prayers similar those in my earlier "To the Land of the Saints" series (i.e., the Celtic examens).

So, you will need to decide how you might best approach these resources while creating your own unique experience during this retreat and (if led by God's loving Spirit) during your journey through *The Spiritual Exercises of Saint Ignatius of Loyola*:

1. The two Celtic examens highlight God's activity in your day. "A Morning Prayer of Encircling" presents a Celtic encircling prayer in which you look forward to the coming day while "An Evening Prayer of Review" looks back at the events and people you encountered during your day in a litany of gratitude.

Note: In a daily life retreat, these examens should stand alone and take no more than fifteen minutes each. But, in seclusion (where much of your day is devoted to formal prayer), you might find it helpful to integrate these prayers into your daily preparation and review exercises.

These prayerful reviews should focus on the concrete expressions of God's love in your daily life, equipping you – on a direct and emotional level – to discern God's desires in your life and to amend your life to be in harmony with them.

2. The descriptions of imaginative contemplation and the application of the senses provide you with a clear and easy to follow structure for these two types of Ignatian prayer. You will find it helpful to refer to these materials as you prepare your prayer until you are familiar with these techniques. But you also should feel free to adapt these guidelines as you discern your ways of imagining the events in the retreat's contemplations and of speaking comfortably with Jesus about your experiences.

3. "Approaching Prayer during this Retreat" addresses the practical concerns of making this retreat, both the nine day/week retreat in this book as well as the complete journey through *The Spiritual Exercises of Saint Ignatius* presented in the "Finding Your Place of

Resurrection" series. These issues involve scheduling your prayer when conducting these retreats in daily life or in seclusion, selecting the Bible you will use during these retreats, pacing your prayers to avoid mental or spiritual exhaustion during the retreats, and adjusting the retreats to your personality and prayer rhythms.

4. "Honoring Holy Ground" suggests three short rituals you might use to consecrate your prayer. These spiritual gestures will create a mental "common space" that unifies the different times and places in which you pray, strengthening your ability to create good prayer habits and easing your entry into the silence and solitude of contemplation.

A Morning Prayer of Encircling

1. Take a moment to become still. You may want to close your eyes, or you might focus your attention on a specific place or object near you. Become completely focused on this present moment and allow all other concerns or problems to dissolve and fade from your consciousness.
2. Become aware of your desire to know the fullness of God's love for you and pray for the grace to see God's actions in your life more clearly, to understand God's desires for you more accurately and to respond to God's guidance to you more generously.
3. Then, imagine the coming day, seeing that God's love is enfolding and encircling every situation. Imagine what you will do during the morning, during the midday hours, during the afternoon, and during the evening. Allow God's love to fill these events as you turn your attention to specific moments during the day.

(a) In your imagination, see the remaining morning hours. Imagine the moments when you expect to be alone and when you anticipate meeting other people. Experience your thoughts while you are alone and your words while speaking with others. Ask God to reveal the divine love shaping and sustaining these moments. Then, rest awhile in the awareness of that love and consider the people you are with before encircling them in God's love and protection, saying:

O Father who sought me,
Encircle and protect us!

(b) Imagine the events and people of the coming midday. Again, see the moments when you expect to be alone and when you anticipate meeting other people. Contemplate your thoughts while you are alone and your words while speaking with others. Once more, ask God to reveal the divine love shaping and sustaining these moments. Then, rest awhile in the awareness of that love and consider the people you are with before encircling them in God's love and protection, saying:

O Son who bought me,
Encircle and protect us!

(c) See the coming afternoon, imagining the moments when you expect to be alone and when you anticipate meeting other people. Consider your thoughts while you are alone and your words while speaking with others. Again, ask God to reveal the divine love shaping and sustaining these moments. Then, rest awhile in the awareness of that love and consider the people you are with before encircling them in God's love and protection, saying:

> *O Holy Spirit who taught me,*
> *Encircle and protect us!*

(d) Finally, in your imagination, see the coming evening hours. Once more, imagine the moments when you expect to be alone and when you anticipate meeting other people. Contemplate your thoughts while you are alone and your words while speaking with others. Once again, ask God to reveal the divine love shaping and sustaining these moments. Then, rest awhile in the awareness of that love and consider the people you are with before encircling them in God's love and protection, saying:

> *O Blessed Trinity,*
> *Encircle and protect us!*

4. Now, as you put these images aside, express your gratitude for the ways God's love will touch you in the depths of your being as it surrounds, protects, and guides you in the coming day. Then, consider how you are the instrument of God's loving presence in the world and ask how you might share that love with family, friends, neighbors, colleagues or even strangers during this day.

5. After taking time to hear God's response, conclude by praying this ancient hymn of Saint Hilary:

> *From heaven has fled the starry night,*
> *And startled sleep has taken flight;*
> *Dear God, to you, our prayers we bring;*
> *To you rejoicing hymns we sing.*
>
> *Lord, be our hearts and hopes renewed*
> *In light and love and gratitude;*
> *May our deeds, illumed by you, be*
> *Worthy of your love and glory.*
>
> *We praise you, Lord, forevermore;*
> *You, with the Son my soul does adore,*
> *And with the Spirit, three in one,*
> *Reigning while endless ages run.*
> *AMEN.*

An Evening Prayer of Review

1. Take a moment to become still. You may want to close your eyes or you might focus your attention on a specific place or object near you. Become completely focused on this present moment and allow all other concerns or problems to dissolve and fade from your consciousness.

2. Become aware of God's goodness and of the many gifts that God has given you, sustaining you and the world around you. Consider the times when you do not reflect God's goodness, the times when you squander or misuse the gifts God has given to you and the times when you feel abandoned by God.

3. Review this day in your memory. Become aware of the gifts and of the needs you have experienced during this passing day. Allow yourself to feel God's presence in the events and emotions of this day as you consider your actions and reactions during it. Ask for the grace to gratefully acknowledge the gifts you received today and to recognize with deep remorse the gifts of God you ignored during the passing day.

    (a) Remember the beginning of this day. Did you awaken quickly or slowly? Did the day begin easily or with difficulty? Did you feel happy or sad? Relaxed or tense? As you awoke this morning, did you feel God being present to you or distant from you? Take a moment to consider these feelings as you ponder and pray:

> *O Father who wrought me,*
> *O Son who bought me,*
> *O Spirit who sought me,*
> *Yours alone let me be!*

    (b) Remember your preparations for the day. Did you dress quickly or slowly? What did you think about as you prepared for the day? What were your feelings? Was God involved in your preparations for this day? Take a moment to consider these events and feelings as you ponder and pray:

> *O Father who wrought me,*
> *O Son who bought me,*
> *O Spirit who sought me,*
> *Yours alone let me be!*

    (c) Remember your morning. Did you eat breakfast or go without? Remember the other events of your morning. Were you alone or with other people? What did you do? What did you think or talk about? What emotions did you feel during the morning hours? Was God present to you or distant from you during the morning? Take a moment to consider these events and feelings as you ponder and pray:

> *O Father who wrought me,*
> *O Son who bought me,*
> *O Spirit who sought me,*
> *Yours alone let me be!*

    (d)   Remember your midday. What did you do? Did you eat lunch or go without? Were you alone or with other people? What did you think or talk about? Did you feel happy or sad? Relaxed or tense? Was God present or distant? Take a moment to consider these events and feelings as you ponder and pray:

> *O Father who wrought me,*
> *O Son who bought me,*
> *O Spirit who sought me,*
> *Yours alone let me be!*

    (e)   Remember your afternoon. Were you alone or with other people? What did you do? What did you think or talk about? What were you feeling? Did God feel present or distant? Take a moment to consider these events and feelings as you ponder and pray:

> *O Father who wrought me,*
> *O Son who bought me,*
> *O Spirit who sought me,*
> *Yours alone let me be!*

    (f)   Remember your evening. What did you do? Were you alone or with other people? What did you think or talk about? Did you feel happy or sad? Relaxed or tense? Was God present or distant? Take a moment to consider these events and feelings as you ponder and pray:

> *O Father who wrought me,*
> *O Son who bought me,*
> *O Spirit who sought me,*
> *Yours alone let me be!*

4.   As you put these images aside, consider the present moment. What are you feeling toward God? Allow yourself to think or say a short one-sentence prayer in response to the memories or feelings of this day. Be completely honest in this prayer since God already knows your deepest desires, joys and pains.

5.   Then, after taking a moment to allow the thoughts and feelings of your prayer to linger on your mind and in your heart, ask God to sanctify

the blessings – and heal the wounds – of this passing day using these words of Saint Ambrose:

> *God of creation, wondrous Might,*
> *Eternal power that all adore,*
> *You rule the changing day and night.*
> *Yourself unchanging are evermore.*
>
> *Pour light upon my fading day,*
> *So in my life no dusk shall be.*
> *So death shall bring me to the ray,*
> *With you, Lord, of heavenly glory.*
>
> *Unto you, Father of Mercy,*
> *I lift my voice in prayer and praise,*
> *And to the Son and Spirit be*
> *Like glory to the end of days.*
> *AMEN.*

Notes on the Prayerful Review of the Day

These two prayerful reflections on the day – a preview and a review, both called examens – come from the spiritual teachings of the Spanish mystic Ignatius of Loyola, who developed this prayer to heighten a person's awareness of God's presence in the commonplace experiences of daily life. However, these types of prayers would have felt familiar to the ancient Celtic saints who also saw God's presence woven into the mundane events of their lives. The morning examen uses the Celtic practice of encircling people and places with God's protection and love – a prayer called a *caim* – and the evening examen uses the imagination to highlight the pervasive and protective presence of God that surrounds each person in the same manner as the distinctive breastplate – or *lorica* – prayers of the ancient Celtic saints.

All these forms of prayer, whether in these examens or in their Celtic counterparts, cultivate an awareness of God's loving activity in one's day-to-day life and foster a dynamic relationship with God based on one's trust in God's guidance and protection

Used during the morning and in the evening, each examen will require 10 or 15 minutes to complete. The morning examen focuses on the coming day, allowing the person to ask for God's guidance, protection and wisdom during future meetings and activities. The evening examen looks backward, eliciting gratitude for God's gifts during the day while also inviting repentance and a desire for personal change by heightening the individual's awareness of moments of personal sinfulness. These two prayers are meant to be done together so they may complement each other. By balancing a cautious anticipation of a new morning with the realistic awareness of human frailty in the evening, they teach us to reach out confidently to God for love, care, and forgiveness.

These exercises are designed to become habits of prayer that remain integrated into one's daily life, rather than moments where one puts his or her daily concerns aside to pray. Because of this, individuals approaching these devotions will find it helpful to:

- Memorize the Core Prayers

It will be useful to memorize the central prayers used in each of these exercises, in much the same way that the original men and women who composed these prayers used them in their own lives. While this may seem a bit daunting, be assured that the rhythm of the prayers makes it possible to memorize them quite easily. However, individuals who are not able to memorize these prayers may write them on a small card or place them in a notepad on their mobile phone so that they may consult them when they are needed. But it is important to record only the prayers so that the surrounding exercises become natural to each individual person.

- Integrate the Examens into Daily Routines

While many people set aside 10-15 minutes in a quiet space to conduct the examen, individuals may find it better to coordinate their prayerful consideration of the day – either that which is coming or which has already passed – to a daily activity, such as dressing and undressing (i.e., putting on and taking off the concerns of the day). This will take time and effort since routine daily activities are often filled with distractions, but the effort will be rewarded since the individual will always have time devoted to the examen while also rendering that daily activity sacred.

The instructions for these exercises are not intended to be a rigid set of rules. Instead, they are designed to help individuals create a framework which will ultimately be adapted to their needs. Each person will need to decide how much time to devote to the exercises as well as to each part of them. Individuals may find that certain parts of the exercises may move slightly, depending on their own desires and needs. Trust that God is present in these decisions and will make the exercises unique gifts to each individual person.

Imaginative Contemplation

connecting imagination and prayer during your retreat

An excerpt from A Pilgrimage to the Land of the Saints.

In his *Spiritual Exercises*, Ignatius of Loyola (the founder of the Ignatian spiritual tradition) lays out a basic pattern for the imaginative contemplation. This involves asking God to give you a specific grace during your time of prayer, carefully reviewing the basic elements of a particular scriptural episode related to your spiritual needs, and then using your imagination to enter those events. For Ignatius, it is important that you allow your imagination (and not your pre-existing desires or expectations) to guide you into prayer – opening an emotional and spiritual space for the Holy Spirit to bridge the divide between your unique personal experience and the universal message revealed in the scripture. In many cases, Ignatius also suggests you discuss the fruits of your contemplation in a casual imaginary conversation with Jesus before concluding with a formal prayer.

Ignatius also emphasized the careful review of prayer afterward, listening for patterns of openness and resistance in your conversations with God. Humbly listening to these clues in your prayer – and in your daily life through the examen – sustains a quiet movement toward becoming what Ignatius called a "contemplative in action" as you learn to recognize the patterns of God's presence in every aspect of your life.

You may find it helpful to use the following approach to your prayer during the retreat:

1. Begin your prayer by relaxing into the moment. Take time to center yourself and become completely aware of your feelings and thoughts in the present. When you have properly prepared yourself, take a moment to consider the specific gifts you wish to receive through this time of prayer and present these needs to God.

Note: You also should allow space for God to help you discern other spiritual and emotional needs you might have, remembering that these leadings will come from a loving and nurturing God.

2. Read the scriptural selection you will be using in your prayer. Do this slowly and meditatively, allowing it to seep deep into your consciousness.

As you review the passage of Scripture that you will use during this time of prayer, visualize the main elements of the story that is being told and the physical environment in which that story takes place. Take your time to slowly see the people involved in the story, their surroundings, and objects relevant to their actions, and what they are doing.

Note: *It is important to make certain that you understand the key elements of the story and their significance as you compose in your imagination the contemplation for a specific prayer period.*

3. When you are ready, imagine yourself in the story being told to you. Become aware of whether you participate directly in the events of the story or observe them. Become aware of what the environment feels like and how you are affected by the different people and events of the story being told to you in prayer.

Depending on how you use your imagination, this can mean many different things. Some people are able to "see" very strong visual images from the scriptural story while others "hear" the conversations in the passage and still others have strong emotional impressions during imaginative contemplations. You will need to find – and trust – your own way of imagining yourself in the scripture passage you want to contemplate.

Allow your imagination to guide you during the contemplation and do not try to control the images of the prayer. Sometimes, a distraction may reveal powerful insights or hidden desires you want to share with God. Or if you find yourself expanding on the story at the heart of your prayer – by connecting it to other scriptural passages or adding details from your own life – these "expansions" may be God's way of communicating with you.

Note: *Still, do not strain to hold onto your prayer if you find yourself unable to stay in the imaginative realm. Feel free to refer to the scriptural account (or any notes you prepared for your prayer) if necessary, taking a few deep breaths after putting these materials aside and allowing your imagination to guide you forward from the point where you became distracted.*

4. After completing the contemplation, allow your personal needs and desires to come to the surface of your consciousness. Then, gather

them and express them in an informal and friendly conversation with Christ. Speak as you would to a close friend, being certain to allow space for Christ to speak to you about his needs as well.

Ignatius called this prayer the colloquy, an exercise of the imagination in which you share the deepest desires of your heart with a loving and interested God. Like the Celtic saints, Ignatius believed that God actively engages us – in our prayer and in the world around us – in a conversation intended to fulfill God's desires for a redeemed creation.

<u>Note:</u> *Sometimes, this conversation constitutes the bulk of a prayer period.*

5.   Conclude your imaginative contemplation with a short formal prayer, such as Lord's Prayer or one of your own favorites.

6.   Review your prayer. Write down the significant moments from your contemplation and the colloquy shortly after leaving the space in which you prayed. You might find it helpful to compare notes from different contemplations since this will help you understand the ways your imagination guides you in prayer. Also, by helping you mark the growing presence of God in your life, these acts of review will nurture your capacity to discern God's will for you and deepen your gratitude for God's loving presence in your life.

The Application of the Senses
a quiet prayer of emotional and sense memories

An excerpt from **A Pilgrimage to the Land of the Saints.**

The primary form of imaginative contemplation outlined by Ignatius of Loyola in his *Spiritual Exercises* reflects his active and vigorous spirituality. It requires that you use your thoughts, feelings and imagination to enter into an active conversation with God. But, also in his *Spiritual Exercises*, Ignatius suggests a very different type of imaginative prayer which he called the "application of the senses." It is a prayer of memory in which you gently listen for God's voice in the emotions and physical sensations of your earlier prayers.

Ignatius of Loyola places the application of the senses at the end of the day when you might be tired or need to relax. For this reason, the application of the senses might be considered the Ignatian counterpart to traditional compline, a night prayer intended to draw together the strands of one's contemplation during the preceding day. However, unlike the forms of Christian contemplation which try to empty the consciousness of sensual images, this prayer uses the memory in concert with your emotions and five physical senses to gently reflect on God's presence in you and in your world.

With this in mind, you might find it helpful to use the following approach when making an application of the senses:
1. Begin your prayer by relaxing into the moment. Take time to center yourself and become completely aware of your feelings and thoughts in the present. When you have properly prepared yourself, allow the memories of your earlier prayers to ebb and flow in your consciousness without trying to guide or control your reminiscences.
2. When a particular moment of prayer comes into your consciousness, remember the grace or spiritual gift you desired in the initial prayer. Then gently consider in turn the images, sounds, smells, flavors, and physical feelings associated with your earlier prayer. Recognize that one of your senses may dominate the way that you imagine a moment in your prayer, so allow this sense to "lead" you into the events of your prayer – and toward other sense memories.

<u>Note:</u> Allow these sense images from your memory to surface in your consciousness without trying to control or interpret them as they

emerge. Simply find pleasure as these images and feelings come to you in what has been described as "a gentle soak in meaningful impressions". It is a highly visceral and, very often, pleasant experience.

3. Repeat this process with another prayer experience as it comes into your consciousness. Without constraining your thoughts, allow different memories from your earlier prayer to ebb and flow as you re-experience the feelings associated with different prayers.

4. When you are ready, allow these various memories and feelings to fade from your consciousness as you allow an image or object that encapsulates all these experiences to form in your mind. Take some time to speak with God about the meaning or significance of this object.

5. Conclude your imaginative contemplation with a short formal prayer, such as the Lord's Prayer or one of your own favorites.

6. Write down any significant memories or feelings from this prayer shortly after leaving the space in which you prayed. You might find it helpful to compare notes from different applications of the senses since this will help you understand the ways your imagination guides you in prayer. Also, these acts of review will nurture your capacity to discern the growing presence of God in your life.

Approaching Prayer during this Retreat

An excerpt from* A Pilgrimage to the Land of the Saints, *with variations and additional materials.

During your spiritual journey, you should listen for the rhythms and patterns of prayer that will mark your journey. Most of these will emerge during the retreat through your conversations with God, but some will be shaped by the design of the retreat and the patterns of prayer used in it.

Note: Before you consider the following suggestions regarding your prayer, you will find it helpful to review the other resources in this section. These include the texts for the examens used during this retreat, discussions of the types of Ignatian prayer used during this retreat, and rituals you might use to create a sacred space for your prayer.

In a daily life retreat, you will pray the morning examen each day before going out into the world and the evening examen each night before going to bed. At an appointed time on each day of the week, you will use the following order for prayer:
- Day 1 – Preparation
- Day 2 – 1st meditation
- Day 3 – 2nd meditation
- Day 4 – 3rd meditation
- Day 5 – 4th meditation
- Day 6 – The Application of the Senses
- Day 7 – Review

In a secluded retreat, you begin you your day with the morning examen and the preparation of your prayer for the day. These two activities may be integrated or conducted separately. Then, it is suggested that you pray using the following daily order:
- Late morning – 1st meditation
- Midday/early afternoon – 2nd meditation
- Late afternoon – 3rd meditation
- Early evening – 4th meditation
- Late evening – The Application of the Senses

Before going to bed, at least half an hour after the application of the senses, you should review your prayer and conduct the evening examen. Again, these activities may be combined into one exercise if you wish.

> *Note: To integrate the examens into your preparation for each day or week, complete the exercises as they are explained in each section of the retreat and then replace the long prayers at the end of these reflections with the appropriate examen.*

With these schedules and concerns in mind, it would be helpful to reflect on the following issues before beginning a retreat:

Selecting a Bible Translation

You should decide which translation of the Bible will best help you hear God's voice during your prayers. It is important to remember that you will be using the Bible for prayer, not as an aid for your study of the biblical selections in the retreat. So, you may choose to use a different Bible than the one you regularly consult in your daily life.

Also, both the Ignatian and the Celtic spiritual traditions believe in an intimate relationship between Christ and his disciples that balances familiarity with deference. So, you will be asked during the retreat to speak with Jesus in a conversational tone like when you speak to your closest friends. Using a more contemporary translation of the Bible would help ease any discomfort you might feel as you approach Jesus in this way.

> *Note: This retreat is not intended as Bible study, so you need to avoid referring to biblical commentaries or other reference materials while preparing or reviewing your prayer. You will have ample opportunity after the retreat to confirm the spiritual leadings of the retreat through study and discernment.*

Using *The Spiritual Exercises of Saint Ignatius*

All the materials from *The Spiritual Exercises of Saint Ignatius* used (or referenced) in the retreat are provided in this book. So, you do not need to have a copy the full Ignatian exercises during your prayers. Still, if you find the language of the version used in this book challenging or off-putting, there are many excellent translations available for purchase. The translations by Michael Ivens, SJ, and George Ganss, SJ, are especially noteworthy as are an older translation by Louis Puhl, SJ, and a "contemporary reading" prepared some years ago by David Fleming, SJ.

However, as with your use of the Bible, it is important to remember this retreat should foster a spiritual and emotional encounter with God. For this reason, you should only refer to the material in the *Spiritual Exercises* referenced (and numbered) in the prayer instructions of this retreat and not read additional materials (including other exercises presented by Ignatius or the translator's commentary until after you complete the retreat. Also, to preserve the emotional and spiritual impact of this retreat, you should avoid any secondary sources about the *Spiritual Exercises* until after you have experienced them directly.

<u>Keeping a Retreat Journal and Using a Notebook</u>

Both during the retreat and the retreat exercises afterward, you should keep a journal of your experiences. Many of the benefits of the retreat will become evident in the months after you complete it, so it is very important to preserve your memories of the retreat as you connect them to the subsequent changes in your spiritual life. This journal should include reflections on each of your prayer periods, especially the review sessions, and any special prayers or insights that seem significant "in the moment". You also should collect any artwork you create during the retreat (e.g., poetry, drawings, etc.). Like your journey through the retreat, this journal should be uniquely suited to your spiritual needs and personality.

However, it is important that you not use your journal while preparing your prayers. Instead, you should record your preparatory notes in a small workbook (or on separate pages collected in a folder). These notes will present your thoughts and desires as you approach different topics during the retreat, while your journal will record the effects of your conversations with God – which may change your perceptions of the various issues and concerns you initially bring to your prayer. Keeping these two records of your retreat distinct and separate from each other will help you better understand the inner dynamics of this special time of prayer and self-discovery.

Preparing for your Prayer

The time you spend preparing for prayer during your retreat, whether in daily life or in seclusion, should occur after you attend or read the prayer sequences. While vital to the successful completion of your retreat, the preparation of your prayer should never become a chore. Instead, it should be a relaxed and pleasant time of listening for God's voice in the readings that will shape the coming day or week of prayer (depending on whether you are making your retreat in daily life or in seclusion). This will allow you to maintain a contemplative disposition as you prepare for your prayer during the retreat.

The focus of your formal preparation time at the beginning of each day or week of the retreat should be the final section, where you express your desires and needs to God. These petitionary prayers will open your mind and your heart to hear what God has to say to you through the readings when you pray with them later. The rhythms – and, occasionally, specific words – of these prayers at the end of your preparation time need to be remembered so they may shape the beginning of each prayer period during the following day or week.

Contemplations, Meditations and Considerations

While most of the prayer periods during this retreat (and the other retreats in this series) use the techniques of imaginative contemplation, the different prayer types have different goals. The prayers designated as contemplations involve a direct experience with Jesus Christ or the characters of stories told by Jesus. On the other hand, prayers designated as meditations involve the Celtic saint associated with each retreat usually provides a narrative setting for otherwise non-narrative scriptural selections. As such, contemplations should involve a direct contact with Jesus or the characters of the stories while meditations should focus on the lesson being taught by the Celtic saint.

Considerations are prayerful reflections on a particular idea or spiritual concern. While considerations are thought-driven, it is essential that they remain prayerful by making certain that time and space remains available for God to illuminate the spiritual truths and desires at the heart of the exercise.

Adapting the Instructions for Prayer

The instructions for this retreat cultivate habits of prayer by delineating clear structures for the different prayer exercises and employing consistent language when guiding each type of prayer presented in the retreat. The various movements within a particular time of prayer are marked by numbers [surrounded by brackets] and the phrasing for each type of exercise uses the same language – with variations for the content of the readings and the spiritual gifts desired in each meditation. In this way, you will become more confident in using different styles of prayer as the retreat progresses.

With time and practice, and as your confidence in using these prayer techniques grows, you may want to revise the activities within a prayer exercise to better suit your own personality. If so, it would be best if you begin by adapting the instructions used to set the scene for your imaginative prayer before changing any of the other sections. Also, you should not alter more than one bracketed section in the instructions at a time. In this way, you will be able to return easily to these instructions if you find that your adaptations disrupt your prayer.

However, if you choose to amend these instructions, it remains very important that you not change the movements of prayer delineated by the bracketed numbers. These stages within each prayer exercise shape the rhythm of your prayer, fostering spiritual habits that encourage an open disposition toward God and his desires.

Repeating Seminal Prayers

During your retreat, you will be asked to repeat and extend earlier meditations. The purpose of these repetitions is twofold: they help you deepen in your appreciation of the material at the heart of your prayer, and they help you understand yourself as you respond to God through your prayers. Repetition will allow you to discern those aspects of your life where you are most receptive to God as well as where you resist God's presence.

So, it is important that you treat each moment of prayer as a new experience of God. Try to allow each time of prayer to remain unique, even as you return to a familiar reading. With time and effort, you will find that you are able to enter your conversation with God more quickly and express yourself more comfortably.

Pacing your Prayer

Whether in seclusion or in daily life, it is essential that you be consistent in the moments of your day devoted to prayer and reflection. You will be more likely to succeed if you remain mentally prepared for the spiritual and physical demands of the retreat and give them the energy and attention they require. Also, by faithfully honoring the times you designate for these spiritual activities, you will be able to relax and find pleasure in the rhythms of your retreat. Remember this time is an opportunity for you to have an extended conversation with a loving God. Feeling the familiarity created by the repeating patterns of the retreat will enhance this conversation as you become more comfortable in your prayer.

Also, it is important to remain faithful to the amount of time you commit to your prayer. You may be tempted to shorten a prayer period when you feel distracted, only to find that God breaks through your distraction. Or you may feel tempted to lengthen a powerful contemplation, only to find your thoughts diverted away from God. This retreat will be a very delicate time, so you need to be careful not to disrupt your emotional or spiritual equilibrium through erratic behavior. These suggestions are particularly important in the daily life retreat, where you have a very specific amount of time with God each day. But, during a secluded retreat, when your prayer permeates your entire day, you may be more flexible – allowing yourself to follow these leadings informally between prayer periods.

Note: *It is important that you do not allow yourself to become too tired to remain faithful in your prayer while in seclusion. So, if you find this happening, you should eliminate one of the repetitions in your daily order until you feel called by God to pray all five suggested meditations.*

Reviewing your Prayer

Learning to listen to God requires a willingness to assess honestly our disposition during our prayers and in our lives. By reviewing the prayers of your day or week, you learn as much about yourself as you do about the scriptures with which you pray. So, as you take time to review your prayer, allow space in your thoughts and feelings for God to speak to you about the gifts you have received and the graces that you still need.

Ultimately, the review periods in your retreat are not about thought. They serve as another opportunity for prayer in which your consciousness of God's presence in your life takes tangible shape. While you certainly will remember seminal moments from the retreat long after it is finished, the deeper currents of God's activity during your prayer will become most evident through your careful consideration of the details of each moment you spend with God during the retreat.

Honoring Holy Ground
rituals for creating a sacred space

The consequences of incorporating personal rituals into our prayer often exceed our expectations. The consistent use of private rituals helps us develop bodily habits that allow us to put aside our daily concerns more quickly and enter into a prayerful conversation with our Creator. But these rituals also remind us that we are invoking protection and guidance while seeking communion with a loving God. With each successive act of ritual, we invite God to consecrate our time with him and reconfirm our desire that he transform us into signs of his presence in the world.

With these goals in mind, you may find one or more of the following three rituals (using early Christian hymns familiar to the ancient Celtic saints) helpful:

<u>Note:</u> *These are variations of rituals presented in my earlier* A Pilgrimage to the Land of the Saints, *so they may be familiar to anyone who made that journey of prayer. If you find the earlier rituals helpful to your prayer, you should feel free to use them even though those rituals use different source materials than the retreats in this book and the other books in this series. Whatever the source of these prayers, they all share in the same Celtic Christian heritage.*

#1 – Bowing Before Jesus Christ

<u>Note:</u> *For this ritual, place three candles at the focal point of your prayer space – along with an image of Jesus or a cross, if you like.*

After relaxing into your prayer space, bow before reciting this prayer:

> Jesus, our heavenly Lord and King,
> Thou didst the world's salvation bring,
> And by thy death upon the tree,
> Didst out of bondage make us free.

Bow again before lighting the first candle while reciting:

Hear now our prayers, O Son of God,
Preserve the gifts thy hand bestowed,
Unto thy love all nations draw,
And bring mankind to know thy law.

Bow again before lighting the second candle while reciting:
Word of the everlasting Sire,
Seal us with faith, with love inspire:
Confirm our hope, O Holy One,
True God and sole-begotten Son.

Bow again before lighting the third candle while reciting:
The tongues of all creation call
And hail thy name as Lord of all:
Their life arose from God's command,
Their living hope, from thy right hand.

After completing your prayer, as you prepare to leave your prayer space, extinguish the candles in the same order you originally lit them while repeating the following prayer

Then, bow before reciting this prayer:
Mid heavenly splendors ranged on high,
To thee angelic choirs outcry;
And bands of bright archangels praise
Thy name in never-ending lays.

Bow again before extinguishing the first candle while reciting:
"Forevermore hosanna sing,
To David's Son, our conquering King;
To thee be ever love and laud
Who earnest in the name of God."

Bow again before extinguishing the second candle while reciting:
To thee shall rise the song and psalm,
O Victim meek, O spotless Lamb,
Whose blood has washed all earthly taints
From the white vestments of the saints.

Bow again before extinguishing the third candle while reciting:
> Lord, guide us by thy blessed light,
> And bring us to thy heavenly height,
> Enroll us with thy blessed throng
> To sing thy praise in deathless song. Amen.

Source:
"Jesus, Our Leader" by Saint Ambrose.

#2 – A Litany of Repentance

Note: This ritual does not require any objects, but you may want to use a crucifix or other image of Jesus as the focal point of your prayer space.

After becoming comfortable, open your hands – palms up – in front of you or pick up and hold the image of Jesus. Then, looking at your palms or the image, offer the following prayer:
> *I am not worthy, Lord, mine eyes*
> *To turn unto thy starry skies;*
> *But bowed in sin, with moans and sighs,*
> *I beg thee, hear me.*

Now, while allowing an image to form in your imagination or looking at the image in your hands, slowly say:
> *My duty I have left undone,*
> *Nor sought I crime or shame to shun,*
> *My feet in sinful paths have run,*
> *Sweet Christ, be near me.*
> *I beg thee, hear me.*

> *O, fill my soul with grief sincere*
> *For mine offences; let the tear*
> *Moisten my pillow; Father hear,*
> *And grant repentance.*
> *I beg thee, hear me.*

For all my many crimes, O Lord,
The pains of hell were just reward;
But thou, O God, my cry regard,
And spare the sentence.
        I beg thee, hear me.

Redeemer, sole-begotten Son,
Father and Spirit, three in one,
Thou art my hope; as ages run
Be thine all glory.
        I beg thee, hear me.

If in the balance thou shouldst weigh
My crimes, there were nor hope nor stay,
But Lord, thy clemency I pray,
To grace restore me.
        I beg thee, hear me.

Dear Jesus, I acknowledge thee,
Thou gavest thy life upon the tree;
Who takes from thy Divinity
Is a blasphemer.
        I beg thee, hear me.

All godless errors, proud or vain,
The false belief and murmuring strain
Insult thy love, thy law profane,
Gentle Redeemer.
        I beg thee, hear me.

When you are finished, return the image of Jesus to its place or move your hands to where you will hold them during prayer while saying:

Sweet Lord, I love thy holy name;
I hear my mother church proclaim
The Spirit, Sire and Son the same,
One God eternal.

Power, love and glory be to thee,
O high and holy Trinity;

Be ours the bliss thy face to see
In light supernal. Amen.

Source:
"A Hymn for the Penitent" by Saint Hilary.

#3 – An Act of Contrition before Prayer

<u>Note:</u> *In this ritual, the focal point for your prayer space should include a candle placed before a cross or crucifix. You also will need some matches or a lighter.*

Begin by saying:
O Word of Might, that springing forth
From out the Father's heart, wast born
To raise our fallen state on earth,
Bring help, and leave us not forlorn.

Light the candle before continuing with this prayer:
Illume our breasts with heavenly light,
And set our souls aflame with love,
That we, forsaking things of night,
Shall lift our hopes to joys above.

Make the sign of the cross as you say:
Let not our souls on that dread day
Be rolled in seething pools of fire;
Let mercy melt thine ire away,
And be thy love our sole desire.

After concluding your prayer period, recite the following prayer while you extinguish the candle:
When from the awful judgment throne
Dread doom unto his foes the Lord
Shall send, and call in tender tone
The just unto their sweet reward;

Conclude by making the sign of the cross as you say:
Then to the Father and the Son
And Holy Spirit, one in three,
From first to last, as ages run,
Eternal praise and glory be. Amen.

Source:
"O Word of Might" by Saint Ambrose

About the Author

A former Jesuit, **Timothy J. Ray** brings a diverse background in creative writing, cultural studies, theology, and the history of ideas to his work in spiritual direction and formation. He received his Bachelor of Arts, *magna cum laude*, in a multi-disciplinary program focused on the cultural history of law, economics and politics from Niagara University before earning, with distinction, both his Master of Fine Arts in Dramaturgy and Dramatic Criticism from Yale University and his Master of Letters in Theology from the University of Saint Andrews.

In addition to this Celtic journey through *The Spiritual Exercises of Saint Ignatius of Loyola*, he has published *The Carmichael Prayerbook*, *A Journey to the Land of the Saints* and *A Pilgrimage to the Land of the Saints, Nurturing the Courage of Pilgrims* and *Seeking our Place of Resurrection*.

For more information about Timothy and his activities, please visit http://www.silentheron.net.

Printed in Great Britain
by Amazon